50 *hikes* in the Hudson Valley

From the Catskills to the Taconics,
and from the Ramapos to the Helderbergs

PETER KICK
BARBARA McMARTIN
JAMES McMARTIN LONG

Photographs by the authors

Second Edition

Backcountry Publications
Woodstock, Vermont

An Invitation to the Reader

Over time trails can be rerouted and signs and landmarks altered. If you find that changes have occurred on the routes described in this book, please let us know so that corrections may be made in future editions. The author and publisher also welcome other comments and suggestions. Address all correspondence to:

Editor, 50 Hikes™ Series
Backcountry Publications
PO Box 748
Woodstock, VT 05091

Library of Congress Cataloging-in-Publication Data

McMartin, Barbara.
    Fifty hikes in the Hudson Valley : from the Catskills to the Taconics, and from the Ramapos to the Helderbergs / Barbara McMartin, Peter Kick, and James McMartin Long; photographs by the authors. —2nd ed.
       p.   cm.
    Includes index.
    ISBN 0-88150-292-8
    1. Hiking—Hudson River Valley (N.Y. and N.J.)—Guidebooks. 2. Hiking—Catskill Mountains Region (N.Y.)—Guidebooks. 3. Hudson River Valley (N.Y. and N.H.)—Guidebooks. 4. Catskill Mountains Region (N.Y.)—Guidebooks. I. Kick, Peter, 1951– . II. Long, James McMartin. III. Title.
GV199.42.H83M36   1994
796.5'1'097473—dc20   94–9722
                                                           CIP

Second Edition: fourth printing, 1996

Published by Backcountry Publications,
A division of The Countryman Press, Woodstock, VT 05091
Distributed by W.W. Norton & Company, Inc., 500 Fifth Avenue, New York, NY 10110

Some of the map sections that appear throughout this book are from the series "Catskill Trails," © 1983 and 1989; "East Hudson Trails," © 1993; and "Shawangunk Trails," © 1990; all published by the New York–New Jersey Trail Conference. Reproduced by permission.

Pages 138, 139, 184, and 193 contain excerpts from *The Catskills from Wilderness to Woodstock* by Alf Evers; © 1972 by Alf Evers; published by The Overlook Press, Lewis Hollow Road, Woodstock, NY 12498; $32.50. Quotes on page 197 are from the letters of Thomas Cole, published in Reverend Charles Rockwell, *The Catskill Mountains and the Region Around*. Cornwall, NY: Hope Farm Press, 1972.

Book design by Glenn Suokko
Page composition by Chelsea Dippel
Trail overlays by Richard Widhu, © 1994 The Countryman Press
Frontispiece photograph: Kaaterskill Falls
Cover photo by Barbara McMartin

in the
Hudson Valley

ACKNOWLEDGMENTS

While the hikes in this volume have been chosen for their scenic value, their selection was not only a matter of personal choice based on our experience; it also represents the favorites of regional experts, mapmakers, hiking friends, and members of various clubs and organizations. Their advice was essential to our planning and writing.

Of those who helped bring this guide to life, special thanks must be given to those friends who walked with us and shared their own love of nature with us. Thanks also are due to those whose special contributions were such an integral part of our project: W. Alec Reid, taking such care to print our photographs; Daniel Chazin, Maurice Avery, James C. Dawson, Paul Leiken, Bleecker Staats, and Hugh Neil Zimmerman for reading parts of the work, hiking along with us, and helping to make sure that the written word corresponds accurately to the trails we enjoyed; Jack Karnig and Ray Donahue for background on trails; Justine L. Hommel, President of the Mountaintop Historical Society for access to archives and research material; the Huguenot Historical Society, the Dutchess Historical Society, and the Putnam County Historical Society's Foundry School Museum; the very generous staffs of the Cold Spring, Newcastle, Haines Falls, and Olive free libraries; R. Laila Alberga, Elizabeth Kick, Eydie King, and Stephanie Steyer for typing.

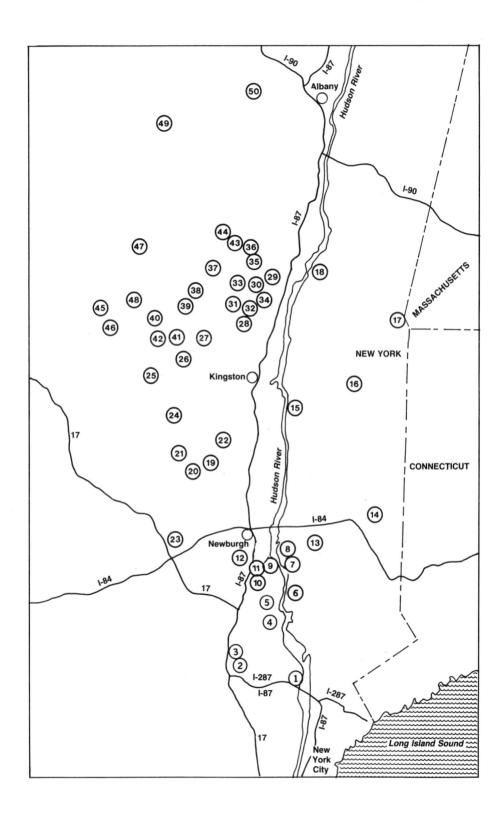

CONTENTS

INTRODUCTION

SOUTHERN HUDSON VALLEY

CENTRAL HUDSON HIGHLANDS

EAST OF THE HUDSON

THE SHAWANGUNKS

EASTERN CATSKILLS

WESTERN CATSKILLS

NORTH OF THE CATSKILLS

INTRODUCTION

Southeastern New York State is dominated by the Hudson River, which flows past the wonders of its cities and industries. At the same time, the river touches some of the state's wilder lands, where the hiker can quickly escape the centers of civilization that dot the Hudson's banks. The wilderness at the Hudson's Adirondack headwaters needs no introduction. Some of the wild lands near the Hudson's southern cities are well known, while others are almost undiscovered. This guide includes a variety of day hikes that will introduce you to the best of southeastern New York's wild lands not far from the Hudson.

The first visitors to the Hudson were mightily impressed by the rocklike fortresses of the Palisades, the rugged Hudson Highlands, and the mysteries of the distant blue Catskills. It is these rocky hills and mountains bordering the Hudson where most of the hikes described in this guide take place. The book will lead you to the northern Palisades, the Ramapos, the Highlands, the isolated lump of Schunemunk, the white cliffs of the Shawangunks, and the recesses of the distant Catskills. It reaches west to Delaware County, east to the Taconics, and north to the fortress of the Helderbergs. It brings you to the tops of this series of ranges, which stand as if designed to give the best views of their succession and of the Hudson and Mohawk valleys.

THE HISTORY OF THE ROCKS AND MOUNTAINS

The drama of the southeastern New York landscape has a second story in the very rocks themselves. From the resistant limestone of the Helderberg Escarpment, to the dissected plateau of the Catskills, and into the crystalline Hudson Highlands lying beside the younger folded rocks of the Appalachians, you can see the parts of the puzzle that make up the region's geological history.

The largest geological province described in the guide is the Catskill region, occupying 1,500 square miles. Next to the Adirondacks, these are New York's highest and most rugged mountains and have the highest elevations. Slide Mountain (4,205 feet) is the highest peak, and there are over a hundred other peaks with elevations over 3,000 feet in the Catskills. Three distinct regions—the escarpment (northeast), the southern, the central—define the Catskill plateau. There are several smaller topographic regions as well, many of which run east-west or perpendicular to the southward movement of ice during the Pleistocene Age.

The profusion of streams that formed when the vast thickness of ice melted and retreated resulted in the erosion that produced the rugged character we see in the Catskills today. The plateau is drained to the north by the Schoharie Creek, a tributary of the Hudson via the Mohawk. To the east the Rondout, Esopus, and Kaaterskill rivers join the Hudson. To the south and west the Delaware and Neversink rivers are the major watersheds.

The rocks found in the Catskill plateau are relatively soft, consisting mainly of the sands and gravels deposited in the rivers and shallow seas of the Devonian period, about 350 million years ago. These sands and gravels became the sandstones and conglomerates that have been uplifted and tilted. However, they have not been significantly folded, faulted, or changed by igneous and metamorphic activity. Thus they differ from many other mountain ranges such as the Appalachians or the Adirondacks.

The Catskills may have been a peneplain (almost a plain) at sea level before they were uplifted to their present elevation. The deep dissection (erosion) occurred when streams were rejuvenated during uplift. The resistant rocks remained, while the softer strata washed away. In some regions joint patterns in the rock controlled erosion to produce the deep cloves (clefts) and wildly scenic hollows that steeped the Catskills in mystery and romance and contributed to the art and literary imagination of early America.

The uplift of the Devonian sediments took place in several stages, and the Miocene and later stages were influenced by several episodes of Pleistocene glaciation. Today the higher peaks are located where the uplift was greatest and where their conglomerate sandstones were able to resist erosion by the advance of the continental ice sheets and later by glacial meltwaters.

What is perhaps most interesting about the underlying geology of the Catskills is the soil and hence the vegetation that flourishes there. The region represents the southernmost occurrence of boreal coniferous forests on glaciated uplands in North America. In contrast with this summit forest of spruce fir and paper birch is the valley forest type, known as the Carolinian zone forest, which consists of oaks, hickories, occasional black birch, tulip trees, and, until recently, chestnut. According to Catskills ecologist Michael Kudish, "The proximity of the Carolinian and Canadian zones, especially in the eastern Catskills, together with the effects of man over two centuries, produces a rich, diverse flora, and creates a vegetation so complex that it nearly defies explanation."

While they are unique floristically and geologically, the Catskills have yet another distinguishing characteristic: their youth. All the surrounding ranges are considerably older. To the east lie the 450-million-year-old Taconics, formed during a continental collision that displaced older sediments in a period called the Taconic Orogeny.

South of the Catskills are the Shawangunks, and although they are close to the Taconics in age, their evolution is more related to the Catskills. Extensive sands and quartz-rich gravels were deposited in a shallow sea during the Silurian period, about 450 million years ago. Much later the resulting sandstones and conglomerates were uplifted and differentially eroded.

The Hudson Highlands to the south are a series of granitic and metamorphic rocks. They were intruded and metamorphosed at great depth over a billion years ago. Later, about 450 million years ago, during the Taconic Orogeny, the rocks were folded, faulted, and uplifted to their present form.

HIKING IN SOUTHEASTERN NEW YORK

By combining walks in these geologically interesting mountains—the best of the East Coast's scenery, in our opinion—with a few walks in the Hudson Valley itself, this guide offers the hiker an excellent range of opportunities.

For residents of southern New York State, the special appeal of most of these trails is their proximity to New York City. The majority of the trailheads lie within two hours of the city.

There are two ways to enjoy these walks. The social hikers will find many walking groups that offer regularly scheduled hikes and trips. The New York–New Jersey Trail Conference (NY–NJTC) will put you in touch with many of these groups. Organizations such as the Catskill 3500 Club, the Appalachian Mountain Club, and chapters of the Adirondack Mountain Club all offer outing schedules for a variety of hikers. Each organization also fills a second role by providing mechanisms for the hiker to return something to the land. With programs of trail maintenance, conservation, planning to prevent overuse, and education to promote wise use, these organizations help protect our wild lands.

Those who seek quiet in the wild lands also can find that. Some of these routes are never heavily used. Others are, but, even here, early-spring and late-fall trips will mix solitude with expanded vistas in ways sure to please any wilderness seeker.

There are relatively few hikes on the east side of the Hudson. Its gentler hills were settled early, and although the farms are shrinking, the settlements have grown to fill most of the open land. In contrast, the forests on the west side of the Hudson have been preserved as the valley's water source and as part of the New York State Forest Preserve, whose unique state constitutional protection ensures they will remain "forever wild." Lands within the Blue Line of the Catskill Park offer the largest group of hikes in this guide.

Almost all the lands traversed by today's trails were once settled and used by farmers, miners, loggers, and romantics. Their presence inevitably is reflected in the lore that surrounds the trails, and we explore that history as well as the natural scene. While this guide serves as an invitation to the mountain ranges and valleys of the southern part of the state, it cannot even begin to probe the vast history that enlivens each route. For further information, consult the bibliography at the end of this book.

BEFORE YOU START

There is an enormous range of hikes in this guide, from easy strolls to strenuous climbs. The information about distance, time, and elevation change should help you gauge the difficulty of each hike and your preparedness. Almost all hikes follow clearly marked trails, although this can change. The greatest source of confusion seems to be the constant revisions in trail designation for the more southerly trails, where interconnecting routes can be confusing and color changes in the markings are in progress.

The area offers many more walks than are described in this book, and references to some of the best of the other guides are given in the bibliography. In order to discover other hikes, or to become better prepared for outdoor adventures, you may wish to join one of the hiking groups listed at the end of the introduction.

Preparedness is key to your enjoyment, and you should be well equipped before you start. This should include beginning to understand the use of map and compass to complement the information in this guide. If you are new to hiking, it is definitely a good idea to join a hiking group and learn from those with experience. The more background you have in the woods, the greater will be your safety as well as enjoyment. Do not count on the following summary of what you need to know to prepare you for every situation you are likely to encounter. While this guide includes excursions for all ranges of experience, this introduction is not a primer for beginning hikers. Treat it instead as a checklist and a set of reminders.

THE WEATHER

Whenever possible, wait for a sunny day—the pleasures are much greater and the problems more predictable. But even on sunny days you should be prepared for changes and extremes. It can be 20 or more degrees colder on the mountaintops of the Catskills than in the nearby Hudson Valley. Storms can appear on short warning.

It often can be too hot in summer for strenuous hikes. There are many who prefer walking in southern New York State in fall and spring, and these are the most changeable times. Extremes from heat waves to snowstorms can occur. But the rewards of fewer people and expanded distant vistas in the leafless season make it worthwhile.

PREPARATIONS

Even with the best of forecasts, your watchwords should be *plan for the unexpected.* Possible changes in temperature mean you should take extra clothing, especially rain gear. Experiment with layers of light, waterproof gear. In the mountains you will want a layer of wool, even if in summer it is only a sweater in your day pack. Places to swim are mentioned, so take along a bathing suit.

Many of the trails are as smooth as a sidewalk; some are as rubble-filled as a rock pile. For most of these hikes a sturdy pair of well-broken-in, over-the-ankle boots is essential. The light-weight Gore-Tex or similar-material boots are wonderful, they give good traction and support, and they are all you need, except when hiking on the higher mountain trails in early spring or winter. Wear two pairs of socks, an inner lightweight pair and a heavy outer pair that is at least partly wool.

Carry a sturdy day pack, large enough to hold your lunch and a few necessities. The separate pouches along the side of our packs always contain a whistle, a case with dry matches, a jackknife, a small can opener, lip balm, and a space blanket. We have used them all.

Carry a map and compass, a flashlight in case you are delayed beyond dusk, and a watch so you do not panic if that happens. You also need a small first-aid kit, containing a few bandages, first-aid cream, and moleskin for the unexpected blister.

Take along a small squeeze bottle of insect repellent, one that contains DEET (N-diethylmetatoluamide). There are black flies in early spring, although not the legions that endure so long in the Adirondacks. Fill a plastic bag with toilet paper and throw in a few towelettes to use before lunch on those dry mountaintops.

It is strongly recommended that you wear a pair of unbreakable glasses—light, tinted sunglasses even if you require no prescription. It is all too easy to run into an overhanging branch or twig.

You will enjoy the hikes more if you carry binoculars and learn to watch for birds. Besides, binoculars are essential for identifying distant sights. A small magnifying glass can add to your discoveries of nature. You may even enjoy carrying a small, lightweight altimeter that works according to barometric pressure. On relatively steady days it is a good clue to progress on a mountain; on unstable days it can alert you to sudden changes in the weather.

Of course, you should always carry water when you hike. These mountains are dry much of the year, and few springs exist. It is becoming increasingly dangerous to trust open water sources because of the spread of *Giardia*. And, remember to take enough water. Dehydration on summer days is quite possible; it can even happen on a sunny, leafless spring day or in winter. Those lightweight fuel bottles of durable aluminum with deep screw tops are wonderful for carrying liquids, but to avoid confusion, their contents should be clearly marked.

Remember, hiking should be fun. If you are uncomfortable with the weather or are tired, turn back and make the complete hike another day. Do not create a situation where you risk yourself or your companions.

And, never walk alone. Be sure someone knows your intended route and expected return time. Always sign in at the New York State Department of Environmental Conservation (DEC) trailhead registers where they are available. The unexpected can occur. Weather can change, trail markings can become obscured, you can fall, and you can get lost. But, you will not be in real danger if you have anticipated the unexpected.

LYME DISEASE
Lyme disease is caused by a tick-borne spirochete that may produce a rash, flulike symptoms, and pain in joints.

If untreated it may cause chronic arthritis and nervous-system disorders. It is difficult to diagnose but treatable if diagnosed early.

The deer ticks that transmit Lyme disease are now found north and west of Westchester County, where the problem has reached epidemic proportions. Their range is expanding rapidly north and west, and users of this guide should take preventive measures.

There is no foolproof way to protect yourself from these minute ticks. Check yourself frequently; tuck pants into socks and boots; put insect repellent containing DEET on your pants, shoes, and socks (note that DEET does weaken elastics); and wear tightly woven and light-colored clothing (making it easier to see the ticks). Above all else, we strongly recommend that you shower and change clothes at the end of your hike; this is the best time to make a complete body check. Change out of your hiking clothes to prevent any ticks present from biting you. If you suspect you have contracted Lyme disease, call your physician right away.

BEHAVIOR IN THE WOODS
So, now you are safe in the woods, but what about the woods? The environment that may threaten you can be just as fragile as you are, and you are the only one who can protect it.

Trail erosion is becoming a serious problem in many areas. Please stay on the main trail at all times to minimize damage to soils, tree roots, and vegetation. Use steppingstones whenever possible to cross wet areas of the trail. Don't pick wildflowers or dig woodland plants.

Leave no sign of your presence. Use pit privies if available. If not, bury your wastes at least 200 feet from water or from a trail or path. When you

A view of the Catskills from the Hudson River's east bank

camp, do not bathe with soap in lakes or streams; when picnicking or camping, carry wash water and dishwater back from the shore. If you are camping, carry a stove for cooking, and do not build fires unless they are needed. In most parks, fires are prohibited. These are very fire-prone areas. If you need to build a fire on a Catskill hike, for instance, build it on dry stones, gravel, or sandy soil surfaces, surrounded by a fire ring to protect duff, leaf mold, or organic soils from burning. Remember, only dead and down wood can be used.

Respect the rights of others and help preserve natural areas for future hikers.

NOTES FOR USING THIS GUIDE

Summaries at the beginning of each hike list hiking distance, vertical rise, time on the trail, and United States Geological Survey (USGS) topographic map (or maps) or the NY–NJTC trail map for the area the hike traverses. Unless otherwise noted, distances are for the round trip or circuit. Distances are given from state markers where available and correct (incorrect signs are noted in some instances). Where measured mileage information has not been available, distances have been computed from the USGS and are correct to within 10 percent.

Vertical rise refers to the total change in cumulative elevation for the hike. In cases where the terrain is relatively level, a numerical figure has not been used.

Hiking time is given for the total time at a leisurely pace, but it is simply the minimum needed to walk the trail as described. The text often tells you to allow more time for sightseeing.

Most of the hikes in this book are accompanied by sections taken from the topographic map (or maps) mentioned at the beginning of each hike description, so it is not essential to have an entire map with you on the trail. These maps, however, do give the larger picture, and you will have more fun on a mountaintop if you can identify surrounding countryside. A cautionary note on the USGS maps: While contours and elevations are by and large reliable, some of the human-made features, including trails, are seriously out-of-date. The New York State Department of Transportation 7½' quadrangles, which correspond in area and name to the USGS quads, tend to have more recent planimetric information, but they have the disadvantage of being printed in only two colors (USGS maps are in four colors). More than half the hikes in this book are accompanied by small sections of maps published by the NY–NJTC. These maps are more convenient and up-to-date than either the USGS or department of transportation quads, and we recommend acquiring them (see page 16). With the exception of Mohonk (hike 22), all hikes using a topographic base map have a trail overlay and—in the case of loop hikes—arrows showing the direction of travel. A few of the hikes are in state parks, and, for reasons of scale, a sketch map instead of a topographic base map has been provided for Olana (hike 18).

If you do not know how to read a map, you should learn to do so before hiking all but about a dozen of the simplest trails in this guide. Spend time walking with someone who does know how to read a map. The same instructions are appropriate for the use of a compass. You may not need either on the easiest of this guide's trails, but walking the easier routes with map and compass will allow you

to become comfortable with their use so you can extend your hikes beyond the ones described or to more difficult hikes.

OTHER HELPFUL INFORMATION

The New York State Department of Environmental Conservation (DEC)
50 Wolf Road
Albany, NY 12233-4255

The DEC, through its Division of Lands and Forests, manages the New York State Forest Preserve lands of the Catskills and detached parcels of state land outside the Catskills. The DEC is responsible for Search and Rescue, planning for management, supervision of campsites, and issuing of camping permits. (Unless expressly prohibited, campers may stay for up to three nights in one location on state land without a permit and may apply for a permit for longer stays. The DEC is considering implementing regulations that would require permits for groups of 10 or more.) The DEC also publishes regional sketch-type trail maps. It is easiest to obtain local information from one of the regional offices listed below.

DEC Region 3 Headquarters
23 South Putt Corners Road
New Paltz, NY 12561-1601
914-255-5453

DEC Region 4—Lands and Forests Sub-Office
Jefferson Road
Stamford, NY 12167
607-652-7364

DEC Region 4—Lands and Forests Sub-Office
HC#3 Box 903
Cairo, NY 12413
518-622-9743

Taconic State Park and Recreation Commission

Mills–Norrie State Parks
Staatsburg, NY 12580
914-889-4100

The Taconic State Park and Recreation Commission manages land assigned to the Office of Parks and Recreation on the east side of the Hudson. It is responsible for state parks and historic sites there, including Hudson Highlands, South Taconic, and Fahnestock state parks.

Palisades Interstate Park Commission (PIPC)

Bear Mountain, NY 10911-0427
914-786-2701 or 718-562-8688

The PIPC issues permits and trail information and supervises Harriman and Bear Mountain state parks and the state land of the Shawangunks.

Mohonk Preserve, Inc.

1000 Mountain Rest Road
New Paltz, NY 12561-9493
Preserve: 914-255-0919

The Mohonk Preserve supervises access to preserve lands, collects an access fee, publishes a brief natural history of the Shawangunks, and manages this unique natural resource.

New York–New Jersey Trail Conference (NY–NJTC)

GPO Box 2250
New York, NY 10116
212-685-9699

The NY–NJTC coordinates the construction and maintenance of some 1,100 miles of hiking trails, including the Appalachian Trail in New York and New Jersey and the Long Path, which connects the metropolitan area with the Catskills and beyond. They also publish regional maps of the Catskills, Northern New Jersey, West and East Hudson, Harriman State Park, the South Taconics, and the Shawangunks. They have published *Hiking the Catskills* and *Harriman Trails*, trail guides to the region, available for $14.95 each. Small sections of conference maps have been reproduced in this book, and the complete map sets may be purchased from the conference. The "Catskills Trails" five-map set is $11.95, the "East Hudson Trails" three-map set is $7.95, and the "Shawangunk Trails" four-map set is $7.95. Some 85 hiking clubs and conservation organizations belong to the conference, along with 10,000 individual members. Applications for individual membership are invited, and the $18 annual fee includes, among other things, a subscription to the *Trail Walker*. This bimonthly publication describes the activities of the member clubs and features timely articles, book reviews, and trail updates. It is a reliable source of information on trail closings, relocations, and other potential problems associated with the hikes described in this book.

Appalachian Mountain Club (AMC)

New York City office:
202 East 39th Street
New York, NY 10016-0962
212-986-1430

The AMC, like most clubs, helps build and maintain trails in southern New York, including some sections of the Appalachian Trail and trails in Harriman and Hudson Highlands state parks. The AMC is also a leader in conservation, canoeing, and bicycling in the metro area. For the area covered by this book, they have a Catskill Chapter and a New York/North Jersey Chapter.

Chapters of the Adirondack Mountain Club
RR #3, Box 3055
Lake George, NY 12845-9522
518-668-4447

The Adirondack Mountain Club (ADK) can supply information about their Ramapo, North Jersey, Mid-Hudson, Long Island, Knickerbocker, New York, Mohican, Albany, and Schenectady chapters, all of which schedule regular hikes in the area described in this guide. Membership is currently $35 a year.

The Catskill 3500 Club
c/o Cyrus Whitney
41 Morley Drive
Wyckoff, NJ 07481-3322

The Catskill 3500 Club is primarily a hiking organization. Candidate members receive notices of trips and outings. A membership patch is given for completing climbs of 35 summits over 3,500 feet, 4 of which must be climbed a second time in winter.

The Catskill Center for Conservation and Development, Inc.
Route 28
Arkville, NY 12406-1010
914-586-2611

The Catskill Center for Conservation and Development is a regional advocate for land-use planning and environmental management, and it is active in natural-area and historic preservation, community revitalization, and public review of regionally significant projects. It publishes general-interest books and technical studies as well as a newsletter on conservation issues affecting the Catskills. The center also publishes a map entitled "The Catskill Region." Offices are in the Erpf House on Route 28 at Arkville, and applications for membership are welcome.

The Nature Conservancy, New York Field Office
251 River Street
Troy, NY 12180
518-272-0195

The Nature Conservancy manages and protects natural areas throughout the United States. Two hikes in this guide are in conservancy preserves.

Map Information Unit, New York State Department of Transportation
State Campus, Bldg. 4, Room 105
Albany, NY 12232
518-457-3555

The state publishes and sells a variety of maps, including topographic maps based on the USGS quadrangles.

Map Distribution Branch
US Geological Survey
Box 25286, Federal Center
Denver, CO 80225
800-USA-MAPS

Many sporting-goods stores sell USGS maps, but for the occasional one that is unavailable, it is good to be able to order from the source (which can take many weeks, however).

Legend for "Catskill Trails" Maps

Marked Trail and Terminus . . . . ———→
Trail Name and Color . . . . **DP(R)**
   See reverse for Trail name and description
   Trail Color
   (R) — Red **(B)** — Blue **(Y)** — Yellow
Unmarked Trail . . . . — — —
Parking . . . . **.P**
Viewpoint . . . . ★
Leanto . . . . **.L**
Water (Spring) . . . . **.W**
New York State   Forest Preserve
   Forest Preserve Lands . . . . ———————
                   Private Land
Keep Out (private land) . . . . **KO**
Marked elevation . . . . △⁴⁰⁴⁰
Unmarked elevation ₓ3810
Primary Road . . . . ———
Secondary Road . . . . ———
Route Markers (State, County) . . . (214) (16)
Bus Stop . . . . **.B**

1

The Hook

Distance: 11.7 miles

Time: 6 hours

Vertical rise: 1,200 feet

Maps: USGS 7½' Haverstraw; USGS 7½' Nyack

The towering cliffs of the Hook have awed travelers to southern New York State for centuries. Henry Hudson and the sailors who followed made note of this impressive headland as they made their way up the Hudson. The constructed cliffs of abandoned quarries further etch the skyline into sheer red-brown walls that appear to continue the Palisades. Whether walking to the high point in spring or fall to watch the hawk migration or bicycling along the paths that hug the shores, you will find much to enjoy in the parklands run by the Palisades Interstate Park Commission that stretch from Nyack to Haverstraw on the Hudson's western shore.

A portion of the Long Path takes the high route from Nyack across the Hook and the hills called the Seven Sisters. With a bit of bushwhacking, you can make a circuit walk along the hills and back on the shore path, enjoying the best of views of woods and water. Probably you will find it best to leave a car at either end, however, as the southern ends of the two portions are not connected easily on foot, and any connection involves crossing private lands.

Leave your return car at Nyack State Park at the end of Broadway in Nyack. Return south on Broadway to Birchwood Avenue, then head west to US 9W. Drive north on US 9W, and as you leave the village, just beginning to climb the hill behind the Hook, you will see a place to park on the west side of the road. There is another turnout at the crest of the hill, from which you can walk back to the trailhead. The trail, marked with turquoise blazes, begins on the east side of the road, a little north of the first turnout.

A 15-minute walk brings you to the top of the Hook with views toward New York City and north to the quarry behind Rockland Lake. Beyond the quarry lies the massif of Dunderberg that ends in the Timp. Farther north and on the other side of the river lies

The Hook

the ragged contour of Breakneck Ridge leading up toward South Beacon. The river, wide here at Tappan Bay, is pinched to the north by Croton Point. Farther north it opens out into its widest segment at Haverstraw Bay before becoming choked into the narrows of the Hudson Highlands.

You are standing on the 736-foot peak of the Verdrietege, or tedious headland, so-called by early Dutch sailors who struggled to sail upwind around it. But the landscape at your feet is not what the Dutch sailors saw, and the history of that landscape accounts for a good portion of the preservation movement that resulted in the parks now lining the Hudson's shores.

The Palisades' traprock, diabase that is volcanic in origin, surfaces here through the base of Triassic sandstone and shale. Quarries along the river to the south were active in the 1820s, and the columnar cliffs of the Hook were quarried extensively in the 1870s and 1880s with the introduction of dynamite and heavy earth-moving equipment. The basalt columns were crushed for traprock for macadam roads and, later in the 1890s, for concrete for Manhattan buildings. Angered at first only by the ear-shattering explosions heard up and down both sides of the river, residents of both New York and New Jersey began to speak out against the quarries. It was not until 1894 that a well-organized group opposed the visual desecration of the cliffs caused by the quarrying.

Finally in 1900, after several years of legislative debate that was fueled by the argument "that preservation would largely benefit those who enjoyed the view from the New York side of the Hudson," a study commission report was accepted. It called for a permanent interstate park commission and the acquisition of land along the Palisades for recreational purposes. With both private and public funds, the acquisition program progressed from acquiring lands from the top of the cliff face to the river to adding cliff-top lands north to Nyack. The Hook was still threatened until the Palisades Interstate Park was extended northward in 1906. By 1915 all of the Hook was acquired by the Palisades Interstate Park Commission.

The cliff-top trail continues north through Hook Mountain State Park by first heading down the incredibly narrow and sinuous ridge. Trees block the views here, but you will climb a handful of open summits before the day is over. One opening discloses Rockland Lake and the landing from which the lake's ice was shipped to New York City. A 40-minute walk brings you into a valley, and shortly beyond is the second hill with several view spots on its summit.

The descent from this hilltop is marked by a left fork that takes you across an old roadway that once led toward Rockland Landing. Beyond the low point another roadway comes in from the left. As you start to climb you will be amazed at the amount of rock work that was used to construct these old roadways, making an especially lovely base for the trail to follow. Gentle ups and downs follow. The curved stone wall and old foundation beside the trail are sure to intrigue you.

As you begin to climb again, about 1 hour and 40 minutes into the trip, watch for a path that leads up to the right to a promontory overlooking Croton Point, unquestionably one of the best views of the day.

This is a good place to observe the clues to the second major industry of

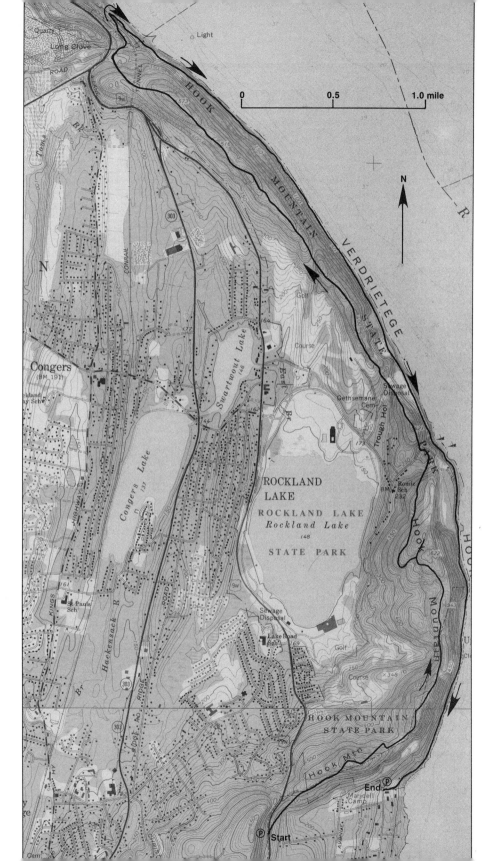

the region's past, clues that are much less obvious than those of the quarries. At the shore below are the remains of old docks, the successors to Slaughter's Landing, a settlement begun in 1711 by John Slaughter from Rockland Lake. An ice business was started at Rockland Lake in 1831 when Moses G. Leonard impressed New York City hotel keepers with the cleanliness and purity of the lake's ice. In 1855 the business became the Knickerbocker Ice Company, the largest in New York, employing as many as 1,000 men. Ice was cut from the lake and stored for shipment south to New York City. It was moved from the lake via an endless conveyor cable to the landings, where three pairs of tracks led across the docks whose ruins are guarded by an old lighthouse. Four-hundred-ton loads were carried south on barges.

Return to the trail, and within a few feet you meet what appears to be a trail intersection. The way right is steep and unmarked. Turn left for an almost equally steep descent behind a row of houses and old foundations; follow it to a road that could provide an alternate trailhead for a portion of this walk. This point also can be reached by car from Rockland Lake State Park, which is to your left (west). Rockland Landing is on the waterfront to your right. The 3-mile walk to this point along the summits should take just over 2 hours.

Immediately north of the stanchions that bar vehicular traffic into the park, the turquoise-marked trail continues, first passing an early-nineteenth-century cemetery. The first hilltop with a view is scarcely 5 minutes from the road, a perch atop the first in a string of smaller quarries north of the landing. Just beyond, you will be amazed to see Dutchman's-breeches blooming in spring only a short distance from the prickly pear cactus that seems to enjoy this dry location. The trail continues on the west side of the ridge, emerging to a series of more or less obscure views, depending on the season. At one spot, you look down on red-brown cliffs and pine seedlings that are filling in a second quarry.

The trail descends, turns left past a filtration plant, and heads up the next ridge bordered by vine-covered stone walls. For a short time the trail follows the park boundary. Just beyond, a side trail (right) leads to a lookout with spectacular views atop a third quarry. A series of gentle ups and downs ends in a sharp, short drop into a hemlock-filled valley. Immediately you emerge with views to the north and northwest. The next downhill leads off the ridge.

The way out of the small valley is viewless, its taller trees making the segment feel like a remote woodland trail where the roller-coaster effect of the ridge continues for a delightful 45-minute walk. There is one summit that yields views of narrow DeForest Lake. As the trail turns sharply east and heads steeply down toward the river, almost above the railroad tunnel, you feel suspended above the water. The hemlock-covered bank parallels the shore 400 feet above it. The trail descends along the ridge, then lies exposed beneath power lines, where you have a view of Stony Point beyond Haverstraw Bay. You see an old bridge and a roadway and could turn left to an alternate trailhead with limited parking at the junction of NY 304 and US 9W. This point is 3.2 miles from Rockland Landing Road. Your trek from the Hook across the hills of the Seven Sisters—and surely twice that number of small knobs and crests—has taken about 4 hours.

Unfortunately, without walking into Haverstraw, there is no good way to cross to the waterside trail. You can turn right and walk north for 0.3 mile, first heading down the roadway and out to the railroad line. Cross it, after being certain no trains are around, and walk north along the tracks to find an easy descent to the waterside path. Bicyclists, joggers, and strollers will join you for the return, but the lack of privacy does not detract from the pleasant route. The level 5.2 miles back to Nyack State Park are easily walked in 2 hours, unless you stop to examine the quarries en route.

Note: If you find the parking lot on US 9W closed, drive 0.9 mile north to the southern entrance to Rockland Lake State Park. In winter turn right, then park in 0.3 mile at the gate to the Executive Golf Course and walk 0.3 mile uphill to the turning loop. In season drive to the parking area, but park away from the clubhouse. A yellow-marked trail heads east from the turning loop. It winds uphill, passing a small pond in 0.2 mile. In another 200 yards it intersects the blue-marked trail in a draw on the ridge, less than 0.4 mile north of the summit of Hook Mountain. Turn right and pass two small lookouts on the 160-foot climb to the summit.

2

The Southern Ledges of Harriman State Park

Distance: 8 miles

Time: 6–7 hours

Vertical rise: 1,000 feet

Maps: USGS 7½' Sloatsburg; NY–NJTC Harriman–Bear Mtn., #3

The Ramapo Mountains run from northern New Jersey into Rockland and Orange counties. Their eroded slopes have risen above nearby seas for nearly 600 million years, making them among the oldest land masses on the continent. These mountains are part of the Reading Prong, which extends from Reading, Pennsylvania, to the Hudson Highlands and north to the Green Mountains of Vermont. This Precambrian formation is the result of periods of intense folding and metamorphism of sediments deposited more than a billion years ago and of intrusions of magma that occurred several times in the Precambrian era. While these forces leave a complicated picture for the geologist, later events, the Ice Ages, are much clearer. The striations and polished rocks and the ubiquitous erratics are obvious to the hiker on any walk through the Ramapos.

Whether the name *Ramapo* derives from a Native American name for the potholes that mark the Ramapo River, or whether it comes from a Leni–Lenape word that means "place of slanting rock," is not known. The latter is certainly more descriptive, for the views of uplifted faces of various metamorphosed layers are also a part of each hike.

Bear Mountain and Harriman state parks span most of the Ramapos in New York State. Their origins are curious. In 1908 the state proposed building a state prison at Bear Mountain. Among the many who protested this desecration of beautiful and historic lands was Mrs. Edward H. Harriman, widow of the railroad tycoon, who offered to give the Palisades Interstate Park Commission 10,000 acres, the nucleus of the modern parks. In return it was agreed that the commission's jurisdiction would be extended north along the Hudson, and plans for the prison would be

A stream in southern Harriman State Park

dropped. Subsequent gifts and purchases have enlarged the park to its present 51,000 acres and allowed for scenic parkways and the building of dams to create or enlarge the numerous bodies of water that dot the park.

The parks are managed now for the hordes of people from the metropolitan area who enjoy the ski jumping, skating, waterfronts, and picnicking in the more developed areas. It is often difficult to escape the crowds, but it can be done. There is a dense honeycomb network of trails that covers almost every mountaintop and follows every handsome stream. This wonderful network, built over a period of many years by hikers and club groups of the New York–New Jersey Trail Conference (NY–NJTC), can be a problem with those unfamiliar with the park. It is difficult to know how to combine these segments into interesting loops convenient to places where parking is permitted. Trails, their names, and the color and style of their markings have multiplied over the years in response to a growing tradition that sometimes defies logic.

The four walks described in Harriman and Bear Mountain state parks provide great loops made up of segments of many different trails. Although difficult to describe, these loops offer a greater variety of hikes from a single access than any single trail in the parks.

Hikers seeking a measure of solitude in the parks should walk during the off-season or during the week, if possible. Parking is permitted only in designated areas; you may not build fires or disturb flora and fauna.

A walk along the southern ledges of Harriman State Park takes you away from the crowds. The loop starts at the parking area adjacent to the Reeves Meadow Visitor Center, which is less than two miles northeast from the park boundary on Seven Lakes Drive. Walk east on a roadway through the field behind the center for less than 100 yards to a right fork marked with three white squares. This marks the beginning of the Reeves Brook Trail, which heads uphill and to the south, following a small tributary of Stony Brook.

The Reeves Brook Trail winds a tortuous course over almost every convolution of the terrain. It passes beautiful rock ledges and crosses a small stream. In 15 minutes the road the trail has been following forks right. Follow the white-blazed trail left, climbing some more to pass a small cascade. You pass a huge erratic on a knoll to the right and then a wet swale to the left. Zigzag south and then east, across a small valley and then up. As you ascend, watch carefully for the trail markers along this serpentine stretch of trail! The trail threads through a very handsome hemlock grove and continues to climb. Still climbing, you become aware of the bare rock escarpment ahead, to the east.

After 45 minutes you reach a four-way intersection where the Seven Hills Trail crosses; it is marked white with blue squares. The left branch of this trail heads steeply up slope; its right branch is slightly less obvious. For this loop you can follow the right branch or stay on the white-marked trail for another 10 minutes. The white-marked trail continues paralleling the cleft beneath the cliffs to the east. Soon the trail ends at a T with the Raccoon Brook Hills (RBH) Trail, which is marked with black dots, squares, or R's on white blazes. Turn right on the RBH Trail, heading up slope for 10 minutes to a wonderful view west.

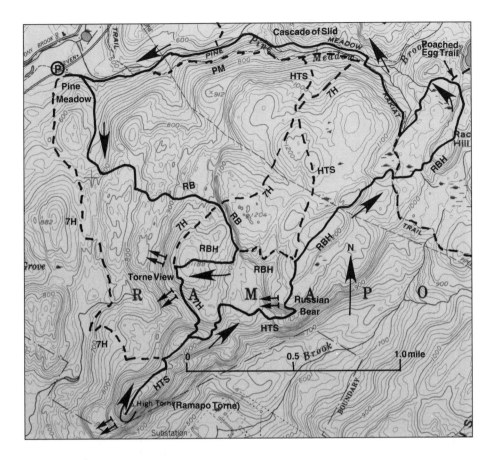

Follow the trail downhill for another 75 feet; you reach a second T intersection, this one with the blue-marked Seven Hills Trail, which would have been a slightly shorter route.

Turn left on the Seven Hills Trail and enjoy more views, some of them across to Ramapo Torne, your next destination. Head, very steeply at first, down to a deep draw, then up a rubble-filled hillside at a scramble that ends at the intersection with the Hillburn-Torne-Sebago (HTS) Trail, marked with white. This last section is about 0.5 mile, but with the rough walking it may take you more than 20 minutes. Just off the trail on the ledge

above you is an overlook with views south to New York City. At this intersection, you could detour south along the joint HTS and Seven Hills trails, staying left on the HTS Trail when the trails split. The HTS Trail climbs to the rock knob of Ramapo Torne, which has more southerly views. Return north on the HTS Trail to the intersection and fork right.

Continuing the loop from this intersection, follow white markers east on the HTS Trail. You descend, then climb a small ridge around boulders to a bare, fire-scarred expanse, beyond which you can see the deep gorge that lies between you and the Russian

Bear, which is the southern tip of the sharp escarpment to the east. You descend from this broad ridge, steeply at first, then cross the head of a draw with its small stream. As you get closer to the jagged cliffs, look up to discover a cave. As the trail turns to climb the promontory, you see a free-standing rock slab that has fallen from the cliffs of Russian Bear. At this point you also have views back to the knob of Ramapo Torne.

The trail swings back left on top of the cliff to a vantage to the southwest and a pretty view back to the ridge you were on about a half hour earlier. The white markings lead you across the broad hilltop through tall oaks on high ground, for a 15-minute walk to an intersection with the RBH Trail. Turn right on the white-with-black-marked trail, which leads you northeast on high ground, across bare rock through another fire-scarred area. This trail is a route of fire and ice: strange, yet beautiful, compositions of fire-ravaged trees and stumps in a landscape punctuated by huge erratics and boulders dropped by the glacier.

Ten minutes from the intersection, as you begin to descend, you can glimpse the cliffs of the Raccoon Hills through the trees. The trail crosses the slash of a gas pipeline, then makes a rubble-strewn, sharp descent to intersect with the white-marked Kakiat Trail. This last segment on the RBH Trail takes almost a half hour. If you are tiring, turn left on the Kakiat to shorten the loop by over 1 mile. To make the loop, turn right through a lovely laurel glade to follow the combined Kakiat and RBH trails. (Kakiat is the contraction of a Native American name for the patent granted by the governor of the province of New York in 1696. The patent encompassed much of northern New Jersey and southern New York.)

Stay on this part of the Kakiat Trail for only 100 feet, and turn left on the continuing RBH Trail, which heads downhill to a rubble-strewn draw beneath the cliffs, then across open rock and up behind the cliffs. Winding east of north along the hilltop, the trail offers several views across the deep valley to the east. Pine and hemlock shelter knolls where you walk on bare rock. Twenty-five minutes from the cliff top, you begin to descend and overlook Pine Meadow Lake with Pine Meadow Mountain in the background. A short, steep descent brings you to an intersection with the "Poached Egg" Trail. A detour of 200 yards on this yellow-on-white-blazed trail leads you to the lake. Caves to the right of the trail have yielded Native American artifacts. Marvelous cliffs line a promontory to the north across the lake.

Returning to and continuing on the RBH Trail, you cross another knob and descend southwest, into a draw and across a deep, rubble-filled valley. A steep descent follows the next height of land, then the trail leads up to a marvelous circle of erratics, a veritable Stonehenge built by the glacier. You meet a small stream coming in from the left—you will follow it, as it grows and joins with others, all the way back to your car.

Across the stream the RBH Trail climbs 30 feet to end at its second intersection with the Kakiat Trail, after making a 1.4-mile loop. Turn right—downhill on the easier footing of the Kakiat—high above the amazing mass of boulders below. This trail gradually swings northwest, descending constantly to the deep, cool valley of Pine Meadow Brook. After less than 10 minutes on the Kakiat, you reach a major intersection with both a red- and a blue-marked trail. Turn right to follow the union of all three trails across the bridge over Pine Meadow Brook. At this point you are under an hour from your car, and you have several choices for the return, including the red-marked Pine Meadow Trail, which stays on the south side of the brook for the return by clinging above it on the steep hillside.

For the most spectacular return, turn left on the white-marked trail, the continuing Kakiat, on the north side of the bridge and stay on it after the intersection 100 yards downstream where the Seven Hills Trail forks right and uphill. The Kakiat here is close enough to the brook that you can enjoy its quiet pools and rock cliffs. In 10 minutes the valley of the brook begins to fall away quickly. Your white-marked trail crosses a second white-marked route, the HTS Trail, just north of a bridge that carries that trail across the brook.

Stay along the brook as it enters a deep gorge and plunges through the Cascade of Slid for the best part of the walk. Hemlocks shroud the cliffs and shelter small waterfalls, making them too dark to photograph except in late afternoons near the summer solstice. In less than 15 minutes, the cascades end at a bridge that crosses the brook, just upstream from its confluence with Stony Brook. Looking downstream from the bridge you can see a second bridge that crosses Stony Brook. Cross to the south side, pass the bridge that carries the Kakiat north, and continue on the old roadway.

Stony Brook descends fairly steeply. The roadway crosses the gas line, then picks up the red-marked Pine Meadow Trail, which joins at an acute angle. Two huge erratics frame a small waterfall on the brook and mark the place the brook becomes quiet. From the boulders it is but 10 minutes along the roadway back to the beginning of the hike. The ease of this stretch should take the kinks out of your legs, kinks that are inevitable when you consider the tortuous route this loop makes through the southern border of the park.

3

The Iron Mine Walk– Harriman State Park

Distance: 6.5 miles

Time: 5 hours

Vertical rise: 1,050 feet

Maps: USGS 7½' Monroe; USGS 7½' Popolopen Lake; USGS 7½' Thiells; USGS 7½' Sloatsburg; NY–NJTC Harriman–Bear Mtn., #4

Harriman State Park is full of historical walks, and the one that touches on a few of the region's nineteenth-century iron mines blends good hiking with the annals of that time. Iron mining in the Ramapos actually dates back to 1742, although the colonies had been an exporter of iron ore since 1718; and at the onset of the revolutionary war they were producing 14 percent of the world's iron. The iron ore of the Ramapo Hills, the nearby watercourses to power the bellows for the furnaces, the heavily wooded slopes whose timber yielded the necessary charcoal—all attracted entrepreneurs. The furnaces at Sterling near Mon-

roe, at Greenwood near the Ramapo, at the Queensboro Furnace, and at the Forest of Dean Furnace all produced iron for guns for the American Revolution and the Civil War. Mines were scattered throughout the Ramapo Hills, furnaces were built, and settlements grew up around the furnaces.

The mines varied in depth from 10 to 6,000 feet, the deepest being the Forest of Dean Mine on US Military Reservation property. That mine's entrance has been sealed. Many of the mines are water-filled and dangerous. This walk takes you past a few of the mines that can be inspected safely from the trail.

The mines you will walk past are in the Greenwood group, suppliers of the Greenwood furnace at Arden. This and other furnaces are described in *Vanishing Ironworks of the Ramapos* by James M. Ransom, a book to read if you wish to delve deeply into the history of the area. The Greenwood furnace was established about 1810 and supplied cannonballs to the American forces during the War of 1812. Robert Parrot acquired an interest in the furnace and surrounding lands in 1837, and he and his brother Peter managed the ironworks and became

The view south near the end of the mine walk

sole owners of it. With coal brought by the newly built railroad through the Ramapo Valley, the furnace's output increased until yearly production reached 5,000 tons of pig iron destined for fine hardware and stoves. During the Civil War the iron was used for the famous Parrot gun, the most effective artillery weapon of the Union army. This gun was made at the West Point foundry at Cold Spring under the direction of Robert Parrot. The ore supplied by the Greenwood, Surebridge, Pine Swamp, O'Neil, and Clove mines was hauled to a kiln about a half mile above the Greenwood furnace, where the ore was roasted to drive off sulfur, stamped to reduce it

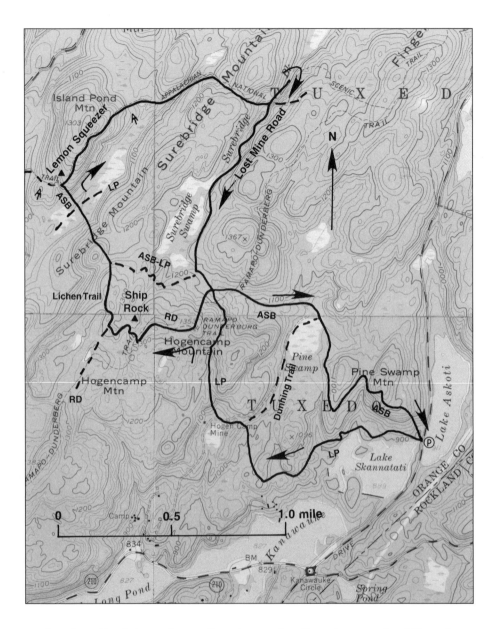

to the size of a "pigeon's egg," and then smelted in the furnace, which was built in the charming glen beside the outlet of Echo Lake.

To start the mine walk, find Seven Lakes Drive, which winds through the section from just north of Sloatsburg to the Long Mountain Parkway (US 6) on the park's northern edge. Drive south from the Tiorati Circle on Seven Lakes Drive and turn right, opposite Lake Askoti, to a parking area for boating on Lake Skannatati. Two trails begin in the northwest corner of this lot, one marked with three red dots on a white blaze and the other with the turquoise-blue rectangle of the Long Path. Take the latter, which begins along the lakeshore, leaving it near a northwest bay, to make a hop-a-rock crossing of an intermittent stream about 20 minutes from the trailhead.

A gentle uphill climb takes you to a gorgeous rock ledge; the route runs through an open parklike area of tremendous oaks with laurel and blueberries beneath. Over a second ridge, half an hour from the start, you reach an abandoned roadway. Turn left on a road marked with the yellow of the Dunning Trail as well as the blue of the Long Path. Within 100 yards turn right, away from the road, following the Long Path as it angles along the rocky hillside. The next half an hour takes you over that hill, across ridges, and beside a lovely hemlock-forested gorge with balancing rocks along the trail to a second intersection. Turn left to join the Arden-Surebridge (ASB) Trail. Your route is marked with the red of the ASB Trail as well as the blue of the Long Path.

In 200 yards you reach the large erratic of Times Square. Six roads or trails intersect in the vicinity of Times Square. The continuing blue-marked Long Path and the red-marked ASB Trail fork left from the intersection, following an old road. A second red-marked trail, the Ramapo–Dunderberg (RD) Trail, also crosses the intersection. For this loop you want the red-marked RD Trail, which is a left fork just south of the erratic.

The RD Trail heads southwest, up steeply through a hemlock draw. In 10 minutes you reach bare rock and an area that was ravaged by fire in 1988. You pass wonderful rock ledges, climb again over bare rocks with glacial striations, and enjoy views, mostly south over lovely rolling terrain falling away from Hogencamp Mountain at 1,353 feet. Many additional markings guide you through the burn area.

From the broad summit the trail zigzags down across a ridge with signs of glaciers and fire everywhere. In 10 minutes you reach Ship Rock, a bottom-up prow of a boat. Just beyond it the trail makes a sharp right turn.

Watch for a second right turn, this one marked with a blue L on a white blaze, which indicates the Lichen Trail. This 0.5-mile connector will take you to the combined red-marked ASB Trail and the blue-marked Long Path. The picturesque Lichen Trail features tall laurel, ledges, and hemlock, with occasional openings with views. The trail drops sharply through an evergreen-covered hillside to intersect the ASB Trail. Turn left beside a swamp and head down a very pretty hemlock-covered hillside with a stream. As the trail levels out at the bottom of the hill, it makes a sharp right turn to pass a wet area and reach another intersection, where the Long Path forks right (northeast) and a white-marked trail forks southwest. Stay straight on the red-marked ASB Trail, the middle route, which crosses a little stream, follows it briefly, then begins to climb beside cliffs with handsome rock formations. The tiny stream contrasts with the violent forces of water and ice that over the years have created this scene with its impressive overhangs. Such a variety of impressions in only 2 hours of walking! The hill to your right now adds to the drama as it is beginning to recover from the devastation of the fires.

Five minutes from the intersection, your route intersects the white-marked Appalachian Trail (AT). Turn right (north) on the AT (and the continuing red-marked ASB Trail). This route quickly splits. The right fork leads you on a scramble through the Lemon Squeezer. After you squeeze between sheer rock walls and pull yourself over ledges through this miniature chasm, you find that the two routes rejoin. The left fork is the easier way. Continue following the blazes to the peak of Island Pond Mountain. In winter there are views south of Island Pond and east to the valley between you and Surebridge Mountain.

Just beyond the summit, near an old foundation, the red-marked ASB Trail forks left. Stay straight on the white-marked AT as it descends into a valley beside a dry streambed and then north for a 5-minute walk to a right turn up through a draw. Near the top of the draw, a hemlock perches on a rock like a brontosaurus on a giant egg.

Beyond the tree the trail may be hard to follow as you continue climbing through the rocky draw. Just about 3 hours into the hike, you cross a hill beyond the draw, through a broad open forest. A short descent through a small draw brings you to an abandoned roadway below ledges that define the eastern side of this small valley. From this intersection with the Surebridge Mine or Lost Mine Road, you can see the tailing pit of the Greenwood Mine. Walk left (north) for a short distance along the road to examine its pit, which, between 1838 and 1880, produced ore from three veins.

Turn south along the road for one of the more charming parts of the walk. The roadway passes a handsome swamp, where signs of mining abound; tailing piles are everywhere, and a few pits of the Surebridge Mine lie to the east of the road. As the road bends right it follows a causeway built up of tailings and heads south across Surebridge Swamp. An arch of rhododendron shades the causeway, from which there are glimpses of the twisted stumps and wildflowers in the sphagnum bog.

A small rise leads to an intersection just short of Times Square. A brief detour north on the red-marked RD Trail takes you to a half-round glacial pothole dripping with moss. Returning to the erratic of Times Square, turn left on the red-marked ASB Trail, which follows another old mining road past charcoal pits and more mine areas. You can stay on this road by forking right (south) on the yellow-marked Dunning Trail. The very pretty road follows the western border of Pine Swamp for a 20-minute return to the Long Path, ½ mile from the start.

Alternatively, you can stay on the red-marked ASB Trail for one more mountaintop view. The ASB Trail continues along a roadway, passing another mine hole near the intersection with the yellow-marked trail. A quarter mile beyond that intersection, the red-marked ASB Trail leaves the roadway to follow a narrower path that winds up and over Pine Swamp Mountain. This 20-minute climb offers an overlook across the lakes where the walk began, and a steep, 15-minute descent brings you to the trailhead.

4

Dunderberg Mountain and the Timp

Distance: 6.8 miles

Time: 5–6 hours

Vertical rise: 1,200 feet

Maps: USGS 7½' Popolopen Lake; USGS 7½' Peekskill; NY–NJTC Harriman–Bear Mtn., #4

Cliffs of the Timp

The eastern end of the Dunderberg massif pinches the Hudson River to create the entrance to the narrows at the southern end of the Hudson Highlands. Its western end is sharply defined by the cliff-faced Timp. The mountain stretches three miles in an almost east-west direction to form the northern border of Haverstraw Bay. This ponderous hulk inspired Washington Irving in *The Storm Ship* to tell of the Dutch goblin who "keeps the Donderberg [*sic*]" with speaking trumpet. Sailors reported hearing him in "stormy weather . . . giving orders in Low Dutch, for the piping up of a fresh gust of wind or the rattling off of another thunderclap." Hikers will find that the loop walk along Dunderberg's summit ridge to the Timp and back is one of the favorites in Bear Mountain State Park, especially if their trips are planned to avoid the goblin's storms and give clear weather for the spectacular views.

You can arrange the circuit from a parking area, with only a short walk of 0.35 mile along busy route US 9W. The parking area is four miles south of the Bear Mountain Traffic Circle and opposite Jones Point Drive.

Walk south of the parking area for

100 yards to the blue-marked beginning of the Timp-Torne Trail. Follow it along the level, then steep, incline, as it begins to climb the flanks of Dunderberg. Within 10 minutes you zigzag up the beautiful cut-stone tunnel of the failed Dunderberg Railroad. Your walk today will take you across many sections of that incline railway, 13 miles of which were completed in the early 1890s before the failure of the project to construct the line to a hotel and restaurant that were to be built on the top of the mountain.

You continue zigzagging in tight S-curves up the steep flanks, then make a long traverse south below the crest. Already through-the-trees views reveal Haverstraw Bay, High Tor, the Hook, and Verplank Point, although the Indian Point Nuclear Plant and other power and resource recovery plants intrude on this wonderful vista.

Turning to climb again, within half an hour you cross another section of the incline railway and make a hairpin turn at the head of a deep hemlock draw. Rock work and the parallel tracks of the railway are visible. At about 1 mile, you are following a track along an almost-level stretch when double trail markers point you uphill to the higher level of track at a point where the railway was supposed to emerge from a tunnel cut into the hillside. Stop to explore this partially cut tunnel. The trail then returns to the lower level where it is built up into a sharp curve from which there are excellent views. The curve ends in a cut, then the trail crosses a stream and a roadway and heads steeply uphill into the woods.

This trail was constructed to take advantage of the views and points of interest along the railway, and the route at times seems illogical. Stay with it as it sometimes follows roadway, sometimes narrow footpaths that are impossible to find without the markers. Be careful not to stray from the trail in these sections.

From a distance, Dunderberg appears as a smooth hillside, but it is covered with rock outcrops, cliff-faced knobs, and various geological warts. You do a lot more climbing up and down than the 1,200-foot vertical rise indicates, so just enjoy the way the trail seems to wind over so many bumps. The New York–New Jersey Trail Conference (NY–NJTC) map shows many of the intersecting roads and trails, but its 100-foot contours give few clues to this contorted terrain.

The climb through the woods takes you steeply up to a viewpoint on top of the ridge. From here you look back northeast. You are about an hour into the walk, and at this point you start zigzagging steeply again, passing a balancing rock, then heading north on the almost-level trail. In another quarter hour you reach a lookout that is the sum of all those preceding it. At this point, just short of a deep draw separating your ridge from a northern part of the mountain, you make a hairpin turn to head southwest, zigzagging again, and in 10 minutes you reach an opening beside a balancing rock, where you have a breathtaking view down the Hudson, past Croton Point and the Tappan Zee Bridge.

After descending from this knob, you climb along a narrow path to a high point, marked with a cairn and winter views to the north. A series of rugged ups and downs follows. In one cut between little cliffs you can see Bear Mountain. The tortuous route

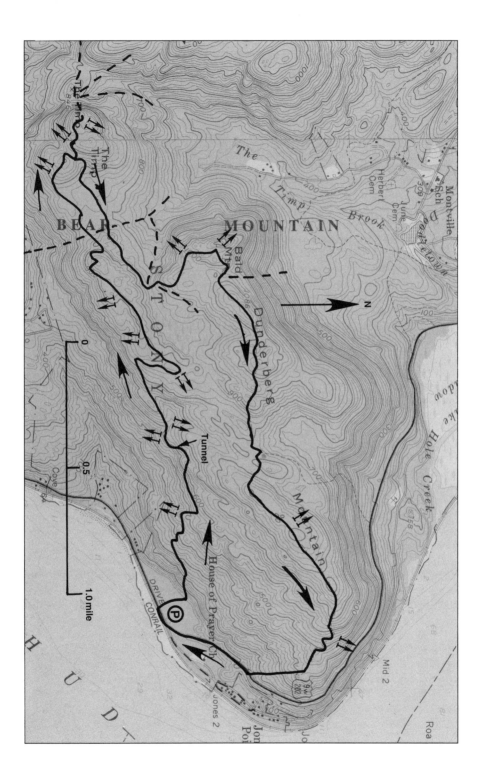

reaches a vehicle track. Downhill from the track and about 2 hours into the hike, the blue-marked trail crosses the 1777 Trail. The trail's name commemorates the roadway used by the British on their march to capture Fort Montgomery.

More jagged ups and downs follow, then a minor lookout and a descent to a valley with an intersection with the Ramapo–Dunderberg (RD) Trail, marked with a red dot inside a white square. Turn left, following the red-with-white and the blue markers for a 10-minute climb to the Timp, that wonderful overlook that encompasses the Bear Mountain Bridge, Bear Mountain itself, several small lakes with islands, and the New York City skyline.

With the NY–NJTC map, you can extend this loop by descending the Timp to the north—a real cliff scramble that ends in Timp Pass. From here you can climb via the blue-marked trail to another superb overlook on West Mountain. However, there are no great loop routes for the return from there, so you will have to retrace your steps to the Timp or improvise a route using old roads and marked trails. Because you have nearly 3 hours of walking left, you should save this for another day or a different approach. (Note that this blue-marked trail continues all the way to the Torne, hike 5—something you might want to attempt with a map, two cars, and some experience in this area.)

From the Timp, 2.5 miles from the trailhead, retrace your steps to the intersection, but this time turn left along the RD Trail. You head steeply down, through stands of laurel, and 25 minutes from the Timp you cross the 1777 Trail again.

Your route now heads over a knob, then winds through tall laurel around the head of a draw, where a half hour from the Timp it crosses a small stream and joins a roadway. Shortly the roadway turns right, and the trail continues straight ahead and up the sides of Bald Mountain. There are several overlooks along this stretch—the northernmost looks straight down at the Bear Mountain Bridge. Bald Mountain's slopes at this western end of Dunderberg are precipitous.

Bald's summit is 1.3 miles from the Timp. To the north of it is a rubble-and-tailing pile that marks the Cornell Mine. The trail east hugs the very steep northern slopes of Dunderberg, quickly intersecting the blue-marked Cornell Trail that forks left and heads sharply downhill. Within 10 minutes you reach another summit in the chain, this one with views to the northwest as well as up the Hudson. The trail winds over a wooded summit, descends to a marsh in a swale, then reaches a second draw, this one with a roadway. Forty minutes from Bald's summit, the trail crosses a portion of the incline railway, climbs, descends to a deep draw with a tiny, dark pond, then climbs to a knoll with a lovely view to the north, with glimpses of Taurus, Beacon, and Storm King.

The trail then briefly joins a roadway to climb another knob. This point, an hour from Bald, marks the end of climbing along the ridge. The trail follows a narrow course through the woods, traversing across the head of a steep ravine and up a short grade to a knoll with a view northeast across Iona Island with its bird sanctuary. The island was once known as Weyant's Island after its first owner. Dr. C. W. Grant inherited it from his father-in-law in the 1850s. He farmed choice fruits there, maintained a vineyard, and gave it its curious name when he claimed "I-own-an-island."

Below the knob the trail begins its steep plunge off the mountain. The route is rubble-strewn and dangerous. It leads out to a knob with a superb lookout north and east. There is a second, similar view spot just beyond.

Below the second outcrop the trail bends sharply south and descends even more precipitously, reaching US 9W in just over 20 minutes. Be watchful of traffic on the 5-minute walk downhill to your car.

The distance between Bald's summit and US 9W is 2.5 miles, and the 3.8-mile return from the Timp along the RD Trail takes upwards of 3 hours.

5

Popolopen Gorge and the Torne

Distance: 8 miles

Time: 5½ hours

Vertical rise: 700 feet

Maps: USGS 7½' Popolopen Lake;
USGS 7½' Peekskill; NY–NJTC
Harriman–Bear Mtn., #4

Popolopen Torne has one of the Hudson Highlands' most surprising views. Popolopen Gorge, early in spring with high water and few visitors, is one of Bear Mountain State Park's most charming spots. Put them together and you have a splendid walk.

Park, for a $2.50 fee, in the lot off US 9W near the Bear Mountain Inn, and walk north along the shores of Hessian Lake and out to US 9W. Walk cautiously along the highway to the traffic circle, and cross both lanes of the Palisades Interstate Parkway. Walk on the grass along the triangle that separates the parkway from the US 9W access road, and cross that roadway. Directly opposite, a road closed

to traffic by a gate leads north. Take it to the intersection with another roadway from US 9W, where, unfortunately, there is no parking. Follow this roadway left (west), guided by red markers that lead you to a trail beside the Hell Hole on the Popolopen Gorge.

East of here, Popolopen Brook flows between two "rocky promontories on which stood Forts Clinton (south) and Montgomery (north), within rifle-shot of each other. The banks of the creek are high and precipitous, the southern one covered with trees; and less than half a mile from its broad and deep mouth in which large vessels may anchor, it is a wild mountain stream— rushing into the placid tyde-water through narrow valleys and dark ravines." Here at the foot of wild cascades, Benson J. Lossing, chronicler of the Hudson, sat in the 1850s to sketch the scene. "A short dam has been constructed there for sending water through a flume to a mill a few rods below. This stream . . . presents a thousand charming pictures, where nature woos her lovers in the pleasant summer-time." The forts disappeared long ago, but Lossing's description is still appropriate.

The forts played a pivotal role dur-

Popolopen Brook in spring

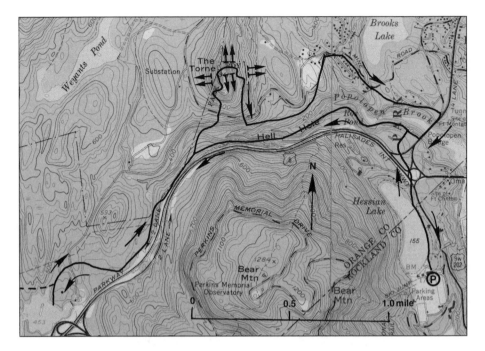

ing the Revolution. They were constructed at the beginning of the revolutionary war, and a chain was strung between Fort Montgomery and Anthony's Nose across the Hudson to stop British ships that tried to reach West Point. In October 1777, under the command of Sir Henry Clinton, the British attacked, making an arduous trip over Dunderberg. A skirmish at Hessian Lake led to its nickname of "Bloody Pond;" the forts were overcome, and the Americans suffered 300 casualties, the British, 150 casualties. American ships, two frigates, two galleys, and an armed sloop tried to escape upriver, but there was no wind and they were abandoned by their crews, who set them afire to prevent the British from capturing them.

Your walk along Popolopen Brook is west away from the site of the forts. The Hell Hole, a pool below a triple waterfall with deep pools and cascades below, greets you as you reach Popolopen Creek, a delightful place to photograph. Beyond the Hell Hole the trail continues its western course, climbing behind the dam that holds back a lovely hemlock-shrouded pond. The western edge of the pond is punctuated by a small waterfall, upstream from which the gorge narrows and deepens. The trail continues west following the course of the creek, interrupted by trail intersections, old roadways, and informal paths to the pools and rapids along the stream's course, which is best seen in high water. Sharp, moss-covered rocks, dark hemlocks, and white-barked sycamores frame the frolicking stream. The crash of water drowns out all road sounds, for the highway is not that far away. You pass a fork to the right; it is not clearly marked, but it is in sight of a bridge over the stream. You will return here later to follow the blue-on-white-blazed Timp-Torne Trail, so mark the spot. The Torne is clearly visible here to the north above the gorge.

The continuing route west is now variously marked with the red of the Popolopen Gorge Trail; the blue of the Timp-Torne Trail; a diamond with a blue 79 denoting this as part of the route the Americans followed in 1779 when they attempted to regain control of the Hudson River; and a diamond with a red 77 that indicates this was part of the route used by the British in 1777. All these routes have different courses, but for a while they coincide.

Within an hour and a quarter, even if you dawdle, you find that the trail swings left, uphill and away from the gorge. You may want to bushwhack farther along the stream, although the steep ledges often make the going rough. The stream levels out beyond a pool. The joint trail continues along the now-quiet watercourse. Within sight of the parkway, you cross a promontory to a bridge over the stream, which now has been forced into a narrow sluiceway.

The trail meets a roadway at this point. The way right leads to West Point lands and the Queensboro Furnace, but this area is not open to the public. The trail follows the roadway left toward Queensboro Lake, but you will follow it only briefly before making a right turn from it to continue on the red-marked Popolopen Gorge Trail, which leads across the north edge of Queensboro Lake and on to Turkey Hill Lake. At Queensboro Lake you will find a choice picnic spot on a laurel-covered promontory overlooking the water. To reach the spot, turn off the trail within sight of the lake

and head right (north) for 200 yards.

For the return walk stay on the trail with its blue and red markers. The trail takes the high road nearer the rim of the gorge. When the trail turns to descend into the gorge, begin to look closely for the fork to turn left toward Popolopen Brook. You cross the brook and begin to climb to an abandoned roadway, following it briefly to climb again to cross an aqueduct and finally to reach Mine Road. The trail continues across the road, leading up the Torne. There are views almost from the beginning along this short scramble. Bear Mountain blocks all views south, but Anthony's Nose is prominent to the east beyond this narrowest bend in the river. A 20-minute climb from the roadway brings you to the summit. On the open rock of the Torne you find both white and turquoise blazes, which mark a trail leading north for a view over West Point lands to an easier descent that is less steep after the first ledge.

On the return to the roadway, watch for where an old dirt road forks toward the gorge. Here, you can easily climb down to follow the aqueduct east toward Fort Montgomery. This side of the gorge is so steep you will not be tempted to leave the aqueduct route to walk closer to water level. The aqueduct trail emerges near the intersection of Mine Road and Cedar Drive. Follow Mine Road for ¼ mile until a sign on a lamppost directs you back onto a hemlock-shaded road on park lands again. At a fork on this roadway, a right choice would lead you steeply down into the gorge near the Hell Hole. The way left leads up to another roadway within sight of US 9W. Walk carefully along the shoulder of US 9W back to your car.

6

Canada Hill and Sugarloaf South

Distance: 7 miles

Time: 4 hours

Vertical rise: 1,300 feet cumulative

Maps: USGS 7½' Peekskill; NY–NJTC East Hudson Trails, #1

The Hudson Valley is rich in revolutionary-war history. The Beverly Robinson House, built by the Philipse family in 1758 on part of the Philipse Patent near Sugarloaf South, was confiscated and used as headquarters by Generals Israel Putnam and Samuel Holden Parsons in 1778 and 1779. In 1780 the house was used by General Benedict Arnold as his headquarters, and it was used as a military hospital during Arnold's command of West

Sugarloaf South from Bear Mountain Bridge

Point. Aboard the British ship *Vulture,* loyalist Beverly Robinson planned with Benedict Arnold and Major André to deliver West Point to the British. When Arnold learned that André had been captured and that discovery of his treason was imminent, he fled from the house down a path to the river and then downriver to the *Vulture;* General Washington arrived only an hour or so later.

Most of the land described here was private until recently and is now part of Hudson Highlands State Park or federal Appalachian Trail land. Many of the trails are easy-to-follow carriageways and old roads and are suitable for novice hikers. The vertical rise from where you park to the highest point is only 620 feet, but the hike traverses a couple of hills and makes a circuit around a trail called the Osborn Loop. The New York–New Jersey Trail Conference (NY–NJTC) named the Osborn Loop in honor of the previous owners of this land, the Osborn family. This is an old, settled farm area with narrow roads that make roadside parking problematic. You can reach Sugarloaf South and the Osborn Loop from NY 9D at the Castle Rock Unique Area, from NY 9D at Manitoga Nature Preserve, or from near US 9. The hike described commences at the Castle Rock Unique Area.

The Manitoga Nature Preserve, the estate of industrial designer Russel Wright, is worth a visit in its own right. The preserve is located 2.5 miles north from the Bear Mountain Bridge on NY 9D. In *Garden of Woodland Paths* Wright wrote, "The land which I bought . . . was a nondescript piece of woods . . . the remains of firewood operations. It was uninviting, dry and impenetrable woods, with no view or vistas. Today the land contains miles of paths, many vistas of the river and mountains, a natural pool, and a waterfall. I am amused and pleased to often be asked, 'How did you ever find such an unusually beautiful site?'—pleased because they think that I found it this way, and therefore I know that it looks natural." He designed his house to fit with the land around it, using the glacially deposited stone "sculptural masses" as the "pattern for masonry around the house." Manitoga, now a nonprofit organization, is open weekdays year-round and on weekends from April through October, 9:00 A.M. to 4:30 P.M. From one of the trails Wright created, the trail to Lost Pond, you can reach the Osborn Loop.

The entrance to Castle Rock Unique Area, 4.2 miles north of Bear Mountain Bridge on NY 9D, is flanked by two stone pillars marked "Castle Rock 1881" and "Wing&Wing 1857." This entrance leads to the castle W. H. Osborn built. The castle and five acres remain private; the remaining property is Castle Rock Unique Area state land. As of this writing, a sign directs hikers to park behind a red barn and then to walk 100 yards south to the start of the trail on state land. Note that while the entrance roads are on state land, they are the sole access routes to some private parcels, so please do not block any roads! In the future the state may build more adequate parking.

Turn left at the Taconic Region trail marker and cross an open field. Above you towers the castle and to your left is a farm. In 5 minutes you enter the woods to find a decaying gazebo above you. You'll be following an old road as it heads right, but pause a moment to take in the view behind you of West Point, Storm King, Break-

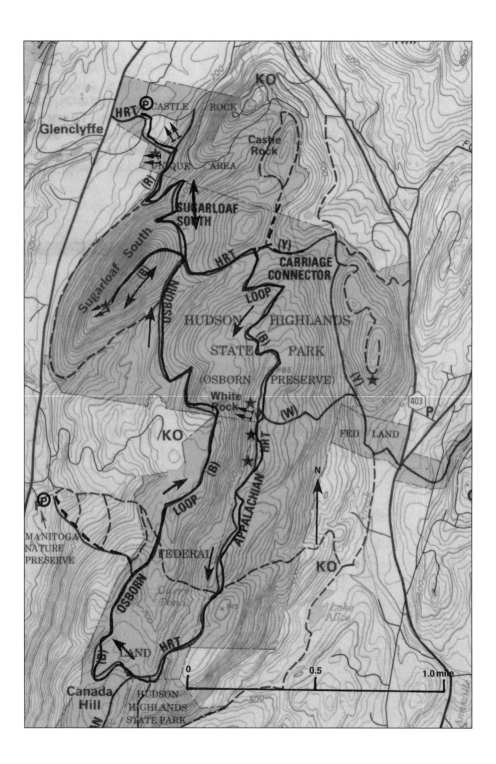

neck Ridge, and Taurus, unobstructed by trees in the field you just crossed. The views continue for a few more minutes until you make a sharp bend to the left to leave the road and ascend on another road. This road is easy walking, but the bridges over gullies are deteriorating and should be crossed with care. In the next 10 minutes you pass switchbacks to the right and left before reaching a small impoundment on your left. Just a few minutes farther and you reach a four-way intersection and the blue blazes of the Osborn Loop.

Take a sharp right and follow the red blazes for a short, steep side trip up Sugarloaf South, so-named because its conical profile resembles a sugarloaf. The trail follows a narrow ridge over the top and then descends slightly. The conifer-covered western flank of Sugarloaf is remarkably steep. After 15 minutes, you reach the best summer views to the south. Anthony's Nose, Bear Mountain, and Dunderberg frame the Bear Mountain Bridge. This is a good spot for a snack.

From Sugarloaf, retrace your route to the intersection with Osborn Loop. Continue with the blue-blazed Osborn Loop trail up an old road. Note the remains of a gazebo above you on the left. Ten minutes after returning to the Osborn Loop, note that the trail makes a right turn. The carriageway becomes the yellow-blazed Carriage Connector path. Take the right turn and continue with the Osborn Loop trail.

After 20 minutes of climbing, you join the white-blazed Appalachian Trail (AT) on a broad ridge known as White Rock. Watch for short, unmarked trails to the right. When foliage permits, these trails lead to views of the Hudson Valley. One short, blue-blazed trail on the right leads to partial views of the valley unobstructed by summer foliage.

After 30 minutes more of walking, you come to the intersection of the AT and the Osborn Loop. Turn right and follow the blue blazes of the Osborn Loop.

After 10 more minutes you see, on your left, the trail to Manitoga Nature Preserve. After descending for a few minutes, you may take a short side excursion to your right to Curry Pond. A three-foot earthen dam once contained the pond, but now water drains through a cut in the dam. What remains is a stump-filled marsh. Double back to the Osborn Loop and continue descending. Twenty-five minutes from Curry Pond, the trail follows an old stone wall and ascends. Deer are prevalent in this col. After passing through the col, you reach the four-way intersection with the red-blazed Sugarloaf South trails. Turn left and descend, retracing your path. Near the bottom, watch for the easy-to-miss sharp right turn.

7

Taurus

Distance: 4.5 miles

Time: 3–4 hours

Vertical rise: 1,400 feet

Maps: USGS 7½' West Point; NY–NJTC East Hudson Trails, #2

Storm King from Taurus

A loop on Taurus, or Bull Hill as the topographic map has it, has been a favorite with hikers for years. Problems with private land on the southeast side of the mountain and the dangers of walking along NY 9D are the reasons for the present loop. The current version incorporates a portion of the historical loop and a portion of New York–New Jersey Trail Conference (NY–NJTC) trails, and keeps you far from private lands.

While this circuit may be walked clockwise or counterclockwise, if you walk a clockwise course, you face the best views throughout the descent. On a hot day, you may wish to reverse the course so you return through the deep valley of Breakneck Brook where you can splash in the cool water; another alternative is to climb through the valley in the later afternoon, enjoy a picnic supper on top, and descend in the cool early evening facing the sunset.

Park near the white-blazed Washburn trailhead, 0.8 mile north of the intersection of NY 9D and NY 301 in Cold Spring. Carefully walk 0.1 mile north along NY 9D to a pair of stone pillars with a metal gate between. Pass through the gate and follow what was the driveway of the Cornish Estate to the left and up. This road is not marked as a trail. After a quarter hour, 0.5 mile from the start, you come upon the stone remains of the Cornish Estate mansion to your left. The property, once owned by the chairman of National Lead, burned in the fall of 1956. Just a few hundred feet farther along are the remains of the greenhouse. Just before the greenhouse is a road circling back to the left you can follow to easily approach the ruins of the mansion and avoid the thick overgrowth surrounding much of it. Do take time explore the ruins of pools, ponds, empoundments, buildings, and bridges in this area. When you have finished exploring you can join the red-marked Brook Trail with a brief descent from the north side of the mansion via a short road that leads to Breakneck Brook. The Brook Trail comes directly up from NY 9D but using the beginning as part of this loop would have required you to walk along NY 9D. Turn right and head up along the red-marked trail, passing some beautiful waterfalls. (You could instead return from the mansion site to the driveway you started on and continue up on it for another 0.5 mile until it joins the red-marked Brook Trail, but then you miss the waterfalls.)

The red-marked trail thrusts up beside the stream. Shortly, the trail forks right, on a narrower roadway that curves around the head of the draw. All along you see immense stone retaining walls and small impoundments in a tributary of the brook. The trail approaches a waterfall, then joins a road that comes in from the north side of the draw. Just beyond, the trail crosses the aqueduct, which heads south to the tunnel through the mountain.

The trail is now close to Breakneck Brook and a bit less steep. Two more faint old roadways join your route; near the second, the red-marked trail bridges the brook. This point is 540 feet above the trailhead; it is 1.5 miles and just over 45 minutes from it. Old stone fences begin to line the roadway 150 yards beyond where the red-marked trail ends at an intersection with the blue-marked Notch Trail. If you detour straight ahead for 5 minutes, you will reach a small pond that is within the park boundary.

The route to Taurus forks right on the blue-marked trail at this intersection and almost immediately crosses another tributary of the brook. The trail wanders beside a shallow gorge, through young stands that mark fields returning to forest. You turn sharply left, pick up another draw, and continue climbing at a moderate rate. A maze of woods roads intersects your marked route. There are several abrupt turns. The first, a jog to the right, is about 20 minutes from the fork, and it is well marked in this direction but could be a difficult turn if the route were reversed. The trail climbs steeply along an old road that now leads through stands of laurel.

Less than 40 minutes from the fork, after another mile and 600 feet of climbing, the blue-marked trail reaches a four-way intersection at another old roadway. This roadway was built to serve a never-constructed hotel on Taurus's summit. Left is the blue-marked route to Nelsonville. To the right the road climbs in sweeping loops toward Taurus's summit. Straight ahead the narrow white-marked trail heads more directly toward that summit.

You can go either way, for the trail and road intersect three more times before they mate for the final approach to the summit. In the last segment the

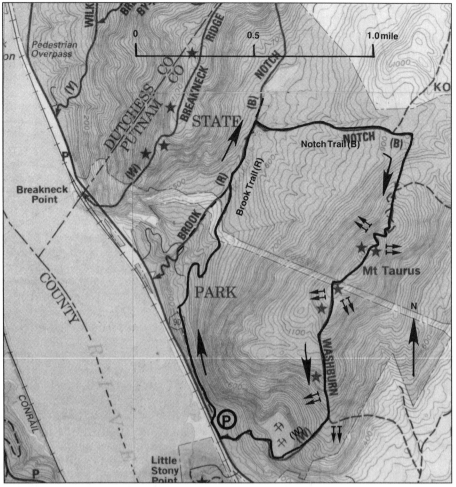

road may be preferable, for as it sweeps north you have the first view, this one to the north and the cut to the east of Beacon. Just beyond, a rock outcrop, where the trail joins from the left, affords a view to the east.

The combined roadway and trail zigzag up; from a curve to the east you can enjoy a lovely view down the jagged face of Breakneck with the Newburgh–Beacon Bridge visible through a cut in that ridgeline. You can see the pond on Breakneck Brook as well as private Lake Surprise, which is farther upstream. The next curve east brings a view expanded to include the northern slopes of Storm King. One hundred feet from this lookout watch for a small path to the left that leads to a sheltered overlook facing southeast. The aqueduct emerges from its mountain tunnel directly below you. The view is right down the Hudson, past the Hook with the Tappan Zee Bridge in the distance. You see Constitution Island and its marshes with West Point across the river, framing the southern narrows of the Hudson Highlands. Above the Highlands you see the distant skyline of New York City. Just north of Constitution Island on the banks of Foundry Brook stood the famous West Point Foundry, referred to in the Iron Mine Walk of Harriman State Park (hike 3) and the walk through Fahnestock (hike 13). The foundry was incorporated in 1818 and produced more than 3,000 cannons from iron mined in nearby hills. The Foundry Museum of the Putnam County Historical Society, just south of NY 301 on NY 9D, has a fascinating collection of local history.

The trail climbs a bit more to the summit where the roadway ends in a circle. The trail, now a narrow footpath, descends a cleft and emerges on open rock. Here you feel as if you are hanging right over the Hudson. The Bear Mountain Bridge, as well as the expanse of Dunderberg and the cliff face of the Timp, are visible to the south. Even with stops for the views, this point at nearly 3 miles is no more than 2 hours from the start. The descent, 1.6 miles, will take little more than an hour, and the views are not over yet.

Arrows point you steeply off this rock outcrop. In just a few minutes, the trail leads beside a south-facing viewpoint that also includes Storm King to the west. As you leave this overlook, immediately turn off the trail to the right (north), where the vista includes not only West Point and Storm King but the peaks of Black Rock Forest, Schunemunk, and the entire Shawangunk range with its white cliffs.

Beyond this point the trail plunges down through the woods, although there are still more viewpoints. The next outlook, after another 10-minute descent and a short climb out of a cleft, is at a much lower outcrop facing Storm King. Imagine the days when the foundry was producing the Parrot guns and testing those rifled cannons by loading them to full capacity and aiming them at the rocky front of Storm King across the river. The bursting shells threw up enormous masses of earth, and the impressions were visible for years.

The trail is rough and rubble-strewn with poor footing for the next 0.5 mile. You zigzag steeply down, reaching another point overlooking Storm King. Then you emerge on the rim of the old rock quarry—an enormous pit on Taurus's lower flanks. The trail circles steeply, following the descending south rim of the quarry. It intersects the road leading into the quarry—turn back to admire the constructed cliffs of the quarry—and briefly follows the roadway down before it turns north from the road into a field that is overshadowed by the sheer cliffs of Storm King. Use care to avoid the poison ivy here. Still zigzagging down steeply, the trail reaches another field with a trail register, then turns from it to emerge on the highway.

8

Breakneck Ridge and Sugarloaf Mountain

Distance: 5.5 miles

Time: 4½ hours

Vertical rise: 1,450 feet

Maps: USGS 7½' West Point; NY–NJTC East Hudson Trails, #2

Storm King from Breakneck

"Eastward a high chain of mountains whose sides were covered with woods up to no more than half of their height. The summits, however, were quite barren; for I suppose nothing would grow there on account of the great degree of heat, dryness, and the violence of the wind to which that part was exposed." Thus, the Swedish botanist, Peter Kalm, observed the Hudson Highlands on the east side of the river in 1749. One highlight of his trip was his discovery and the first botanical description of the American mountain laurel, *Kalmia latifolia,* the shrub that grows on every slope from the Ramapos to the Shawangunks and whose blooms make walking here and everywhere in southern New York in late May and early June so special.

For a time Breakneck was known as Turk's Face. According to the British traveler John Maude, writing in 1800, "The profile of the Face Mountain so strongly resembles the profile of the human face, that I had for some time my doubts whether art had not assisted in improving the likeness. I have seen other blockheads which did not possess so sensible a countenance." According to Benson Lossing, a blast from a quarry on the side of the mountain dislodged the head, complete with a "thick curly beard upon the chin," making it look like a Turk. Sometime after the head disappeared, a runaway bull was rumored to have climbed the mountain and fallen to its death when pursued, giving rise to the name Breakneck. In the first few hundred feet of scrambling up Breakneck's serrated face, you may wonder if the name refers to crazy hikers.

Judging by the cars that line NY 9D two miles north of Cold Spring, near the underpass and trailhead below Breakneck Ridge's cliffs and jagged skyline, it is easy to believe that the mountain is everyone's favorite in the Hudson Highlands. On occasion you will find crowds on the region's steepest scramble, but the higher you go, the fewer climbers you will meet, and if you follow the described loop, you will enjoy not only the fabulous climb, but you also will get away to more remote and especially delightful vantages.

Park at the roadside just north of the underpass, and begin this loop walk on the west side of the road where you will find the white-blazed Breakneck Ridge Trail by climbing south along the road and over the overpass. The well-worn route is a wild scramble of nearly 1,000 feet in 0.4 mile; it is comparable to a climb up the Empire State Building, with views at every level. "Scramble" to me means using your hands, and you will appreciate an old pair of gloves to protect them from the rough and most resistant of the highland rocks, the Precambrian magma intrusion that crests Breakneck Ridge.

In 30 minutes you reach a first knob, the destination of most climbers. Your route is to the right along the cliff top. The trail has been designed to take advantage of the wildest scrambles, and you will note that below the first knob and twice on the way to the second, white arrows and a sign painted "alt." direct you to alternate easier and safer routes.

The first 1.5 miles of the trip is a series of knobs, false summits on the way to the 1,200-foot crest. The second knob reveals a third knob as well as views north to the cone of Sugarloaf. You continue traversing the rock face just above the cliff with the third knob looming above you. This third knob in the sequence is more deceptive than the rest, for, upon reaching it, you discover that the trail dips into a small valley before rising to a fourth knob. This hawk's perch is followed by a deep, wooded ravine, above which the fifth knob looms. Here you have a fine view to the northwest.

Another rise brings you to the west face of the fifth knob, overlooking Bannerman's Island, Sugarloaf, and the Newburgh–Beacon Bridge with the Shawangunks beyond and the Catskills outlining the distant horizon. It takes a pretty steady climb of an hour and a quarter to reach this point. Breakneck continues north as a narrow ridge with the trail winding from side to side to take advantage of the overlooks. Its warty surface continues to offer a series of knobs to climb. A sixth distinct knob is open to the east with views of the heavily wooded Lake Surprise Valley. A walk along the thin ridge separates this vantage from the seventh knob, where the trail first brings you to an overlook to the east and then across the height of land to a western vantage. A gentle descent and an equally short rise bring you to a well-marked fork where the red-marked trail heads west toward Sugarloaf.

This red-marked trail, reached at 1.5 miles after one and a half hours, would provide a shorter alternate loop. It descends 0.6 mile, passing one good overlook, to join the last 0.5 mile of the yellow-marked trail you will follow to complete the longer loop outlined. So, continue straight ahead. A small rise opens to a view of the eastern slope of Sugarloaf. Beyond, the trail dips into a deep valley that lies beneath the eighth knob. As you head steeply down into the valley, a blue-marked trail from Lake Surprise Valley comes in from the right, and blue markers continue with the white. Even the valley has its ups and downs, and a final rubble-filled draw precedes a steep climb to a spot on the knob that looks southwest to Black Rock Forest. A second vantage overlooks Lake Surprise. It takes about a half hour to reach this knob from the red-marked trail intersection. As you start down its northern flank, you view a wooded knob ahead. This one you will not climb, for you will look for an abandoned roadway in the valley between.

The trail continues on the east side of the ridge, descending into the less-exposed region of taller trees. At 2.5 miles, 15 minutes from the last summit, the trail, marked mostly with blue, intersects a roadway. The route right is unmarked while the trail follows the road left for 100 yards and forks right again along the ridge. At this point stay on the unmarked road, which heads generally west-southwest. Don't be too mesmerized by the delights of this woodland road, for you will have to find and follow an unmarked path that leads left away from it. To discover this fork, mark the following clues. If you follow the road down for a 10-minute walk, you will discover an often-waterless brook and

a valley on your right. An equal distance beyond, at about 0.6 mile after leaving the red-marked trail, you cross over the valley to follow the stream on its right bank. After walking along the right bank for 300 yards, you should notice a left fork and a narrow trail heading steeply down to the stream. Take it, for the continuation of the road you have been following leads to private lands.

Across the stream another roadway leads up and to the left, passing a field across which lies Sugarloaf. About 200 yards beyond the stream, the woods road angles sharply right and downhill, following the course of the stream. At this point, a second, less-distinct road goes straight ahead and quickly becomes a roadway choked to a narrow path with grasses and marked infrequently with yellow. Take this route to the western edge of the field beyond a chimney of a long-gone farmhouse and around to the woods beyond where you climb toward the south. One hundred yards up the slope the yellow-marked trail turns right, continuing uphill around the northern flank of the mountain. Along the way you have through-the-trees views of Beacon before reaching an overlook with a broad expanse of the Hudson between you and the gradual western slopes that lead up to the high peaks of the Catskills. The 1.5-mile walk from the ridge north of Breakneck down the valley and up to Sugarloaf's first outlook should take less than an hour.

The yellow-marked trail, known as the Wilkinson Memorial Trail, winds south across Sugarloaf's summit to a second overlook, this one more southerly. The southeast face is a little less steep than the cone's western flanks, but the route the yellow-marked

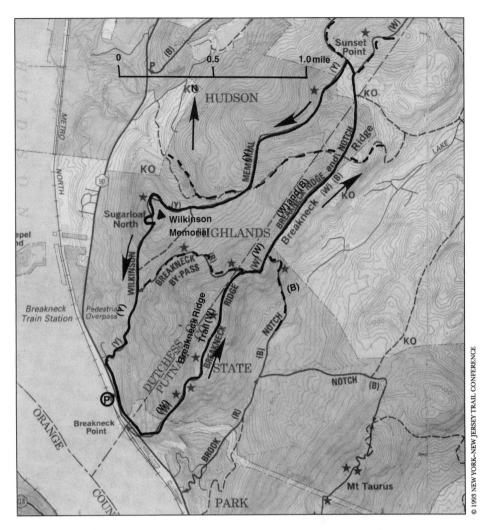

Wilkinson Memorial Trail takes you on is still quite precipitous. As the trail levels out beside a hemlock-filled valley, you turn left into that valley and up to a roadway. Here the trail turns right along the roadway and quickly reaches a giant oak with three red blazes, which indicates the western end of the red-marked trail.

The yellow-marked trail follows the roadway down for the most part, cross-ing a small ravine, and yielding but one view, a glimpse across a ravine toward the top of Storm King. The route is through a field, past a huge stone foundation, and finally out to the highway. The descent from Sugarloaf requires but 20 minutes for the 800-foot, nearly mile-long drop. You reach the highway, NY 9D, 0.3 mile north of the trailhead from which you started.

9

Storm King

Distance: 7 miles

Time: 5½ hours

Vertical rise: 1,200 feet

Maps: USGS 7½' Cornwall; USGS 7½' West Point

A view of the Hudson River from Storm King

"The Montaynes look as if some Metall or Minerall were in them. For the trees that grow on them were all blasted, and some of them barren with few or no trees on them." Thus did Robert Juet describe his view of the Hudson Highlands in September 1609 after his first trip up the Hudson in Henry Hudson's boat, anchored in what is now Newburgh Bay. The centuries have done little to alter the view.

The noble ring of hills through which the Hudson flows south of Newburgh is as impressive as any range in the state. Storm King guards the west bank, and Beacon, giving way to Breakneck Ridge and Taurus on the south, guards the eastern shores. They are all mountains you will climb again and again.

Storm King and Butter Hill form a semicircular crest that Benson Lossing believed the Dutch skippers thought of as a huge lump of butter, hence the original name Boterberg. Nathaniel Parker Willis, who settled at Idlewild at the foot of Storm King in present-day Cornwall, wrote weekly letters to the *Home Journal* in the 1850s describing his bucolic surroundings. It was he who was able to change part of the mountain's name to the more romantic Storm King.

There are several ways to savor the walk on Storm King and Butter Hill. Sometimes the opportunity to get away for a short excursion makes the walk from US 9W across the vantages just west of Storm King's summit seem like a perfect outing. This is a round-trip walk of about 3 miles, with a climb of 350 feet, for a 3-hour excursion. The walk can be extended by a descent toward Cornwall and a visit to the Museum of the Hudson Highlands, with distance, time, and elevation as noted above.

Take US 9W as it climbs the hills north and west of West Point. There is a large parking turnout at the height of land on Butter Hill, just before the highway descends toward Cornwall. From the north of the turnout, and quite close to the highway, the Stillman Trail, with its unmarked trailhead, begins its ascent. Yellow blazes finally appear on the open rock crossings. The trail climbs the ridge near the road to a stone foundation, then winds into a stone-filled valley. A sharp right across the draw at the head of the valley heads sharply up to the first knob with a narrow view of the river.

Notice all along the trail the signs of an old burn that swept this hilltop. Somehow the laurels and many of the oaks survive. A gentle walk to the next knob on Butter Hill yields views of Cold Spring and the quarry north of it on the slopes of Taurus. A few more minutes of walking brings you to the height of land on Butter Hill with its survey markers. This spot, only 30 minutes from the start, has views of the summits of Breakneck Ridge and Beacon.

Good views north and west accompany you as you walk north, especially when the leaves are down, permitting the range from Schunemunk to the Shawangunks to stand out in front of

the distant blue hills of the Catskills. The walk on the northwestern flanks ends in a sharp right marked by yellow blazes as the trail reaches Storm King. The trail continues on the northern flanks of Storm King, with occasional view spots opening up en route. Stunted pines frame the vistas: the broad sweep of river, punctuated by Bannerman's (or Pollepel) Island, which lies 1,300 feet below your perch. This mysterious island has a strange tale. Jasper Dankers, a minister, recorded in 1680 that it was called Potlepels Eylant, Dutch for Potladle Island. General Clinton fortified it in 1777 along with Constitution Island to the south. In the 1850s Benson Lossing reported that it was home to a solitary house that looked like a wren's nest, inhabited by a fisherman with an insane wife who thought herself to be the Queen of England. Francis Bannerman bought the island to house his arsenal of secondhand military supplies, arms captured in the Spanish-American War. It was Bannerman who built the replica of a Scottish castle whose remains you see. He had a thriving military-supply business until the US government made it illegal for citizens to sell arms to foreign governments.

The trail continues, gradually descending, to a final opening overlooking the river east and southeast. It is delightful to picnic here and retrace your steps; but, time permitting, you can continue along the trail for the steep descent, a real scramble at first, to the west.

The trail drops 700 feet in 0.5 mile. About two-thirds of the way through the steepest drop, as the trail seems to level out, you will notice two unmarked paths coming in from your right. You may wish to experiment with one of them on your return. You

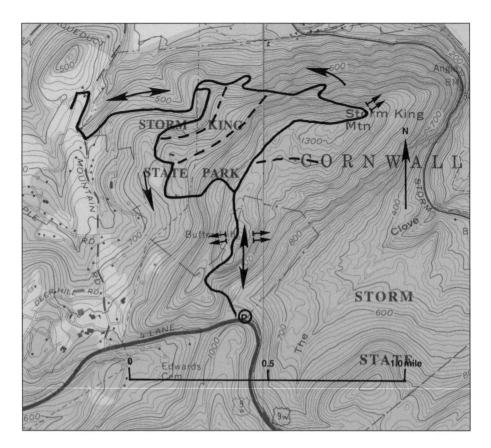

continue the zigzag route of the yellow-marked trail, coming out to a promontory with views up toward Beacon. After a distance of 100 feet, the trail reaches and follows a dirt roadway to Mountain Road. Turn right, then left to reach the Museum of the Hudson Highlands, open Monday through Thursday and weekend afternoons. The museum houses a natural-history collection highlighted by an assemblage of owls and snakes that live in these mountains but are rarely seen. If you have opted for the longer trek, you can enjoy a picnic beside a stream at the rear of the museum.

On your return, stay on the abandoned roadway. It once led to a stone building constructed by Italian stone masons before World War I. The ruins lie at the end of the roadway that zigzags up the mountain. It must have been a handsome place, if the stonework along the road is any indication. Note the beautiful arch that carries the road over a small stream just before the Stillman Trail forks left. And notice too the huge grapevines curled around a nearby tree like a serpent in the Garden of Eden.

The road forks after a 20-minute walk; the foundations lie to the left. Walking through them to a stone stairway in a wall at the far end, you find the start of an unmarked path that contours around the slopes to intersect the Stillman Trail again. From this point it is a stiff 20-minute climb to the crest of Storm King, where you can retrace your steps to the parking turnout.

10

Black Rock Forest– Southern Ledges

Distance: 7 miles	
Time: 5 hours	
Vertical rise: 850 feet	
Map: USGS 7½' Cornwall	

The hiking trails in Black Rock Forest are among the region's least used. They wind around and over a dozen peaks with elevations over 1,400 feet. But these peaks rise generally less than 400 feet from the high plateau that is a westward continuation of the Storm King intrusion of the Hudson Highlands. That plateau drops precipitously to the west and north, with the dark summit of Black Rock Mountain, namesake of the forest, standing out above the valley near Cornwall.

In 1949 the 3,600-acre forest was given to Harvard University for research by Dr. Ernest Stillman. A consortium of New York State colleges has recently acquired Black Rock Forest from Harvard (minus its endowment). Silvicultural research and public access will continue as before. A feature of any walk in the forest is the sight of distinctive plots of native trees, each with differing timber-management techniques. All but one of the half-dozen ponds are parts of water systems for nearby towns, so laws prohibit use of them in any way. Dirt roads connect the different plots and are used by the forest's managers, but public vehicular traffic is not permitted. The Black Rock Game Club has sole permission to hunt the numerous deer that populate the forest, so hiking during deer season is prohibited. As in all the Hudson Highlands, fire is a problem, so there are prohibitions against fires in any form.

There are two eastern entrances to Black Rock Forest from US 9W and one entrance from Mine Road on the west. This hike will start at an eastern trailhead and wind along the southern ledges that border on US Military Academy posted lands. Both hikes in this area combine roads with marked trails.

Drive north on US 9W past an entrance to West Point and over the shoulder of Storm King, and take the first right turn onto Mountain Road. Immediately turn right again, under the highway and onto a narrow road that leads southwest to the parking area at the forest boundary. From this point it is a 0.5-mile walk along the continuing roadway to Upper Reservoir. There is also a trail leading right from the parking area that winds through Black Rock Hollow to intersect the road just west of Upper Reservoir. (If you continue north on US 9W for 0.7 mile beyond Mountain Road, a right turn will take you to the park's headquarters, where maps are available. Drive southeast from the headquarters on Hulse Road under US 9W to the second parking area and an alternate beginning for this loop using the blue-marked Reservoir Trail.)

From either the end of the blue-marked Reservoir Trail or the roadway, walk west from the reservoir on White Oak Road for 5 minutes, then turn south on the yellow-marked Stillman Trail, one of the two principal trails that traverse the forest. Follow this route up Misery Hill. The short, 20-minute climb seems steeper than its 300-foot rise above the reservoir, but it yields views of Black Rock Mountain and Aleck Meadow Reservoir to the west. An equally steep descent follows, through rugged and rock-strewn terrain. The trail is composed of the latter. As the yellow-marked trail levels out, you see on the left the three white blazes of the Scenic Trail. Take the left on the white-blazed trail, and in 100 feet or so you pass through a second intersection. Here, at 0.6 mile, you meet the blue-marked Swamp Trail, but you continue straight ahead on the white-marked Scenic Trail.

The Scenic Trail begins another rough climb up the Hill of Pines. You approach an opening with a view below the summit. Double white markers and a cairn direct you up and left to the summit with its view south-south-west over lakes and the fire-tower summit. The white-marked trail leads down through a narrow rock cleft to an open knob with views all around. Notice how flat and equal in height the summits of all the visible mountains seem.

The white-marked trail leads sharply right, down to a draw, then briefly up before the final descent to a dirt road, 1 mile from the start. Turn right on the road and then immediately left, essentially crossing it to begin a climb again. You quickly attain a ridge, then drop sharply down about 50 feet to walk on a relatively level high ledge near the southern boundary of the park. You can see one of the day's destinations, Spy Rock, ahead over ponds and lower hills. As you continue on the ledges, you look ahead to Eagle Cliff, also one of your destinations.

A steep descent follows, circling around and switchbacking down again near the park boundary. At 1.9 miles, a double white marker alerts you to a left turn along Bog Meadow Road. In 0.25 mile a yellow-marked trail forks right from your white-marked route toward Arthurs Pond and the fire tower, but you continue on the road, passing a pit privy at an intersection 2.5 miles and about 2¼ hours into the walk.

Just past the privy, jog right then left on the road, then back to a white-marked trail. After 5 minutes of following this trail, begin to watch carefully for a cairn—it will alert you to an unmarked path on the right that leads 200 yards to a rock outcrop on Spy Rock. Here the Hudson Valley appears incongruously on your left as it bends into the Hudson Highlands. The view beyond the valley is toward the Shawangunks, with the Catskills beyond. South Beacon and Breakneck

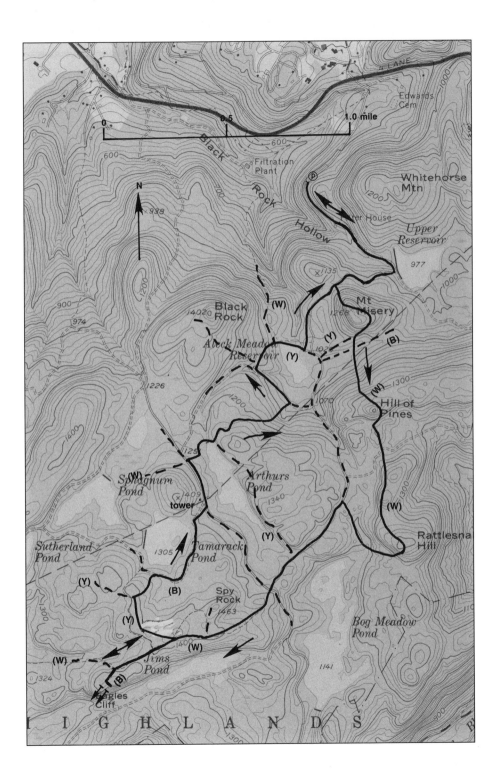

Tamarack Pond in Black Rock Forest

Your Invitation To Join The NY-NJ TRAIL CONFERENCE
GPO Box 2250 ○ NY NY 10116

Hikers and friends who wish to support the efforts of the Conference to maintain and protect 1,300 miles of marked foot trails in the NY/NJ area are invited to join as members. Dues include a subscription to our bi-monthly, The *Trail Walker*, 20-25% discounts on our publications (& 10% discounts at 21 local outdoor stores), and use of our extensive Library ...*and, above all, the opportunity to protect the hiking trails and to get involved!*

Name(s)_____

Address_____

City_____State_____ Zip_____

Phone(s) Day _____/_____ Eve _____/_____

E-mail?_____ (Please PRINT clearly)

Check ✓...	Individual	Joint/Family	
Regular	☐ $18	☐ $23	
Sponsor	☐ $35	☐ $40	
Benefactor	☐ $75	☐ $80	
Student	☐ $12⁵⁰	☐ $17⁵⁰	**1997 Rates**
Senior	☐ $12⁵⁰	☐ $17⁵⁰	
Ltd. Income	☐ $12⁵⁰	☐ $17⁵⁰	
Life	☐ $300	☐ $475 (2 adults)	

Do you belong to a hiking or outdoor club(s)? If yes, please list:

_____

☐ Mailing: Check box to left if you do **_not_** want your name exchanged with others (hiking clubs, etc.)

☐ *Check Here for the NEW MEMBER SPECIAL*: Join before 12/31/98 and take $2 off any of the above dues rates.

Hiking Maps & Guides...

...By the People Who Maintain the Trails...

Map Sets

HARRIMAN-BEAR MOUNTAIN TRAILS / 2 maps
EAST HUDSON TRAILS / 3 maps
WEST HUDSON TRAILS / 2 maps
CATSKILL TRAILS / 5 maps
SHAWANGUNK TRAILS / 4 maps
NORTH JERSEY TRAILS / 2 maps
SOUTH TACONIC TRAILS / 1 map
NORTH KITTATINNY TRAILS / 2 maps
SOUTH KITTATINNY TRAILS / 2 maps
PYRAMID MOUNTAIN TRAILS / 1 map
HUDSON PALISADES TRAILS / 2 maps
HIGH MOUNTAIN TRAILS / 1 map

Books & Guides

THE NEW YORK WALK BOOK
APPALACHIAN TRAIL GUIDE, NY/NJ
CIRCUIT HIKES IN NORTHERN NJ
GUIDE TO THE LONG PATH, NY/NJ
HEALTH HINTS FOR HIKERS
50 HIKES IN NEW JERSEY
50 HIKES IN THE HUDSON VALLEY
IRON MINE TRAILS: NJ/NY HIGHLANDS
BEST HIKES WITH CHILDREN: NJ
BEST HIKES W/CHILDREN: HUDSON-CATSKILL
HIGH PEAKS OF THE NORTHEAST (NY/VT/NH/ME)
HIKING THE CATSKILLS
HIKING THE DELAWARE WATER GAP NRA
HARRIMAN TRAILS: A GUIDE & HISTORY

Full catalog & order form included with membership or on request.
See address on reverse or call us anytime at 212/685-9699.
E-mail info requests: nynjtc@aol.com. Include postal address for reply.

Ridge define the horizon on your right. At 1,461 feet this is the highest point in the western Hudson Highlands.

As you return to the ledge trail and continue quickly along it, watch carefully. In another 5 minutes, at about 200 yards, you should see three yellow blazes on a rock on the right side of the trail. Mark it well, for you will retrace your steps to this spot after a visit to Eagle Cliff. Next, on the white-marked trail, you will see, on your left, a yellow-marked trail to Jims Pond. Very shortly beyond, three blue markers direct you left to the knob of Eagle Cliff, 1,443 feet high, from which you can see the skyline of New York City beyond Anthony's Nose, Bear Mountain, Dunderberg, and the Timp. It takes less than 3 hours to reach this spot, 3.6 miles from the beginning, which makes it ideal for a lunch break.

Return to the white-marked Scenic Trail, and retrace your steps to the three yellow blazes on the rock. A left turn puts you on a narrow path over a rise. A gentle descent brings you in 0.2 mile to an intersection, where the yellow-marked trail makes a sharp left turn. You should turn right onto a blue-marked trail, which leads in 100 yards to Chatfield Road. Turn right on it past Tamarack Pond, which you partly circle.

The next milestone on the road, near the intersection of Tamarack and Continental roads, just over 1 mile from Eagle Cliff, is an old stone building with a beehive oven. It is Chatfield House, built in 1834. The house was gutted by fire in 1908 and restored in 1932 by Dr. Stillman. The lands nearby were once pastures and orchard, and Tamarack Pond, originally called Orchard Pond, was used as a cranberry bog.

Turn left on Continental Road and pass by Chatfield House. After 0.2 mile turn right on the white-blazed White Oak Trail, passing opposite the foot of Arthurs Pond. Pass by the yellow-marked trail on the right and continue on the white-marked trail left. This route takes you to a road beside Aleck Meadow Reservoir. At this point you could go right and back to the road and quickly end the trip, but instead turn left toward Black Rock Mountain. One hundred feet past a stream, observe a yellow-marked trail making a close pass by the road. Head right on the yellow-marked trail, which shortly meets a white-marked trail. Continue on the yellow-marked trail to the right turn, and cross the reservoir's dam. Turn left on the road below the dam, which takes you in 0.6 mile back to the parking area.

11

Black Rock Forest–Northern Loop

Distance: 5.5 miles

Time: 3½ hours

Vertical rise: 600 feet

Map: USGS 7½' Cornwall

There is a small trailhead for the trails in Black Rock Forest on the northwestern side of the forest that is ideal for this loop hike. Drive north on US 9W to Angola Road near Central Valley. Head southwest on Angola Road for 1.6 miles, then turn left on Mine Hill Road and go 0.9 mile to the turnout. The Rich Mine in this vicinity was described in 1837 by Lewis C. Beck, a professor of chemistry at Rutgers. It was part of the Monroe Iron Works, owned by Hudson McFarlan, which produced quantities of nails and hoop iron dating back to 1808.

The trail begins opposite the uphill end of the turnout and is marked by three yellow diamonds. The faint beginning leads sharply uphill on a traverse that immediately offers views

Sutherland Pond in Black Rock Forest

of Schunemunk and the Catskills. The trail is carefully marked, with double diamonds indicating switchbacks.

After a 10-minute climb, a triple marker alerts you to an intersection; the yellow-diamond-marked trail that forks right will be your return route. Take the left fork, marked with yellow circles, to a series of overlooks on open rock ledges. You continue on the ridge on high ground at the border of deeper forests, then descend slightly into them. Cross a small stream by hopping rocks, and walk through a wet area with trout lilies and violets. Beyond, a small rise leads to Hall Road, 1 mile from the start, but just before you reach it, the yellow-marked trail makes a sharp left. It is easy to miss the turn, but if you do, a left turn on the road will do, for the yellow-marked trail reaches the road again in less than 200 yards. Continue on the roadway, which bears yellow markers, for 75 yards to a point where the road angles left and the yellow-marked trail takes off right, uphill.

Follow the trail as it traverses the mountain through a tall oak stand, with glimpses of the roadway below and left. Your route parallels the road somewhat, then climbs, crosses a bridge near a spring, and rejoins the road, which you follow for 200 feet to a road barrier. Continental and Hulse roads intersect here, and the yellow-marked Stillman Trail goes through the intersection. Make a left turn on the road across a bridge for 150 feet to a right fork. The spot is confusing! Immediately on leaving the road at this right fork, the yellow-marked trail makes a sharp left turn through a tall stand of laurel. A gentle climb continues on the right side of high ground, contouring the hill until you see a little rocky knob ahead through the trees—the summit of Black Rock at 1,402 feet and 2 miles from the start. You will want to pause here to enjoy the vista upriver. Yellow-painted footprints on the rock lead you to an opening in which Storm King is framed by Taurus and Beacon.

The continuing yellow-marked route from the summit is most eroded, attesting to the popularity of this section, in contrast to the faint trails you walk in the rest of the forest. You descend to White Oak Road in 10 minutes, and turn right on it as it heads up the outlet of Arthurs Pond. A lovely swampy vista greets you as you cross a bridge, then head into a plantation of pines. A giant white oak marks the triangle intersection, where you turn left, then in 100 feet you turn right onto the white-marked White Oak Trail into a spruce plantation.

Stay on the white-marked trail to pursue a varied nature exploration. This route leads you through a wet sphagnum area with typical bog plants. A large, grassy field off to your right is full of frog and bird sounds. The white-marked trail leads you to and along a small dam beside the very pretty impoundment of the Cornwall water system and Sphagnum Pond.

Beyond the pond the trail crosses Hulse Road. A left on the road provides a pretty walk as it stays close to the shore of Sphagnum Pond. Stay straight ahead at the next road fork just beyond the pond. In a short distance, before the next pond, the road rises and curves. Watch for white blazes that direct you right and steeply uphill toward Split Rock. You can head up slope for a walk along the open escarpment on top of Split Rock or continue on the road.

The road is close to the shore of Sutherland Pond; watch as it pulls away from the road. A guide board with map marks a small path that heads for the shore. The path leads to a rock ledge and a lovely picnic spot. Sutherland is the only pond in Black Rock Forest where you can swim— the others are reservoirs for nearby towns. By the route outlined this spot is 1.8 miles from the summit of Black Rock Mountain.

The jumble of rocks fallen from the escarpment below Split Rock should still intrigue you, so for a second route up it, continue on the road for 0.2 mile to a fork and turn right on Hall Road. It is gated near the intersection; 75 feet beyond the gate a narrow blue-marked trail forks right, uphill, through laurel stands along the crest of the ridge. Within 5 minutes, the trail splits. The way right is the other end of the white-marked Split Rock Trail; it soon leads to the open rock of the crest, past several vantage spots with views of Sutherland Pond and Black Rock tower. A yellow diamond beside one outcrop marks the place to turn left for 100 feet to intersect again the blue-marked trail, near its intersection with the yellow-marked Stillman Trail, which comes in from the right.

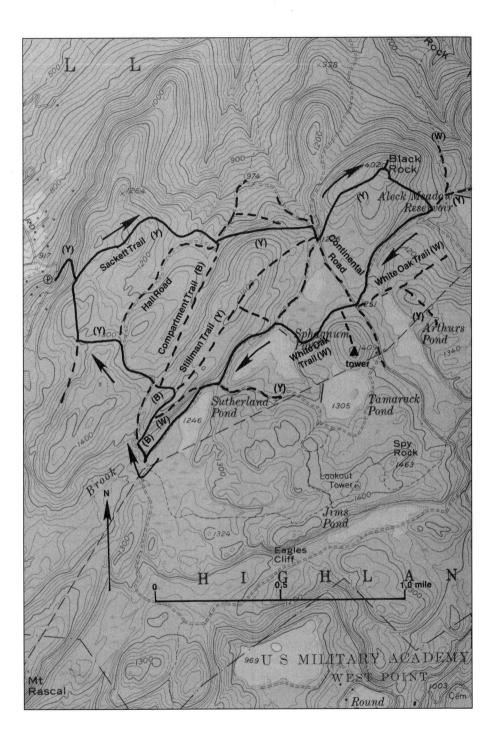

From this apt-to-be-confusing intersection, you want the combined blue-and-yellow-marked trail for the walk downhill (west) to another peculiar intersection. Turn left, 50 feet to Hall Road. Turn right on Hall Road for a 10-minute walk to a left fork where the yellow blazes of the Stillman Trail direct you on a narrow trail. In 5 minutes this trail, marked with yellow squares, reaches a three-way intersection. Go right, now on the Sackett Trail (yellow circles), and traverse the top of the ridgeline heading north, passing a western overlook. In 8 minutes the trail forks. You turn left, following yellow diamonds, for the sharp zigzag downhill to your car.

12

Schunemunk

Distance: 7 miles

Time: 5 hours

Vertical rise: 1,360 feet

Map: USGS 7½' Cornwall

The megaliths on Schunemunk

Schunemunk sits in solitary splendor, its long, gently rounded form isolated from the Hudson Highlands and the Shawangunks as completely as its rocks are separated by ages from their surroundings. Its complexly deformed sedimentary rocks date from the Silurian and Devonian periods, while all around are pre-Silurian formations. The light grayish and pinkish sandstones, shales, and conglomerates that crown its summit were slowly deposited from a landmass to the east. The polished quartz pebbles embedded in the pink and lavender sands could only have been formed by water washing them from the heights of a mountain range. These deposits, the Schunemunk conglomerates, accumulated in a shallow sea. The uplift of the Acadian Orogeny warped and raised this new landmass, so today the conglomerates sit like colored icing on the sandwich of deposits beneath. In addition, the uplift pressed against the long sides of the formation, pushing them up and leaving a deep cleft valley between.

A loop walk from the north will highlight the deep cleft that creases the mountain as well as take you to vantages on both the long eastern and western faces. To reach the trailhead, drive north on NY 32 from Central Valley to Mountainville and a sign that reads Black Rock Game Club. Turn immediately left onto Taylor Road, which crosses over the thruway. On the far side of the crossing, park at a small turnout on the north side of the road. A sign here notes the easement given by Star Manufacturing Company for hikers to park and walk across the private lands at the foot of the mountain to gain access to its public heights. Hikers are warned that they enter these lands at their own risk, and they are cautioned that any use other than hiking is a trespass. Following the example of my companion on this walk, who said that every time he climbed Schunemunk he offered a silent thanks to the owners who have made this access possible, you can show your appreciation by your respect for this property—observe the regulations that prohibit camping, fires, destruction of flora, and littering.

To make a counterclockwise loop, walk north along the road, noting the yellow blazes on telephone poles that denote the Jessup Trail. In just short of 1 mile, past the Taylor home, turn left into the field at the gated entrance. Note that there is no parking here. You walk through the field toward the north end of Schunemunk, and at the edge of the woods turn right onto a road that leads between posted lands. The yellow blazes, posted signs, and thick poison ivy will keep you from trespassing.

After 0.5 mile the roadway briefly follows Baby Brook, and about 100 yards beyond a small waterfall the yellow-marked trail forks right, away from the road and up to a railroad track, across that track, and into the woods again. The trail continues to climb beside an old stone wall through mountain laurel. If your walk is a spring one, wild oat, spring beauty, and trailing arbutus line the way. Farther along, you rejoin the brook where quartz crystals and conglomerates of rounded purple and green rocks brighten the streambed.

You climb about 700 feet in just over 1 mile to arrive at an intersection. Here, about an hour into the trip, the Western Ridge Trail, marked with blue dots on a white rectangle, forks right across Baby Brook to begin the climb of the western ridge. This scramble, over pinkish conglomerates, zigzags quickly up so that within a few minutes you can enjoy views back over Storm King and Black Rock Forest. As you climb higher, the panorama of Beacon and Newburgh Bay on the Hudson emerges. Near the top of the knifelike edge of the western ridge, views northwest to the Shawangunks and Catskills begin, and you have your first glimpse of the eastern ridge.

You pass a trail intersection, but many markings do not quite conform to previous guides. However, it is easy to follow the route along the ridge. There seems to be an intermix of the turquoise-blue of the Long Path and the white-with-red that should only denote the Barton Swamp Trail, which breaks off just after the intersection near Baby Brook to wind through the cleft. Stay on the ridge, in any case, and for about 45 minutes you can enjoy the openness of the walk, the views of the eastern ridge, and the occasional openings to the west. After nearly 2 miles along the ridge, blue markers, as well as the white-with-red, direct you left for a brief descent into the moist realm of the cleft, which you follow south briefly. The red-marked trail continues south, but you want a blue-marked

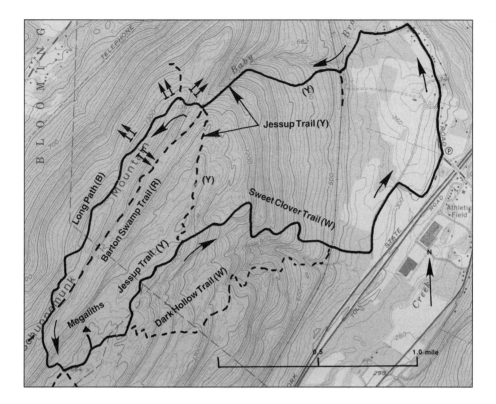

left fork, which shortly begins to climb the eastern ridge. This scramble will take you in 20 minutes to intersect again the Jessup Trail with its yellow markers. Here you turn left (north) to complete the loop. This ridge is broader and more heavily wooded, with fewer views, although from the peak at 1,664 feet you can see the northern end of Harriman State Park.

Just beyond the peak, yellow arrows on the rock slabs point you west to the megaliths, columns of pink and white conglomerate split off from the ridge. Besides the beauty of the area, your 3-hour walk to this point makes it a good lunch spot.

A 15-minute walk north along the trail brings you to the spot where the Dark Hollow Trail forks right, show-ing white-with-black marks. You can take it down if you choose, for it inter-sects the way to be described near the base of the mountain. In fact, you may wish to return to walk this alter-nate trail, as well as others along Schunemunk's crest. For now, con-tinue on the yellow-marked trail along the ridge with its pink and purple conglomerate slabs, a color fantasy of gray-green lichens on mauve. The gleaming white quartz pebbles shine like precious stones.

You will also find two places with views in this just-over-a-mile-long por-tion of trail, which you can cover in less than half an hour. The next inter-section brings you to a right fork onto the white-marked Sweet Clover Trail. Here a sign designates the distance south along the Jessup Trail but makes no mention of the nearly 2.5 miles along which you will follow this trail to your car.

The 40-minute descent is punctuated by tantalizing sounds of rushing water from the hemlock-concealed stream in Dark Hollow, but there are no views into it. The trail emerges beside the railroad tracks, 50 yards north of the cairn that marks the end of the Dark Hollow Trail. Go straight across the tracks and intersect a dirt road, back on private land. The road leads you along the eastern edge of a field, then across it and beside a farm to emerge on Taylor Road opposite your car.

13

Fahnestock State Park

Distance: 7.5 miles

Time: 4½ hours

Vertical rise: Less than 500 feet

Maps: USGS 7½' Oscawana Lake; NY–NJTC East Hudson Trails, #3

Fahnestock State Park, astride the Taconic Parkway in Putnam County, has several lovely lakes, a huge swimming pool, and picnic and boating facilities. It also has many miles of trails that will take you far from the crowds that regularly enjoy the park. Perhaps the best introduction to Fahnestock's quieter areas is a figure-eight walk that loops around its southern hills and ridges. The park, begun with the gift in 1929 of Dr. Ernest Fahnestock in memory of his brother, Clarence Fahnestock, and added to in the 1960s, now totals 6,200 acres.

West of the Taconic Parkway on NY 301 is one of the park's prettier lakes: Canopus. There are two parking areas near the lake, and opposite the western one, on the south side of the road, you will see an old roadway. Walk along it, and you will easily pick up the blue markers for the 3 Lakes Trail; the markers quickly lead you south into a deep forest of tremendously tall hemlocks. The trail begins by following an old roadway, with tailings of an abandoned mine on your right. The mines in this area, especially Sunk Mine, which you will walk near shortly, provided ore to the West Point Foundry at Cold Spring. This ore, with ore from the Greenwood Mines, was turned into the Parrot guns of the Union army artillery. The bed of the railroad built in 1862 to carry ore from the mines makes the handsome route you will follow at the end of this walk.

All the land about you was purchased by Adolphe Philipse in 1691 and established as the Philipse Grant six years later by King William III. The vast and rugged wilderness surrounding the interior range of hills could not be farmed and never had many settlers. Only the eight-mile-long vein of iron ore that follows the ridgeline of the hills south managed to attract settlers and then not until after 1800. Even the early miners regarded these dark woods as foreboding; actually, because they have not been logged for many years, the woods probably look now very much as they did then.

The first mine you pass, identifiable only by its tailing pit, belonged to Richard Hopper who opened it in 1820. The mine remained a small operation until the Civil War, when Philipse heirs sold the mineral rights to Paul S. Forbes, the builder of the railway. The mining survived until the panic of 1873, and the surrounding land was obtained by Dr. Clarence Fahnestock in 1915 after a series of intervening land sales.

Beyond the tailings you will see a lovely marsh with lots of birds. In less than 0.5 mile you reach the first fork; the roadway continues straight, you turn right past fields of hay-scented fern and down to a charming little brook. Again, tall hemlocks cool the small ravine. The trail crosses the brook and arcs back north along the stream almost to a meadow before it turns left, uphill. A zigzag in the trail brings you to a ridge in the impressive forest, certainly one of the more handsome second-growth forests in southern New York.

It will have taken no more than 35 minutes to walk the mile-plus distance to the intersection with the white-marked Appalachian Trail (AT). Cross the intersection and continue on the blue-marked 3 Lakes Trail, watching for Hidden Lake on your right. You may want to wander off the trail to examine this constructed lake, filled with stumps. With its dam breached, the lake has a weird, desolate appearance. At the south end of the lake, you will find a road that detours to the dam.

Continue on a ridge, and barely sense marshy John Allen Pond, again

on your right. Thirty minutes from the AT crossing, you cross the outlet of this second pond. At this point the trail may confuse you, for it forks right to rejoin the roadway, while other hikers have beaten a path straight ahead toward a marshy area. The road, which you will follow atop a causeway, reaches the outlet dam, from which you have your first good view of the pond.

Time has altered the features of the mines and ponds, but a nineteenth-century observer once wrote about a spot not far from here that was the destination of an 1887 picnic. The trip to Pine Swamp was described by E. M. Hopkins, one of the picnickers who spent a summer afternoon exploring the Sunk Mine, an enormous cleft "gently filled with green slimy looking water." All the accessible ore had been removed, and "one end of the cleft terminates at the surface of the sloap; for the other a lateral drift, whose mouth is partly concealed by water extends into the mountains . . . None now living can remember when it was in operation." Two picnickers entered the mine guided by dry birch-bark torches. Inside they discovered the canoe of one Levi Marshall, deceased, who had claimed once to have found a silver mine. Thinking they had discovered Marshall's lost silver mine, they walked deeper and deeper into the mine, until they found a pile of silver objects: teapots, plates, and other objects. Leading up from the cache was a ladder that led the picnickers into Marshall's cabin. The residents at the time were charged with burglary, putting an end to the rumors that silver could be mined with the iron in these hills.

After crossing the outlet of John Allen Pond on a bridge below the

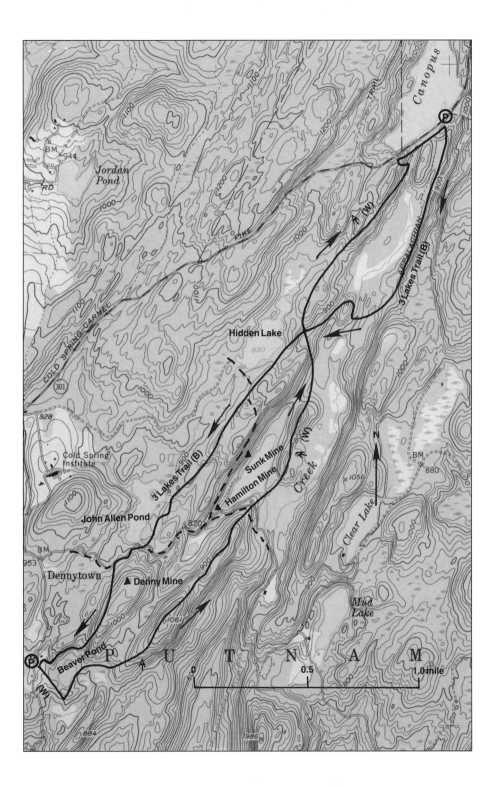

Ruins of a stone church on Dennytown Road

spillway, you climb to Sunk Mine Road, marked also with white blazes. Walk right 200 yards along the roadway until you see the double blue markers of your trail. A left turn onto the blue-marked trail takes you uphill to a ridge, then along the rock outcrops atop the ridge. The final outcrop with a through-the-trees view is a good spot for lunch after a 2-hour walk.

The trail follows a narrow trench downhill to another marsh. Triple blazes direct you to turn right and walk along its western side. Gorgeous maples shade the head of the marsh. At this point the trail enters the woods again, crosses a stream on a small bridge, and emerges in a field beside the ruins of a stone church. Behind a small stone building near the church is a water pump, a safe source on a hot day. Cross the field in front of the church, heading toward the woods and walking west away from Dennytown Road. Watch for a white blaze on a tree. This marks the point at which the AT enters the woods. Follow it for 0.3 mile as it rounds the south side of the marsh. Double white markers indicate a sharp left turn, which leads down through a locust grove and into the woods along the stone walls of an abandoned settlement whose first residents were the Dennys, miners of the southern portion of the vein.

You wind up and down ridges for about 1 mile until the trail meets and follows an abandoned roadway that heads steeply down into a hemlock gorge. At this point, after 1.5 miles on the AT, you cross the road again and head past stone foundations toward the outlet of John Allen Pond. You may want to pause and enjoy the waterfall in this small gem of a gorge, which you reach after a slow hour's walk from the lunch stop. In this area, you will cross a red-marked horse trail several times.

Next you climb to a blueberry knob with no real views and again head down into a hemlock ravine. Beyond lie apple trees and the small grassy meadows of an abandoned home site. The trail continues briefly beside a stream, then heads up a ridge to cross the blue-marked trail, 1.2 miles north of Sunk Mine Road.

About 0.3 mile beyond, the trail joins the bed of a narrow-gauge railway. Admire the wonderful rock work that carried the rails around a semicircular causeway at the head of a ravine. All too quickly the trail emerges on the roadway 100 yards west of the place you began.

14

Pawling Nature Reserve

Distance: 7.2 miles

Time: 4 hours

Vertical rise: 700 feet

Maps: USGS 7½' Pawling, NY–CT; USGS 7½' Dover Plains, NY–CT

The Appalachian Trail traverses Hammersly Ridge from southwest to northeast through the 1,000-acre Pawling Nature Reserve. Combining parts of the trail with a walk on Quaker Lake Road and some of the reserve's other trails makes not only for a fair hike but also gives a delightful chance to observe a variety of flora, from a deep hemlock gorge to wet meadows to swamps. You may see wild turkeys, deer, and an occasional beaver, coyote, or bobcat; but remember to take precautions against the bites of deer ticks when you are walking here.

Three trailheads for the reserve are on Quaker Lake Road, but only one, the main entrance, has good parking. To reach the trailheads, turn east off

Fern glen in Pawling Nature Reserve

NY 22 north of Pawling at Hurd Corners, and continue on County Route 68 for 1.5 miles to Baker Corner, where you turn left on Quaker Lake Road. A figure-eight walk can be started at the main entrance, 1.3 miles north on Quaker Lake Road, just beyond the private lands of Quaker Lake. Three small patches of the reserve line the road, but all the rest of the roadside is posted.

There is no parking at the southern red-marked trailhead near the height of land south of Quaker Lake; this spot is 0.4 mile from County Route 68. There is room for only one or two cars at the northern parking area for the yellow-marked trail at 2.7 miles. But Quaker Lake Road is a quiet, mostly dirt road, so with a 2.3-mile walk along it, you can make a figure-eight loop over the top of Hammersly Ridge. Alternatively, you can walk several shorter loops through the reserve.

A yellow-marked trail from the main entrance immediately enters the gorge with its charming waterfall and lush ferns. The trail continues briefly beside the stream and crosses it before mounting the rocky slopes of the ridge. In 5 minutes you reach the red-marked trail, which forks right. Stay on the

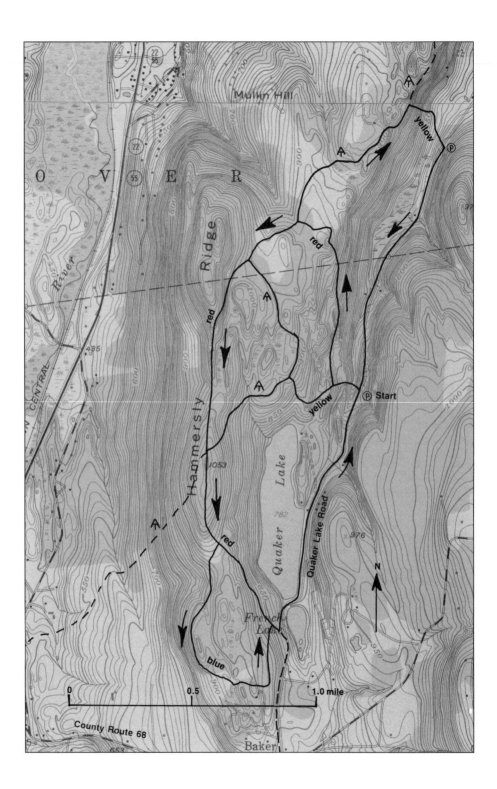

yellow-marked route, and after 0.5 mile, the trail swings along the ridge, then intersects the white-marked Appalachian Trail (AT) at an acute angle. Your continuing walk north has both yellow and white markers. Pinksters, many ferns, and marsh plants fill the wet areas along the ridge, areas that were cleared and farmed sometime before the revolutionary war. In another 0.3 mile the red-marked trail forks right, and you could follow it back to the start for a shorter loop. If you choose to continue on the AT, the next 20 minutes, about 0.9 mile, is a walk along the ridgeline.

When the AT goes straight ahead, take the yellow trail 0.3 mile down the eastern slope of the ridge. The trail crosses the outlet stream on a shaky bridge, then turns right to emerge at the northern parking area. New flagging, mixed with the yellow blazes, makes it possible to follow the route through the brush to the small parking lot. Walk south for 1.3 miles along Quaker Lake Road, past lovely stands of hemlock that line the valley beside Quaker Lake outlet. The ridge is quite close to the road, and when the leaves are off, the steep slopes are clearly visible from the road.

From the main entrance, begin the second half of the figure-eight walk as you started, but this time turn right on the red-marked trail and follow it north to the AT, then turn south on the AT briefly, walking this 0.3-mile segment in the opposite direction from your earlier walk. Near the top of the ridge, watch closely, for the AT makes a sharp turn left; go right on the red-marked trail and enjoy the lovely walk south along the ridgeline. The AT crosses this red-marked trail just below the crest of the ridge. (An alternative entrance to the reserve is along the AT from the large parking area on NY 22, 0.25 mile north of County Route 68.)

Stay on the red-marked trail; it will lead you past small wet places and beside truly wonderful stands of hemlocks as it descends to Quaker Lake Road. Another variation is inviting: A blue-marked trail makes a loop to the reserve's southern boundary, returning to the red-marked trail within 100 yards of Quaker Lake Road. This loop circles more marshes, and its northern leg takes you through a large area of blowdowns. A short walk north beside Quaker Lake, about 1 mile and no more than 20 minutes, takes you back to the main entrance.

15

Mills–Norrie State Parks

Distance: 5 miles

Time: 3 hours

Vertical rise: Minimal

Maps: Available from Taconic State Park Region Headquarters, Mills–Norrie State Parks, Staatsburg; USGS 7½' Hyde Park

The east shore of the Hudson River between New York and Albany was settled by holders of large patents and purchases. Portions of a few of these magnificent holdings survive as modern parks. In the mid–Hudson Valley, the most beautiful of these parks are the great homes and estates built in the nineteenth century. Some, like the Vanderbilt Mansion and the Mills Estate, were the homes of industrial and financial leaders of the time. Clermont, the home of many generations of Livingstons, a family including notable statesmen, dates to the eighteenth century. Frederic Edwin Church, the Hudson River School

painter, designed the grounds of his Persian-influenced castle, Olana, to frame the vistas of the distant Catskills.

Each of these parks has walks laid out by the original owners. Most walks are short and take the hiker through manicured grounds. The walks along the Hudson at the Mills–Norrie state parks are special: They are longer, offering a half-day of outdoor activity, and a portion are directly along the river, for the railroad, which closely follows the eastern shore through most of the valley, lies inland here.

The Mills Estate was built by a great-great-granddaughter of Robert R. Livingston, Ruth Livingston Mills, and her husband, Ogden Mills, a wealthy financier. The Greek Revival mansion, which was designed by the firm of McKim, Mead and White, was completed in 1896. The Louis XV and Louis XVI rooms were richly furnished with art from Europe, ancient Greece, and the Orient.

The estate's formal sweep of lawn and its tree-covered roadway offer a charming beginning to the trails that lead south to the adjacent Margaret Lewis Norrie State Park. To reach the Mills Estate, turn onto Old Post Road, which loops west from US 9 around

Maple-bordered roadways in the beginning of the Mills Estate walk

the village of Staatsburg. You will want to stop at the park offices in the mansion and get a map, although the ski-touring map available there does not show the shore-hugging route that is the centerpiece of this walk. You can follow its red-, blue-, and green-marked trails on your own.

Walk west from the estate on the blue-marked trail, following the roadway toward the waterfront boathouse, enjoying views of the Catskills on the way. The boathouse, architecturally interesting in itself, is a barrel-vaulted stone structure. The roadway curves around the cove beyond; watch for the white-marked trail that forks right to hug the shoreline. Along it, hemlocks shade the small shale cliffs bordering the river with its shingle beach. The narrow trail follows the top of moss-covered ledges, while you have lovely views of water and gnarled ce-

dars. Only an occasional old stone wall will make you believe this land has ever been disturbed by humans.

A 40-minute walk brings you to a picnic area, which also can be reached by a roadway from Norrie State Park. The white-marked route continues on the far (south) side of the parking area but farther inland, leading through a camping area to a roadway. Follow that roadway out until it intersects another park road, not far from the railroad. South on the park road, in about an hour's total walk, you reach the Dutchess Community College's Norrie Point Environmental Center, open Saturdays from 11 A.M. to 5 P.M. and Sundays from 1 P.M. to 5 P.M. You may want to see its exhibits of the plants and animals of this portion of the Hudson shoreline.

As you return north along the road, watch for an underpass below the rail-

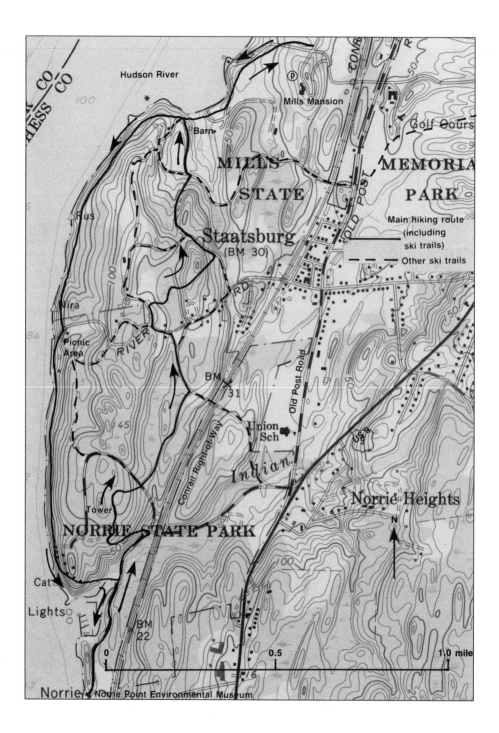

Hudson River

*

Barn

P
Mills Mansion

CONR R

MILLS

STATE

Golf Cours

MEMORIA

PARK

Rus

Staatsburg
(BM 30)

OLD POST

Main hiking route
(including
ski trails)

Other ski trails

Nina

RD

Picnic
Area

RIVER

BM
31

Union
Sch

Old Post Road

US 9

45

Conrail Right-of-Way

Indian

Tower

NORRIE STATE PARK

Norrie Heights

N

Cat

Lights

BM
22

0   0.5   1.0 mile

6

Norrie   Norrie Point Environmental Museum

road. Opposite it, a red post along the road alerts you to an abandoned roadway that serves as one of the park's unmarked trails. Follow this road to the left, as it curves back and then almost disappears on the summit of a small hill with a stone water tower. There are a multitude of such walkways in the park, some of which shortly will be marked as nature trails.

Following the roadway, you intersect one of the park roads (blue-marked) that has been identified as a ski-touring route. Your route back north to the Mills Estate can take any one of the intersecting segments of the ski trails, most of which follow abandoned roadways, but for now follow the blue-marked trail to a T intersection, where you turn left on the red-marked trail.

Your detour through the woods takes you past a marsh, through beautiful forests, and to a memorial pylon noting that this land was given to the people of Staatsburg in memory of Lewis Gordon Norrie, 1901–1923. Just beyond the pylon, turn left, following the ski-touring signs. As the park map indicates, these trails all lead back to the large barn near the point where the white-marked trail headed along the shore. To extend your walk, you may wish to choose different segments of the loop; they are clearly marked and easy to follow. A most delightful way to end the day is with a picnic on the lawn in front of the mansion.

16

Stissing Mountain and Thompson Pond

Distance: 4 miles

Time: 4 hours

Vertical rise: 950 feet

Map: USGS 7½' Pine Plains

Stissing Mountain's long profile so dominates the surrounding flattened fields that it appears taller than its 1,403-foot height would indicate. The fields, remnants of a glacial lake, encircle this dome of Precambrian gneiss, enhancing the mountain's scale. A pair of trails leads to the abandoned firetower summit, making a loop walk possible, although views are limited to openings in the forest cover. A companion walk around Thompson Pond, to the west below the mountain, makes this a lovely, short day's excursion. The pond is part of a kettle lake, formed with Stissing and Mud ponds to the north by the melting of glacial blocks. Now the resulting bog pond, filling with grasses and cattails, is home to many birds. From the path that winds

along its shores, you can not only watch those birds, but you also will be treated to views of Stissing across the marshes, as the mountain rises steeply from the level of the lakebed.

The mountain is unusual in that its Precambrian mass was thrust on much-younger sandstones and shales that form the surrounding valley, completely isolating it from similar landforms that make up the Ramapos and the Hudson Highlands. Its strong profile that dominates the countryside is the result of resistance of the Precambrian rocks to erosion.

The pond and 300 acres are managed as a preserve by the Nature Conservancy. The area is home to many mammals, migrating warblers and marsh birds, and a rich variety of plants that find their niches in areas as varied as the pond and the adjacent wooded slopes of Stissing Mountain.

To reach the trailhead, start at the intersection of NY 82 and NY 199 in Pine Plains, and drive south for 0.4 mile on NY 82. A right turn on Lake Road takes you out of the village, along a lovely stretch of maple-lined road, and across a causeway, 1.6 miles to the Thompson Pond Sanctuary entrance on the left. The trailhead for

The view east from Stissing Mountain

Stissing Mountain is unmarked and 0.2 mile farther, near a bend in the road where the shoulder is wide enough for parking.

There is little or no marking on the trail, but it is easy to follow. The 950-foot climb should take you less than 40 minutes. It begins steeply up a narrow path that intersects an abandoned roadway, which you will meet after a 5-minute climb. Turn left— the way right leads to private lands— and continue uphill. Another 5-minute walk brings you to a fork. The way right follows the old roadway and streambed. It is the much more obvious choice. You will return that way.

Take the left turn up a fairly steep path. Stones heaped beside the trail indicate that this too was once a cleared way, but it is now rubble-filled and eroded. You can see Stissing Pond occasionally through the scrub oaks and birches, tantalizing glimpses that finally open up, after a 30-minute walk, to reveal the northern hills. The sum-

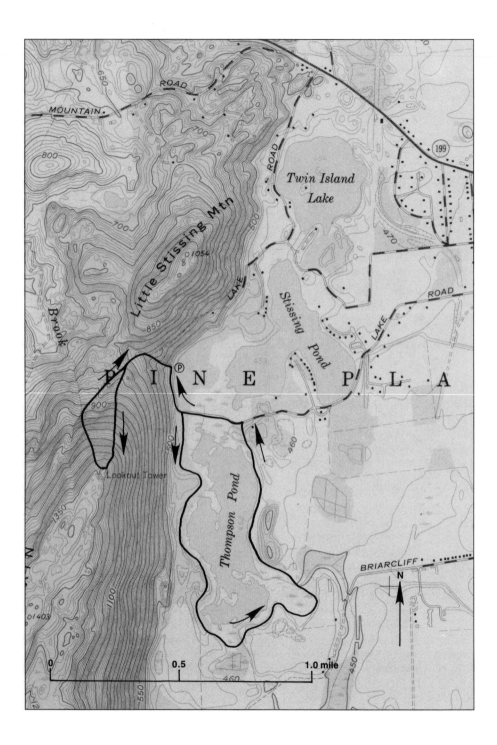

MOUNTAIN ROAD

650

800

700

Little Stissing Mtn

01054

850

Brook

900

ROAD

LAKE

500

470

Twin Island Lake

199

ROAD

Stissing Pond

LAKE

P I N E P L A

453

P

Lookout Tower

1350

700

460

Thompson Pond

1100

460

ROAD

BRIARCLIFF

N

01403

0   0.5   1.0 mile

550

460

450

mit is overgrown; however, the views from the fire tower are almost unobstructed. Climb the fire-tower stairs to the top of the third flight; the stairs above have been removed. You are now just above the tree line. From here you will see a spectacular view of the Catskills to the west. Stissing Pond, Twin Island Lake, and Massachusetts are visible to the northeast. Thompson Pond and Connecticut lie to the east. Portions of the southern end of the Shawangunks are visible to the southeast. The foundations of a cabin lie below the tower on the narrow summit ridge.

Walk beside the tower, heading south on a faint path. The descent is simple if you keep bearing right; left always leads to private lands. The first choice of paths is within 100 yards of the tower, and the way right is steeply down to intersect an abandoned roadway in another 100 yards. At this point a right continues downhill, following the roadway past handsome rock ledges. Below the ledges and another right fork, you can see Little Stissing Mountain through the trees. Thirty-five minutes of walking and a few more right turns bring you back to the fork you passed on the ascent. Retrace your steps for the 10-minute walk to your car, completing the 1.5-mile circuit.

To add to the excursion, walk along the road to the Thompson Pond Sanctuary entrance. An old road leads you south into the sanctuary, and 200 yards from the road is a registration booth and a map of the sanctuary. You scarcely need a map for the counterclockwise walk around Thompson Pond. There is a short loop to the pond from the registration booth, marked with blue arrows. The main trail around the pond, marked with yellow, continues on the abandoned roadway. The only time you might have trouble is at the far southern end where the trail leads briefly to a weed-filled field. Head left along the fence, and the way will soon become obvious again. The trail continues near the sanctuary border, heading down into a swamp toward a decrepit boardwalk. The swamp, outlet of Thompson Pond, marks the headwaters of Wappingers Creek. Lovely views of Stissing follow, then the trail cuts again to the border fence circling around another swampy area, taking you briefly to the edge of a barnyard. The trail then heads back closer to the pond for the rest of the return to Lake Road. An hour or so will take you around the 2.5-mile circuit. With binoculars you will surely want to take longer. There is also a rich variety of ground cover to examine and a series of framed views of marsh and mountain to enjoy.

17

South Taconic Trail

Distance: 9 miles

Time: 7 hours

Vertical rise: More than 2,000 feet

Maps: NYSDT Copake; USGS 7½'
Copake, NY–MA; USGS 7½'
Bashbish Falls, MA–CT–NY

A sentinel line of hills forms the border between New York State and Massachusetts and Connecticut. A 15-mile range trail follows the crest, paralleling the border, much of the time in New York State. The most eastern of New York's great trails is a relative newcomer, built between 1972 and 1976 by Bob Redington and Frank Cary, both residents of Connecticut. This hike takes you on a portion of that trail system, from the Whitehouse Road in the south to the magnificent Bashbish Falls in the north. The route encompasses a chain of vantages that will inspire any hiker and make light the rigors of the long walk with its many climbs.

The Taconics are remnants of a thrust mass of mostly unmetamor-

phosed shales ranging from Cambrian to Middle Ordovician in age. The ancestral Taconics, products of violent upheavals known as the Taconic Orogeny, became eroded away; sands and gravels from the mountains were washed west into a sea whose waves deposited a thick layer of the quartz-pebble conglomerate; its later upthrust became the Shawangunks. By Late Silurian times only the eroded vestiges of the original Taconic Mountains remained. And fine muds and limestones again accumulated in a shallow sea, forming the bed of Upper Silurian limestone near Pine Plains and beneath Stissing Mountain. From overlooks on the Taconic Ridge, this quiet plain contrasts vividly with the forces that created the mountains on which you will walk.

Because of the length of the walk and the advantages of staying on the ridge, a two-car trip is best. To leave one car at the north, turn east from NY 22 at Copake Falls onto NY 344, and drive through Bashbish Park to a parking area on the south side of the road, 1.4 miles from NY 22. After parking your car, examine the water level of Bashbish Brook and decide whether, at the end of the day, you would be

Bashbish Falls

able to hop across upstream. The fork that takes you past Bashbish Falls requires crossing the brook after a 500-foot descent; you won't want to climb back up to the alternate route if you can avoid it.

Drive south from Copake Falls on NY 22 for 7 miles, turn left onto Whitehouse Road, and turn left again in 0.7 mile onto Under Mountain Road. A right turn in 0.3 mile onto Deer Run leads in 0.9 mile to a small parking turnout on the left. Three white square marks denote the trail, which begins by following the edge of the field. The gentle uphill toward the looming mountain quickly ends in 0.4 mile in a scramble beside a small stream. In 0.5 mile the trail reaches a tall but scanty waterfall. The trail then turns and zigzags up the steep face, yielding views along the northern escarpment of the Taconics and south to Stissing Mountain, with the Shawangunks and Beacon beyond.

Within 30 minutes the scrambling ends, and you reach a sign pointing 0.7 mile back the way you just climbed, 0.18 mile to the right to New Point to a lookout, a detour from the projected route, and 1.24 miles ahead to Brace Mountain. Continue on to Brace, past a couple of nice openings with pretty views, then, as the trail turns again to the mountain, you climb a pair of ledges to reach South Brace and a vantage with views south over New Point and Riga Lake and South Pond beyond. Here, at 1.4 miles, a turquoise-marked trail forks back to Riga, a possible loop route for another day.

About an hour and a quarter from the start, you reach the summit of South Brace (2,304 feet), with its superb views. Beyond, the summit continues open with small birches and oaks. You drop into a saddle, then climb to a huge cairn monument on the summit of Brace (2,311 feet), from which there is a 360-degree view. From this point, nearly 2 miles from the start, you see Bear Mountain, the highest point in Connecticut, to the east; Mount Frissell in Massachusetts is to the northeast. The split summit of Mount Adams is on the horizon ahead.

Continuing north, the trail descends about 350 yards to intersect a woods road. The way right leads into Connecticut; your trail continues north, joining the old, shingle-filled road, which follows along the narrow ridge to a signpost pointing to Mount Frissell and the tristate marker. From this point it is 3.71 miles to Alander Mountain. Just beyond this spot you pass a lovely upland pond and continue down, then up to another knob.

Beyond, the trail descends, fairly steeply, crossing into Massachusetts. A side trail left heads toward Boston Corner and another beyond heads right to Ashley Mountain. Your route north continues on the old roadway, bordered with stone walls.

After you pass a gorge with a small stream on your left and enter a park-like area of tall trees, you see a red marker denoting a trail joining from Robert Brook and Boston Corner to the west. This intersection is 2 miles from the summit of Brace. The trail continues with red markers for about a 10-minute, 0.5-mile walk to a fork where a blue-marked trail turns right toward the summit of Alander Mountain, which you can gain by either this blue-marked route or a continuation of the trail you have been following. On the blue-marked trail it takes about 20 minutes to pass through scrubby forests to open ledges. There are lovely green fields of the Harlem Valley beneath and views back to the cairn on

Brace. You circle west to the summit, past a series of strange convoluted ledges and a cleft with a cabin from the days when the fire tower on Alander was manned. It is a fairly leisurely 4-hour walk for the 6 miles to Alander.

From the summit itself (2,250 feet), you view the hemlock-rimmed valley of Alander Brook. West of the summit there is a point from which the capitol in Albany appears against the skyline. To the east of the tower there is a fork in the trail, with marks painted on a rock. Take the blue-marked trail, which leads quickly to the white-marked trail north along the very precipitous northeast ridge of Alander. The descent is fairly steep as it follows the narrow ridge, crossing to the west to overlook a bucolic scene of farm fields and little ponds.

The trail continues high on the ridgeline, descending slightly, occasionally climbing little knobs, punctuated with many lovely view spots. The high point of Bashbish Mountain at 1,980 feet is just under 2 miles from Alander. Just beyond, after 50 minutes of winding across the ridge, you reach an intersection.

Choose carefully here. The way left avoids fording the brook, but it does not take you past Bashbish Falls. Instead, it leads you to a bridge over the brook, and you would have to backtrack through the park to see this choicest part of the trip. If the water is not too high and cold, and probably that would be only in early spring, you can turn right for a wild descent through the hemlock-covered slopes at what seems to be a 70-degree angle. In less than 0.5 mile, the trail takes you down to the railing that keeps you from falling into the gorge. It is a rough descent, but the views of the falls from this side are worth the trip. You continue descending past several tiers of falls that break through the ravine as the brook ends its plunge down 700 feet of this cleft in the Taconic ridge. The falls lie just over the New York border in Massachusetts. Fording the stream just below the falls will lead you up to the stairs constructed on the north side for more sedate viewing of this cataract. The park road leads you along the rim of the gorge, and in 15 minutes you reach your car.

18

Olana

Distance: 7.5 miles
Time: 3 hours
Vertical rise: 300 feet
Maps: Available from the ticket office at Olana

As the romanticism of nineteenth-century Hudson River School painting is exemplified in the works of Frederic Edwin Church (1826–1900), the belief that nature could be manipulated to express that romanticism is summarized in Church's home, Olana. The Olana State Historic Site near Hudson preserves the grounds Church designed and the castle he built that surveys the Catskills and a bend in the Hudson River. Now, a century later, a walk through the grounds and a tour of the castle summarize those romantic notions of nature as eloquently as any river site or any painting.

Olana is on NY 9G, just south of the entrance to the Rip Van Winkle Bridge between Hudson and Catskill. The park grounds are open from dawn

to dusk throughout the year. Tours of the castle are offered Wednesday through Sunday 12 P.M. to 4 P.M. from Memorial Day through the last Sunday in October. There is a fee of $3 for the tour.

Frederic Edwin Church studied with Thomas Cole and painted Hudson River and Catskill scenes throughout his career. For two decades he traveled throughout the west, to Newfoundland, and to South America. In 1867 he and his wife visited Greece, Italy, and Syria. It was the architectural styles of the latter country that inspired the pink stone castle that his wife named Olana, a Latin interpretation of a Syrian word meaning "our place on high."

Olana sits on a narrow ridge 500 feet above the Hudson, a site that inspired Church to write, "About one hour this side of Albany is the center of the world—I own it." The magnificent trees that now edge the sweeping lawn have grown to full maturity, as have the oaks and maples that shade the carriage roads making up the park's trails. From the castle, the view southwest encompasses the northern escarpment of the Catskills, the bend in the Hudson, and a lake Church had con-

A view of Olana, home of Frederic Edwin Church

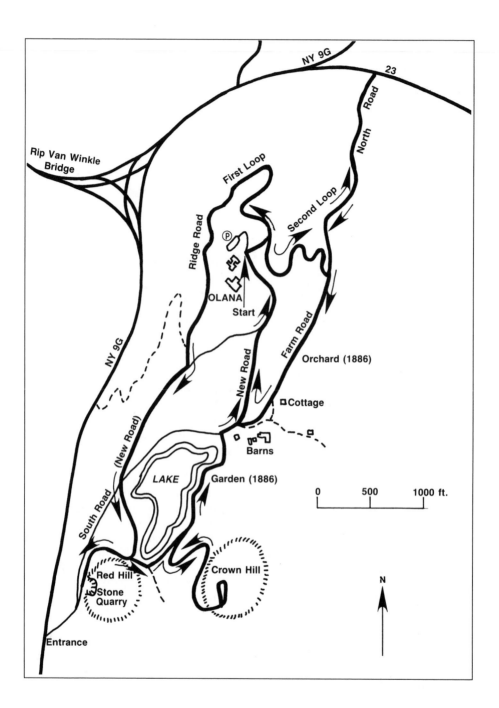

structed as a necessary artistic counterpoint to complete the dramatic view. The castle's windows were designed to frame portions of that view, enabling its owners to command in nature a view as awe-inspiring as Church's painted scenes.

A walk on portions of the 7.5 miles of trails and carriage roads is more of an elegant stroll than a hike, but you can extend it through two lovely loops. A trail enters the woods just below and east of the road to the visitors' parking area. A left fork near the beginning takes you onto Ridge Road, which winds to the north and then below the castle with one vista of the river and the Rip Van Winkle Bridge. Follow Ridge Road, marked with yellow disks, as it circles to the park entrance road (South Road), which you follow downhill (south) toward the lake. Turn left from South Road along the lake. The first right from this trail leads to the southern park boundary. This route continues on private lands along a very narrow ridge that affords glimpses of the Hudson.

Returning to the lake trail, continue north along the lake, enjoying occasional glimpses of the hilltop castle. The next right turn, red-marked, leads to a circle on the summit of Crown Hill, where a cut in the forest reveals the castle again. The entire park is full of such surprising, yet planned, vistas. The lake trail ends at a roadway (marked New Road on the map) along which you can make your way north to the castle.

A second loop also begins near the parking area but goes to the right (south) down through a deep ravine of stately trees to the North Road. Follow this north to the park boundary and back to enjoy more of the noble forest. Retracing the route south to continue on Farm Road, you remain on the ridge overlooking the old orchards. You may wish to turn west from the roads and wind generally west and uphill through the fields toward the castle. If you do, be wary of the poison-ivy patches. Near the intersection of the two paved park roads, a pathway circles below the castle and leads gently up to it via a small but charming Victorian garden that is tucked just below the castle garden wall.

19

The Trapps to Gertrude's Nose

Distance: 8.5 miles

Time: 6 hours

Vertical rise: 800 feet

Maps: USGS 7½' Gardiner; USGS 7½' Napanoch; NY–NJTC Shawangunk Trails, #9

The long ridge edged with sparkling white cliffs visible to the west of the New York State Thruway in the vicinity of New Paltz is the Shawangunk Mountains, pronounced Shon*gum*, also called the Shawangunks or simply the Gunks. For a first look at this geologically intriguing spot, try the hike along the Trapps, a portion of those cliffs, to Gertrude's Nose. Drive west of New Paltz on NY 299 to NY 44 and NY 55, and continue west to park

Erratics on the way to Gertrude's Nose

along the shoulder of the road near the cliffs, which usually are full of rock climbers. Your route will take you southwest along the cliff tops on a trip that for a non–rock climber is as much of a thrill as the climbers get from those famous cliffs, known world-wide as the "Gunks."

Because your route starts on lands belonging to the Mohonk Preserve, there is a fee, $2 per person as of this writing, usually collected by a ranger who patrols the road. The crowds whose vehicles line the road are climbers; you will meet very few hikers on your walk. The Mohonk Preserve office is located on Mountain Rest Road near New Paltz, and there you will find much information on the natural history of the area, a part of which is described in a wonderful little booklet you may wish to purchase.

Walk just south of Trapps Bridge, over which the carriage road from Minnewaska to Mohonk passes, and follow that road northwest for about 100 feet. A well-marked, blue-blazed trail starts steeply up the rock slabs to the Millbrook Ridge Trail.

The beauty of the Shawangunks lies in the way the views continuously unfold, enlivening every few feet of each walk. Still, a sparkling day in early spring or late fall with the leaves off and not too much wind is the best time for this hike. You will be walking along a knife-edge, sometimes so narrow you feel a good gust could give you flight, like the birds you will see soaring close by.

You are immediately aware of the cleft in the Shawangunk ridge—you will walk the eastern ridge until it meets the western one near Minnewaska, a resort whose lands once encompassed most of the central Shawangunks. As you climb you see the cliffs and tower

of Mohonk, a hotel whose grounds, together with Mohonk Preserve lands, make up the northern Shawangunks. These cliffs and the tower of Sky Top frame the high peaks of the central Catskill range—a view that will return many times during this walk.

It is the rock under your feet and what you know of its history that will most impress you on this walk. The Shawangunks were formed about 450 million years ago, first as sedimentary deposits worn from an even older mountain range. The sediments, the shining white conglomerates you now see, were once deposited along the shores of an inland sea, whose waters tumbled and smoothed the quartz pebbles, which were later embedded in the gleaming white rocks you will traverse. These sediments were shaped by heat and pressure, faulted and bent, and uplifted about 280 million years ago to form the magnificent cliffs of the Shawangunks' southwestern face, where the horizontal layers of deposits are worn away. The dip to the north-west gives the long slopes you see; these slopes will be even more evident if you take the Ice Caves of the Shawangunks hike (hike 21). The age of the uplift makes the Shawangunks one of the youngest formations in the east.

So, let's begin the walk along the straight, thin ridges of the sloping face of the Shawangunks' geological history. Scrub oak and pitch pine will be your companions, opening up to offer a series of beautiful vistas along the way.

You climb a first rise, the site of the annual hawk watches, then descend into a little draw, climbing again, this time more sharply, to turn left and return to the exposed slopes of the amazingly narrow ridge. The trail is

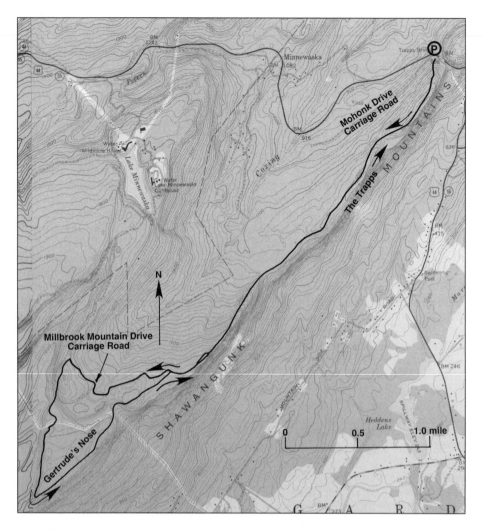

routed along bare rock as much as possible, minimizing erosion of the fragile niches of blueberries and laurels. You zigzag across the ridge to take advantage of the rock walkways and the views, but the lack of evidence of defined foot tread means you need to watch for the trail markers. With your eyes diverted to distant views, it is easy to wander off the trail.

A half-hour walk through a section of tall trees with few views brings you to a deeper valley. As you climb again, you see Millbrook Mountain looming ahead like Gibraltar. About an hour's walk brings you past a big rock slab, cantilevered to create a shelter. Then, passing another protected area of large hemlocks, you scramble left to circle to the edge of the cliffs once more. 5

You look down now on Heddens Lake, whose position will mark your progress through the walk. The view south down the Hudson Highlands reveals Breakneck Ridge and Storm King, while toward the north the Catskills are framed by the cliffs you have just climbed. Observe how the Minnewaska Ridge to the northwest grows closer—when it connects with the Trapp Ridge you are on, their joint thrust forms the prong of Gertrude's Nose, your ultimate destination.

One hour and forty minutes of walking should bring you to the high point of Millbrook Mountain, a wonderfully narrow ridge where the trail emerges several times right at cliff top. The route west continues on a height of land, 1,200 feet above the valley, and 20 minutes later you reach the end of Mohonk property and encounter the loop that marks the end of the Millbrook Mountain carriage road from Minnewaska, about 2.5 miles from the start. For now, take the carriage road. It is easy walking, a bit dull, but the quickest way to make a loop walk around Gertrude's Nose. The carriage roads are the marvel of Mohonk and Minnewaska, miles and miles of graded pathways that today make superb walking. They all are paved with the Martinsburg shale, a 2,000-foot layer of which underlies the Shawangunks. The shale weathers to a dense but surprisingly soft and smooth walking surface. Except on the trails, you will be unaware of the shale, for it is almost everywhere topped with the white icing of the conglomerate.

It takes just over half an hour to cover the mile to an intersection with a red-marked trail that leaves the carriage road on your left. Yellow flags may also alert you to the red-marked trail. Follow it as it descends toward the Palmaghatt Ravine, the deep ravine between you and Castle Point.

The ravine was the site of a "salted" gold mine, which deceived several investors nearly a century ago.

For a time the trail is along the edge of hemlock-covered ledges, sometimes on the white, sloping slabs of the cliff tops yielding views ahead to Gertrude's Nose. A 20-minute walk brings you to an opening under telephone lines and across a little stream.

As you head out to the white slabs, you will have to stop and admire some of the glacial erratics that dot the cliff tops. Observe also the deep clefts that fissure the cliffs, created as the soft shale foundations weathered and became displaced. The 50 minutes it may take you to walk the mile from the carriage road to the Nose includes time for you to pause to admire the sculptured rock wonders. Here the evidence of another geological force is clear: the glaciers that once covered the Shawangunks to a depth of 4,000 to 5,000 feet. As the ice mass moved along the northwestern slopes, the rocks it pushed along scraped the conglomerate, leaving striations, long, thin scratch marks you can see occasionally. The smooth polish of many surfaces is also the work of the glaciers, achieved as the ice mass moved over a layer of mud.

Pause at the promontory of Gertrude's Nose for lunch and views to the east. When you start south along the ridge, you will follow some old brown markers and newer red ones. The way is not well marked as of this writing, mostly because of fire disturbance—a reminder that no fires are permitted in the entire fragile Shawangunk area. Rerouting and remarking is scheduled, so these cautions on trail location may be unnecessary. The way is close enough to the escarpment edge that you will have several good views east and north and even on toward Millbrook Mountain. In little more than half an hour you pass under the power lines, then climb again along ledges amid stunted trees and rocks that form a landscape reminiscent of windswept tropical islands. Just over half an hour of walking should bring you out to the carriage road a few minutes from that road's end. The time for this 1.5-mile loop on the Nose may be increased if you have difficulty finding the trail. About 1 hour and 40 minutes should suffice for the return trip to your car, providing you do not stop too long to savor the views.

20

Minnewaska Scenic Trail

Distance: 11 miles

Time: 7 hours

Vertical rise: 600 feet, plus scrambles

Maps: USGS 7½' Gardiner; USGS 7½' Napanoch; NY–NJTC Shawangunk Trails, #9

The Minnewaska Scenic Trail offers a great walk that combines the best of the Minnewaska carriage roads with interconnecting paths that take you on a moderately strenuous but wonderfully varied trip.

Minnewaska State Park is limited to day use only. Its public lands are now managed by the Palisades Interstate Park Commission, whose rules are clearly posted at all entrances.

You have three choices for starting and finishing this hike. For one, park at the principal parking area at the park entrance, 0.2 mile west of the Minnewaska complex road on NY 44. The hike starts and returns along the 2.4-mile Peters Kill Carriageway, which

is barred to outside vehicular traffic but used by park managers, so it makes a less-than-desirable walking route. You may want to use it, because it is the quickest way to get to the best trails. Your second option, a looping route, is, again, to park at the park entrance, but then walk west and downhill 0.7 mile on NY 44, and head left on the Jenny Lane Trail. This route winds along a long wooden causeway through a marsh surrounding Sanders Kill and, later, through lush laurel stands. The trail is almost entirely shaded. You will return via the Peters Kill Carriageway. Note that it takes an hour longer to make this loop. Your third option is to park 0.7 mile west at the Jenny Lane parking area and enter and return via the Jenny Lane Trail. Allow an extra half hour for this route.

As you start along the access road, variously called Lower Awosting Road or Peters Kill Carriageway, for the lovely stream you hear below and to your left, you will see several paths that could take you to its shaded valley. A stiff pace of 45 minutes brings you to the open field with comfort stations to the right as you enter the field.

A huge pine tree in the middle of the field sports the turquoise blazes

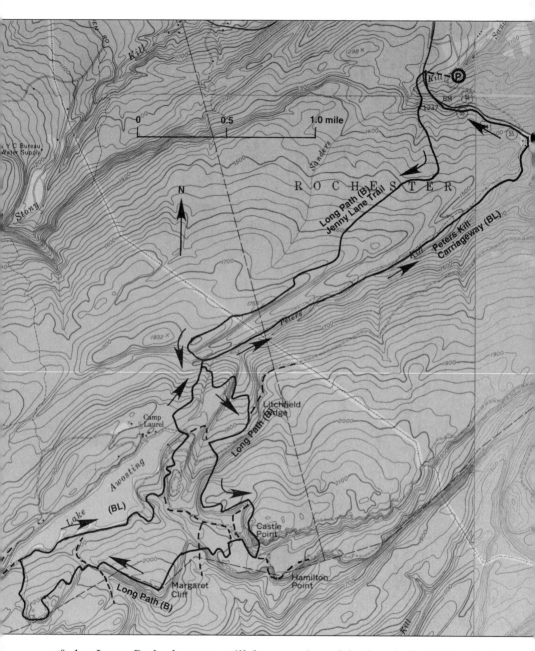

of the Long Path that you will be
following. These turquoise blazes
gradually are replacing the old yellow ones that previously marked this

section of the Scenic Trail. Turn left,
across a sort of causeway, on the road
that leads to Lake Awosting. Immediately across the causeway there is a

left fork to the Scenic Trail.

The route, occasionally marked with cairns, leads up over open ledges and is not always obvious as it zigzags uphill. You cross a stream and pause to look back at a wonderful panorama of the distant Catskills. The path turns to follow a ledge covered with hemlock and laurel, high above a deep ravine on your right. You pass one more pretty overlook that is just off the trail, then start to descend, steeply, into Huntington Ravine, a deep, hemlock-filled valley with a small stream. The path through the ravine leads you up to an overhanging ledge and Rainbow Falls, a small cascade that in spring shoots out over the horizontally faulted cliff.

Below the falls, the path leads down across the stream, then left and up the far side of the ravine. You turn to climb gently out of the valley, then up to Upper Awosting Lake Road. Turn right on it for one of the most beautiful parts of the walk. Those handsomely built old carriage roads are so comfortable for walking, and this one is bordered by the tall, sheltering Litchfield Ledge.

In 10 minutes, you turn left on the more narrow Long Path and begin to climb, then scramble, over ledges through viburnum thickets. There are spectacular views back across the ravine to the Catskills and west to Lake Awosting. As you wind along on open ledges, you catch sight of Castle Point toward which you are headed. You briefly leave the escarpment to intersect a road from Lake Awosting. You could shorten the trip by turning right here toward the lake, but go left instead, curving up around a hairpin turn of Battlement Terrace and out to Castle Point. Somehow, it is possible to spend 1 hour and 40 minutes on the

walk past Rainbow Falls and along the ledges, a distance from the field of not much more than 1.5 miles. On a good day, you will have many lovely impressions to justify the slow pace.

(*Note:* The United States Geological Survey (USGS) map and some previous maps do not show correctly the deep hairpin turn of the Kempton Ledge and Castle Point Carriage Road. You could follow it down to its intersection with the Hamilton Point Road and avoid the scramble that the Scenic Trail now follows.)

While you are contemplating the views from Castle Point overlook, ponder the ledges down which the arrows direct your continuing route. Rock climbing is not for the faint of heart, and while this climb may not be technical, it can be a scary scramble, with the leaf-strewn path at the bottom providing still more slippery footing.

When you meet the Lower Carriage Road (the Hamilton Point and Palmaghatt Road), turn right for just over 100 yards. Just opposite the point where the Castle Point Road joins the Hamilton Point Road, turn left on the path toward Margaret Cliff.

The varied and ingeniously designed Scenic Trail continues down through a cleft between huge boulders and right into a mossy, wet cave that looks for a moment like the end of the line. An arrow left leads through a chute—someone's idea of fun—then out to a rough walk on the conglomerate rock. (Actually, the cave and chute are the work of Maurice Avery, who designed the trail and for a time worked to maintain it.) The trail here is just below the edge of the scarp. There is a small stream to ford in a sylvan dell, then you are out on a carriage road again, this one called Slate Bank Road.

The Catskills from Minnewaska Scenic Trail

Here you merely cross the road and head back into the woods, turning to climb another ledge. You finish the scramble with an oh-wow view back to the two ledges below Castle Point as well as those below Hamilton Point. Margaret Cliff is a choice spot.

The trail continues along the ridgeline through scrubby growth with occasional glimpses of Lake Awosting and the Catskills. You intersect a carriage road again, this one called Spruce Glen Drive; hiking time for the 0.7 mile between the carriage roads is about 30 minutes.

Follow Spruce Glen Drive north for no more than 100 yards to a sharp left turn back and up toward Murray Hill.

Twenty minutes more of following the cliff edge, and your trail again intersects a carriage road. You will walk along it, past the last cliff-top view, which is Murray Hill, and follow it as it turns north for less than 0.5 mile, or a 10-minute walk to the lakeshore. The 1-mile segment around Murray Hill requires a bit over a half hour.

At the lakeshore, turn right and in a very few minutes you reach a lovely point—the perfect rest stop. Lake Awosting, at 1,800 feet in elevation, is a true glacial lake, lying in a trough below the cliffs, as are the others in the chain of lakes that descends from the southwest following the dip of the range.

Your route back is the carriage road along the lakeshore with but one fork. At the fork turn left, continuing north around the end of the lake. The walk along the lakeshore is as pleasant as any part of your day. At the head of the lake, stay left at the intersection with Upper Awosting Lake Road; then, across the outlet, turn right and you return quickly to the field you left to head for Litchfield Ledge. After a few more minutes, you see the Long Path trail markers for the Jenny Lane Trail on your left. If you are returning that way, you will climb and follow a ridge before descending through thick stands of laurel and on to the Jenny Lane parking area. Otherwise, continue on the Peters Kill Carriageway back to the Peters Kill parking area.

The Scenic Trail is such a delight that you must be certain to allow adequate time to enjoy all 6 miles of ledges, views, and quiet spots. The 5-mile round-trip walk to its beginning does make it a long day, but it's a great one.

21

Ice Caves and Napanoch Point

Distance: 7.5 miles

Time: 6 hours or more depending on time spent exploring the Ice Caves

Vertical rise: 1,800 feet

Maps: USGS 7½' Ellenville; USGS 7½' Napanoch; NY–NJTC Shawangunk Trails, #9

There are two ways to approach the Ice Caves of the Shawangunks. Parking can be a problem at one entrance, so this hike is designed to minimize that problem and provide a loop walk with additional destinations that sample other features of the western ridges of the range. The hike starts in Ellenville. From Canal Street near the center of town, head east on Berme Road until you reach the Ellenville Fire House. Park in the firehouse parking lot, taking care not to block the firehouse. Walk east gently uphill until you meet Smiley Carriageway, an eroded dirt track at the edge of the steep forested slopes.

Turn left (northeast), and follow Smiley Carriageway as it heads gradually uphill, with one switchback south 10 minutes after the beginning. The roadway zigzags gradually uphill through tall forests, quite a change from the eastern slopes. It was a real feat to build this road into the side of the hill—you can marvel at its construction as you climb gently toward Shingle Gully. That stream crossing looks to be directly downhill from the Ice Caves where the caves are shown erroneously on most maps—including the United States Geological Survey (USGS) one. The new New York–New Jersey Trail Conference (NY–NJTC) maps and the map accompanying this hike are correct.

The roadway becomes a shingle-filled gully with only occasional views to break up the trek. The coarser rock beneath your feet differs from the eastern slopes you traverse in the other hikes in the Shawangunks. This Shawangunk grit was quarried to create millstones for the first settlers in the Rondout Valley, which lies to the west of the range.

At 2.5 miles, after 1 hour and 20 minutes of walking, you reach a spring tapped by a pipe—the only drinking water on your route. At 3 miles—10 more minutes of walking—you cross a

Ice Caves

crystal-clear stream, the middle tributary of Louis Ravine. Just beyond this, you pass a woods road forking up and back to the right. Note this junction, for you will be doubling back and following the road after you visit Napanoch Point. Continuing on the carriage road for less than 10 minutes, you reach a sharp right turn. To the left is a rock outcrop with views to the north, if you care to leap over a small divide to reach the outcrop. Exactly 2 minutes farther, see a faint sign painted on a stone in the middle of the trail, directing you left to a promontory that lies about 100 yards from the roadway. You follow a series of cairns to the promontory. Some people think the true Napanoch Point is the lower extension of this promontory, a point that overhangs Napanoch Settlement.

Your walks on the Shawangunks cannot fail to interest you in the region's special flora, a transition between the northern boreal forests of the Catskill high peaks and the southern forests distinguished by oaks, hickory, and pitch pine. Patches of laurel and azalea, blooming in May, dot the range. And, on every open spot, blueberries abound. At one time blueberries were harvested commercially, and often the slopes were burned to promote the bushes' growth.

Napanoch Point, at 3.6 miles, is a good place for lunch. From it, you retrace your steps along the cairns to Smiley Carriageway and turn right. After 2 minutes you revisit the sharp bend and rock outcrop. Ten more minutes brings you back to the junction with the old woods road. Turn left on it through a deep hemlock glen. Shortly you come upon a stream to the right flowing on exposed bedrock. Upstream, beaver have managed to flood the roadway, and several detours around to the left will be neces-

sary. Sometime after you pass the new beaver pond, as you begin to climb, look back to enjoy views of the Catskills. Within a 50-minute walk, 1.7 miles from Napanoch Point, High Point looms above you.

From this promontory, by the foundation of what was once a fire tower, the view of Rondout Valley is most impressive, backed as it is by the mountains of the southern Catskills, where the Long Trail crosses Peekamoose and Table from the Rondout Valley. The high peaks are easily identified— the steep slopes of Wittenberg hide Cornell, with Slide behind. The Devil's Path Mountains are north or north-northwest of you, with Plateau, Sugarloaf, Twin, and Indian Head running easterly out of Stony Clove through Mink Hollow. Stony Clove is the deep U-shaped valley; Pecoy Notch and Jimmy Dolan Notch also are visible.

Return to the trail and clearing that lie below the promontory. From here you may retrace your steps back to the Smiley Carriageway, or you may follow the more difficult route to the Ice Caves described below. As of this writing, the path is overgrown and should not be attempted without long pants, map, and a compass.

In the southwest part of the clearing you find a red-marked, overgrown, rough path. It heads down a slope through the strangest terrain of trees, stunted so that you look right over their tops. Gnarled trees intersperse the bare rock openings, sites that are, here in the Shawangunks, often inhabited by rattlesnakes. At times this section of trail can be wet underfoot. And, if you venture off the trail to find dry footing, you will run smack into dense thickets of laurel; now, perhaps, you can understand the feelings of John F. Stokes, the man who originally owned the land that later

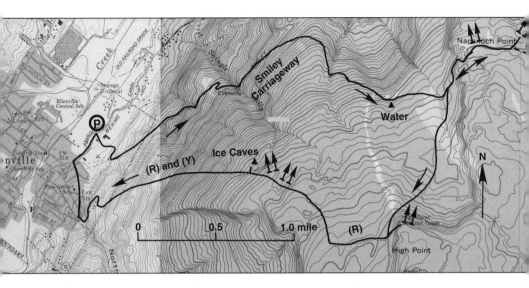

became Mohonk. He protested that "I suppose . . . the creator made everything for someone; but what in the world he ever made that pizen laurel for I can't see. It never grows big enough for firewood and the cattle won't eat it." Yet people travel great distances to see its bloom. Those who do not stop to appreciate the beauty of the laurel and all the other plants, as well as the Shawangunk birds, are missing much the range has to offer.

After a 30-minute gradual descent of about 1.2 miles, you reach the point just below the brow of the hill where it begins to drop off more steeply. You see paths heading right. Be careful, but do follow them—they lead to the edge of the ravines with the Ice Caves. You can follow the crevices downhill until you gain entry to the ravine, or you can follow the crevices as they curve uphill to the northeast. The caves were formed as a whole piece of the mountain pulled away, creating a semicircular ravine, whose major crevice—the grand canyon of the Shawangunks—is hundreds of feet across and a hundred feet deep. South of the crevice are many minor fissures. The northern end of the canyon curves around, reaching close to the top of Shingle Gully. There are many places to explore; and with the early-afternoon sun filtering in, photographs are possible. For some of the deeper crevices, take a flashlight. Ice persists in some places well into summer, so caution is advised. For some, a rope is helpful.

Allow plenty of time to explore the caves. For your descent, return to the red-marked trail, which becomes a narrow woods path as it winds gently down in a just-over-30-minute, mile-long walk to a road. The limited parking along this private road makes this approach to the Ice Caves undesirable. The road S-curves down to a small park beside North Gully Stream. From this point it is less than a 20-minute, 0.8-mile walk through town to your car.

Note: The trail from Smiley Road to Napanoch Point is open to the public. However, the part of the hike to High Point and Ice Caves may be closed in the future, or permission and fees may be required.

22

Mohonk

Distance: *Approximately 7 miles*

Time: *6 hours*

Vertical rise: *Many short climbs, none more than 200 feet*

Maps: *USGS 7½' Mohonk Lake; NY–NJTC Shawangunk Trails, #10 & #10A; park map*

How about a hike that has as much fun as a trip to a county fair? The equivalent of roller coasters, snap-the-whip, a merry-go-round, and intriguing tent shows beckons at Mohonk.

Mohonk Preserve is the gem of the Shawangunks. The Mohonk Mountain House, a private hotel surrounded by the preserve, reflects the leisure and elegance of old-time vacations. The trails and walks that circle round the hotel were laid out with the same nineteenth-century attitude that fostered the hotel. Today they are a marvel of rock climbs, lover's lanes, deep-woods walks, and vantage points that reflect their builders' humor. Every spot is named, every path has been walked many times before, but the fun and

On the trail in Mohonk Preserve

sense of discovery are still there. For a modest fee, you can walk the preserve's trails just as Victorian vacationers did a century ago.

The Shawangunks owe their development to the vision of Alfred H. Smiley, who first saw the escarpment in 1869. Alfred later developed the Minnewaska resort. His twin brother, Albert K., purchased the first 280 acres for $28,000 and began the development of the hotel and grounds. At Albert's death in 1912, the property had grown through over 100 purchases to encompass 5,000 acres. The brothers transformed a "labyrinth of boulders" unfolded into "two fertile valleys with the Catskill range against the western sky" into a premier resort designed "to make accessible the beauty and romance of the mountain. The systematic construction of paths began. Through labyrinth and forest, over ravines and under precipices, through fissures and solemn vales, year after year the trails were made and then widened into walks."

The visitors' parking area at Mohonk is on Mountain Rest Road west of New Paltz. Here you pay a $5 entrance fee that entitles you to park and walk everywhere but in the restricted central area of the Mohonk Mountain House. You will receive a map, and for another dollar you can ride a bus to the visitors' center, open daily in the summer and on weekends in winter for skiing.

You could not possibly walk all the trails, even on a weekend; the guide says there are 128 miles of paths and carriage roads. But, it is possible to sample some of the best and whet your appetite for a return visit to sample more.

Let's start out by following the signs to the Lake Side Path and turn south away from the lodge to Labyrinth Path. A sign warning of "crevices and scrambles which require hiking over and under huge rocks" greets you. You are advised to wear sneakers or nonslip shoes and to carry no handheld articles. The warning continues that the crevice just below Sky Top is deep and narrow, and its ladders and scramble are not for everyone.

And so the fantasy atmosphere of Mohonk's walks begins. You cannot help but wonder at the women in long skirts who flirtatiously clambered through the passages in tumbled rock slabs, with chutes and ladders. Sometimes you are buried deep within the cliffs that seem to peel away from the mountainside, sometimes you emerge to glimpse the hotel across the lake. Arrows point the way, and within 20 minutes you see an intersection where a left fork leads to Sky Top Road. If you are still game, continue straight ahead—the best is yet to come. Red arrows and rectangles point the way over an open rock scramble with views across to the cliffs on the far side of the lake, topped with precariously perched gazebos and, overall, a view toward the Catskills.

Near the end of the scramble, arrows point up to the crevice, which narrows to no more than 18 inches wide and is some 20 feet deep, with a climb over rocks and up ladders that total 30 feet in height. After you have finished this, laughing and groaning, you have begun to savor Mohonk's adult playground.

A sign points to the Pinnacle Path, and another ladder and scramble bring you out on Sky Top Road heading up to the Albert K. Smiley memorial stone tower with its superb views. It takes about an hour for the less-than-1-mile walk from the visitors' center to Sky Top via the Labyrinth. You may surmise that directions here are superfluous, but follow on, to sample Mohonk's best.

Briefly head down the road and turn left, away from the crevice route, onto Pinnacle Path, which turns sharply down at the first overhanging, rustic seat. This precipitous clifftop walk leads you to a fork; take the left turn, down, and follow signs to Pinnacle Rock, a photogenic column separated from the cliff.

Turn uphill, following the Mohonk Path, crossing carriage roads as you climb. Shortly after your narrow path begins to descend steeply, you reach Reservoir Road and turn left beneath overhanging ledges and deep shade. The soft moss base of these old carriage roads makes beautiful walking.

When you reach Sky Top Road, head toward the hotel to circle round to its northern side. Notice the museum, which you will want to visit another day. About 40 minutes suffices for this 1-mile segment of the walk.

Turn onto Eagle Cliff Road with signs pointing toward the Granary and Undercliff. Turn left on Lambdin's Path, where you will walk down and under a bridge to Undercliff Path. At

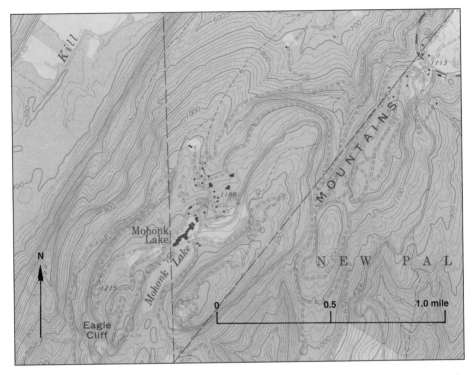

this point turn right, away from the hotel. Stop at one of the gazebos for a brief rest, then continue to the end of the lake and turn away from Undercliff on a faint path through a draw that quickly intersects lovely Woodland Road. Turn right toward Humpty Dumpty and Cope's Point.

You emerge from the deep shade of tall trees to a gazebo with a gorgeous view of the Trapps. Turn here toward Humpty Dumpty and the Plateau Path. From hopping on sunwarmed rocks, you descend into a deep, cool glen with bursts of moist air telling of deeper crevices beneath. Look back at intervals, for at a point you will see an exquisitely framed view of the Trapps. Follow the deep cleft into a hemlock ravine, where lots of scrambling will take you to a fork. Try the blue blazes that continue down—a

nearly straight drop—to Giant's Workshop. You begin to feel a bit silly, like a child in a magical kingdom.

You have traversed so many paths and found such a variety of routes that it is hard to believe it is less than 45 minutes since you left the lake. The path emerges on Minnewaska Road, and turning right, uphill, you shortly intersect Laurel Path Road, my idea of the perfect woodland road. Your map shows that at any point you could continue on the old carriage roads back to the visitors' center. But, to continue the adventure, turn right on Plateau Path, then turn again onto blue-marked Cathedral Path. The way straight, marked with red, circles back to the Giant's Workshop and the trail you have already followed. Cathedral Path will lead you up through a jumble of rocks—doesn't one look like a huge whale?—you may catch the "naming fever" that infected the trails' creators. A red-marked trail joins from the right, you go leftish and up beneath the cliff, then up it to emerge on a rock ledge with a gazebo and views. If that spot is occupied, turn left on Copes Lookout Road.

Beyond the next charming overlook, turn right from Copes Lookout Road to Copes Lookout Path, which quickly brings you back to the Eaglecliff Road near the tennis courts. You will easily spend 2 hours savoring these 2 miles of walks and scrambles. Have you noticed how close the carriage roads and paths are, yet how separated they seem because they circle the mountain at such varied elevations?

A right on Eaglecliff Road gives you a beautiful walk beneath hemlocks and ledges, again in the deep, cool shade. Pause again for the views from Artists' Rock, then turn again downhill. Instead of following the carriage road, look for the red arrow–marked path that weaves between switchbacks on the carriage road and keeps you close to cliff top as you descend. Look across the lake to the crevice below Sky Top that you climbed earlier in the day. The Sky Top loop on Eaglecliff Road and back to the visitors' center is about 1.8 miles and takes 1¼ hours.

You return to the visitors' center; look for the arrows to Mossy Brook Road and signs pointing to the shortest way to the parking area, 1.5 miles and a 40-minute walk. The route takes you past impressive views of the Hudson Valley and again onto a woodland path, this time through an exquisite valley. It leads you up Whitney Road to Huguenot Drive and a short stretch along that road back to the parking area.

23

Wurtsboro Ridge

Distance: 4, 6, or 10 miles, depending on route taken

Time: 3, 4, or 7 hours

Vertical rise: 400, 1,100, or 1,500 feet cumulative

Maps: USGS 7½' Wurtsboro; USGS 7½' Ellenville

Wurtsboro Ridge, part of the Shawangunk Mountains that run from New Jersey to New Paltz, yields unobstructed views along most of the ridge, creating a sense of openness unlike other hikes in the Hudson Valley. The trail, a recent opus of the New York–New Jersey Trail Conference (NY–NJTC), is part of their Long Path and generally lies just below the ridgeline on the western side. Much of it is in newly acquired state land. The state parcel

Looking toward Sams Point and Gertrude's Nose from Wurtsboro Ridge

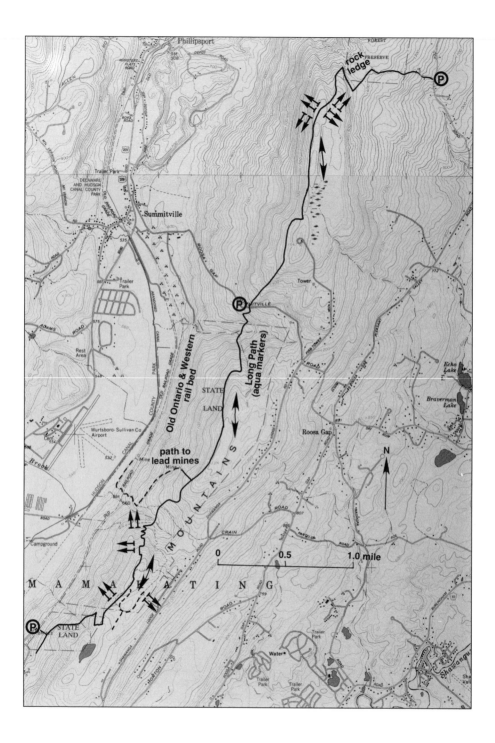

is split by the abandoned New York Ontario and Western Railroad bed a hundred or so feet above the floodplain. The railroad bed would allow you to make a pleasant loop instead of doubling back; sadly, as of this writing, the owners do not permit hiking on the bed. The Village of Wurtsboro below is named in honor of Maurice and William Wurts, developers of the Delaware and Hudson Canal, which runs along the western base of the Shawangunk Mountains.

If you have a single car, starting midway along the ridge, at Roosa Gap Summitville Road, allows you to enjoy all the best views in one outing. A two-car route is described at the end of the hike. To get to Wurtsboro Ridge, take NY 17 to Exit 114 and turn left on County Route 171 (old NY 17). Continue into Wurtsboro, turning right on US 209, and, in four miles, note a yellow traffic warning sign showing a road to the right and the word "Firehouse." Although unmarked, this is Roosa Gap Summitville Road. Turn right here and, in 50 feet, turn right again to ascend on the narrow, paved road. In 1.4 miles from US 209, at a sharp left bend, there is room on each side of the road to park; the trail crosses 100 feet farther uphill. From this road you may hike north 2 miles (or more) and back and, along the way, see spectacular views in all directions. You may also hike south 3 miles (or more) and back, enjoy views all along the ridge toward the Basher Kill wetlands and the valley below, and explore an old lead mine. The ridge is mostly scrub oak, blueberry, and some open rock, with views to the southwest clockwise through north much of the way. If you have time, hike both north and south and enjoy all this ridge has to offer. The route north is described

first, then the route south.

Starting north, following the parakeet-aqua blazes and Long Path disks, the steep, rocky ascent will quickly provide southwest views of Wurtsboro Ridge, Basher Kill, and Wurtsboro Airport. In another few minutes you gain your first postage-stamp view southeast through the Roosa Gap toward Schunemunk. Soon, 0.5 mile from the start, you are walking parallel to the ridgeline, on the northwest side, always a few tens of feet below the ridgeline. Behind you, if the weather is clear, you can see all the way south to New Jersey High Point State Park. Ahead, the Catskills come into view above the scrub oak. On top of the ridge you may see an antenna on what was a fire tower but is now a posted state police relay station. Once you are well past the state police tower, 1 mile from the start, you gain the ridge. Soon, sighting along the ridgeline, you catch tantalizing glimpses of Sams Point through the tops of the scrub oak.

The views get better and better with each rise until suddenly, less than 2 miles from the start, as the ridge starts to descend, the views open up. From here you can see back southwest toward the Basher Kill. To the north the Catskills lie before you, obstructed only by a nearby unnamed peak in the Shawangunks on the Sullivan–Ulster County border. Along the ridge you can see Sams Point, Margaret Cliff, Castle Point, Hamilton Point, and Gertrude's Nose. To the east the expanse of the Hudson Valley opens before you. To the southeast, Taurus and Storm King mark the passage of the Hudson, flanked by Breakneck Ridge and Beacon to the left and Black Rock Forest and Schunemunk to the right. Views continue all the way through southern Harriman State Park.

Perhaps this is a good spot to find a boulder to sit on and have a snack before retracing your steps. You might also continue on down into a col, where, after entering state land, you can see a handsome rock ledge before returning.

Starting south from Roosa Gap Summitville Road, following the parakeet-aqua blazes, you descend quickly into the col of Roosa Gap. You leave private property and enter state land where the path is now marked with blue DEC disks. In less than 10 minutes you cross an old woods road and two forks of a small stream surrounded by laurel. You ascend along the right bank of the second fork. After a half hour's ascent, with a couple of switchbacks, you reach your first views back toward the Catskills, to Roosa Gap, and to the ridge beyond with a tower on top. You continue climbing, but the trail stays 40 to 50 feet below the ridgeline. The valley below remains a constant companion. Just as you start to descend into another col, less than 2 miles from the start, you cross a wide path that leads directly down to the upper of two lead mines, just a couple hundred feet below.

You'll want to make a side excursion to these historic mines. Orange County historian Mildred Parker Seese claims that these mines are the oldest in New York State. It is likely that Native Americans were the first to mine here. The Dutch may have been mining here as early as 1664. The mines have been in and out of operation for perhaps three centuries, hampered by the problem of separating zinc, lead, and smaller quantities of copper and silver. Local historian Pat Moore says the mines continued to operate through the first part of the twentieth

century; only recently were the family-owned mine properties sold to the state.

After 10 more minutes on the trail, as you descend into a col, you cross a road that leads back to both mines and up to an attempted housing development aborted by bankruptcy. You climb steeply through a series of switchbacks to reach the final summit with the valley and Wurtsboro Airport behind you. Wurtsboro Ridge, with a near-ideal 1-to-4 slope, helps make the airport a popular soaring spot. With west winds of 15 knots or more, sailplanes will ride the lift from the ridge wave just above you.

As you near the summit, your view is blocked by taller trees. Continue to the south end of the summit where you meet much open rock. On this summit are your best views of the Basher Kill wildlife area to the southwest. This is a good spot to eat before heading back. If you'd like to make a side excursion to enjoy views to the east, you'll find a gravel road by the eastern edge of the open rock area, near where the trail meets the open rock. There are a series of gravel roads, and if you head east 0.3 mile or so, you'll come to a rock cut from which you can see Beacon, Breakneck Ridge, Taurus, Storm King, Black Rock Forest, Schunemunk, and all the way down to southern Harriman State Park. Don't go beyond this rock cut or you'll end up in the development covering the eastern side of the ridge.

You could continue on the Long Path and it would take you down to the old New York Ontario and Western Railroad station. However, since you've hiked 3 miles, plus any side excursions, it is a good time to turn around and retrace your steps to Roosa Gap Summitville Road.

If you have two cars, you can traverse

the ridge in a 7.5-mile hike to Cox Road. (Sometime in 1994 the NY–NJTC expects to extend the trail 2.5 miles farther to NY Route 52.) At 0.2 mile from Exit 114 of NY 17 on County Route 171 (old NY17), proceed right on Shawanga Lodge Road for 3.2 miles, then right on Roosa Gap Summitville Road for 0.7 mile, then left on Roosa Gap Road (which becomes Pleasant Valley Road) for 1.2 miles, then left on Cox Road for 0.8 mile. There is very limited parking along this narrow dirt road. Leave one car here near an unmarked road and house on your left, and retrace your route back to County Route 171 where you turn right for 0.6 mile and head right on a gravel road. Park next to what was a New York Ontario and Western Railroad station and is now a VFW post. Follow blue blazes uphill and head left at the intersection with the Long Path. The route is as described above. At the northern end, shortly after the rock ledge, you turn right (southeast) on a woods road that you follow for 0.5 mile to Cox Road.

24

Vernooy Kill Falls

Distance: 3.6 miles

Time: 2 hours

Vertical rise: 640 feet

Map: USGS 7½' Kerhonkson

Vernooy Kill Falls is the site of an old gristmill now surrounded by farmlands. A walk to the falls is short and delightful and a time to think about farmers of long ago.

The route to the trailhead passes through farmlands that are giving way to resorts or forest cover. From the intersection of NY 44 and NY 55 with US 209, go north 1.2 miles on US 209 to the traffic light in Kerhonkson. Turn left here on Clay Hill Road, which is unmarked. You reach a stop at 2.5 miles where Pataukunk Road, also designated County Route 3, comes in from the right. Turn left on County Route 3 and then turn left again in 0.2 mile on Cherrytown Road. Again there are no signs to guide you, but there are beautiful vistas back to the Shawangunks.

Cherrytown Road winds west and then north. You will be reassured that

Vernooy Kill Falls

you are following the correct route by the blue paint slashes that mark this stretch of road as a portion of the Long Path. You pass Baker Road 3.65 miles from County Route 3, 6.3 miles from Kerhonkson. Immediately, Upper Cherrytown Road crosses a brook, and just beyond it, before the road crosses over Mombaccus Creek, you turn left again, this time onto Upper Cherrytown Road. Follow it north for 3.15 miles to the trailhead, which is on the left (west) side of the road, with a parking area on the right.

The trail, a portion of the Long Path, is marked with blue DEC hiking disks. It follows an old town road through a lovely laurel stand across a little stream with a rock-hop crossing. Two hundred yards farther you will cross Mombaccus Creek on a snowmobile bridge to the right of the roadway and briefly follow the creek uphill. The road makes a sweeping S-curve as it begins to climb the ridge, rising out of the valley's deep hemlock stands into second-growth hardwoods. The uphill route is steady, gradually leaving laurel behind. You pass through an area of blowdowns, then, as the trail levels out to round the hillside, you may notice a road that forks left.

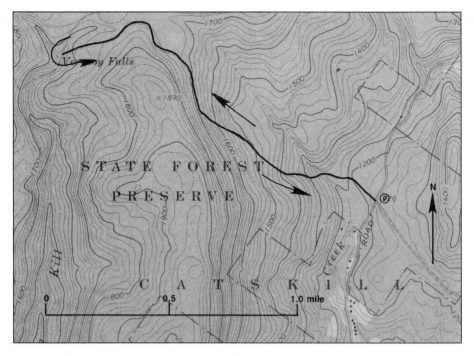

You continue on the obvious route, shortly hearing the falls and beginning a small descent to Vernooy Kill.

The spot is charming, with a bridge across the stream from which you can view the falls. Below, one solid wall of the ruins of the mill extends along the eastern shore, and other rock walls delineate the channel through which water was diverted to power the mill. You can try to discover the way water was used to power the mill or extend your visit in a number of other ways. The hemlock bank to the southeast of the falls is an attractive place to picnic or camp, though it can be crowded on summer weekends. You can walk downstream along the western shore to a lovely picnic spot and more foundations.

Below the mill site, Vernooy Kill continues to tumble over boulders, creating cascades and small falls in the secluded valley. There is short path along the western shore to lead you briefly downstream. You can continue the walk west on the snowmobile trail through a spruce and hemlock swamp with a lovely understory of *Lycopodia* and ferns. A faint path leads north along the stream to other smaller falls and pools. The Long Path continues north along an old road. Wherever you turn, you can explore the foundations of houses and barns and follow old stone fences. And, you can wonder, as we did, about the origins of the mill.

The Kill was named for Cornelius Vernooy, one of the very first settlers in the Rondout Valley. In the early 1700s, he brought the area's first gristmill to Warwarsing, with machinery imported from Holland. But the name of the settlers upstream at the falls remains a mystery.

25

Peekamoose and Table

Distance: 10 miles (from Denning Trailhead)

Time: 5 hours

Vertical rise: 1,750 feet

Map: NY–NJTC Catskill Trails, #43

What will impress you most about Peekamoose and its environs is the remarkable clarity and storybook forests of the Rondout and Neversink Creeks and their valleys. The Rondout is conceived on the south- and east-facing slopes of Rocky, Lone, and Peekamoose mountains and is joined by the malachite waters of Peekamoose Lake as it swells through Bull Run and joins its east branch at Sundown.

Deer Shanty Brook

John Burroughs loved this flashy, pellucid brook, vowing that "if I were a trout I should ascend every stream till I found the Rondout." If you're coming from the west, you follow the Neversink's east branch from Claryville. It, too, is famous trout water.

While you can make this hike as a back-the-way-you-came jaunt, bagging both Table and Peekamoose in what would amount to a strenuous, 1,800-foot ascent from Denning, you also can leave one vehicle at the Denning trailhead and another at the Long Path trailhead for Peekamoose, on Peekamoose Road just east of Bull Run. Or make it an overnighter, camping among the intricate islands and peninsulas created by the confluence of Deer Shanty Brook, Donovan Brook, and the upper reaches of the Neversink's East Branch. This popular spot with its lean-to and untold campsites upstream along the Neversink is certainly as close to heaven as anyone can be—and still be in the Catskills.

Whatever you choose, be warned of the approach directly to Peekamoose Mountain from the south, along the Peekamoose Road above Bull Run. This trail has long been a model of demoralizing ascents, with its 2,643-foot elevation gain within 3.5 miles. The Denning Trail, or Phoenicia–East Branch (PE) Trail, with its crossing at Deer Shanty Brook is the more gentle and scenic option, and it will save you 1,000 feet of elevation. If you wish only to climb Peekamoose (which doesn't have Table's view), are rushed for time, in top condition, and up to an unrelenting, difficult ascent, the trail from Peekamoose Road provides the shortest route.

If you choose the yellow-marked PE Trail, start at Denning. From Big Indian, west of Phoenicia, travel south on County Route 47 through Oliverea, Winnisook, and Frost Valley, and turn left in Claryville onto County Route 19 (Denning Road). Follow this straight into Denning to the trailhead parking area, a total distance from Big Indian of some 30 miles. A more complicated route is from Boiceville on NY 28A south to West Shokan, turning right onto County Route 42 (Peekamoose Road), passing the strenuous blue-marked trail (and Long Path) access 10 miles from West Shokan. Then bear right into Grahamsville, Unionville, and Curry on NY 55, turning right at Curry to Claryville, and again right into Denning and to the trailhead, also a total of 30 miles. From NY 17, the shortest approach to this area from the south, take NY 55 east from Liberty, turning north on County Route 19 at Curry. Bear right (staying on County Route 19) at Claryville, and follow Denning Road to the trailhead. Use your map to navigate the last several miles from Claryville.

Park at the road's end where trail signs to Slide Mountain and the Denning lean-to are posted. The setting is a high farming-valley plain with frequent plots of old-growth forest. You may see deer feeding close to the road here. Once we even rolled apples from roadside trees to waiting deer, who munched them happily.

Follow the trail through a hemlock woods over a crude road, crossing a small plank bridge and a small seasonal brook. Within 25 minutes you will reach a trail junction, where you turn right toward the Denning lean-to. Go downhill into a wet area (seasonal), keeping an eye on the markers (blue) and continuing steeply down across two bridged streams, one of

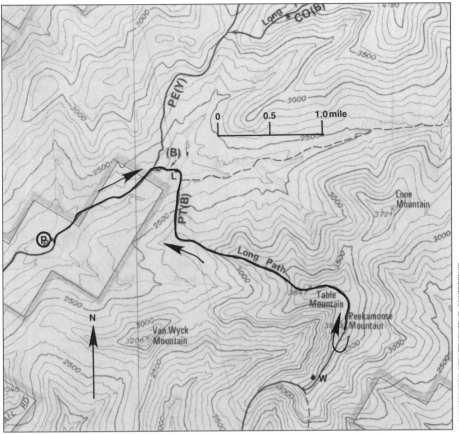

which could be a dry bed at various times of year. The trail will bring you to the lean-to within a few minutes.

There are many campsites upstream from the lean-to, perhaps hundreds, with several campfire rings constructed along the creek's edge. These primitive sites continue seemingly without end, along the banks of both Deer Shanty Brook and the Neversink. It is possible to cross these streams on rocks without difficulty. The blue markers are good as the trail leaves opposite the lean-to.

Go uphill through a lush forest of fern, oxalis, club moss, and huge birch.

Within a half hour the trail will level somewhat, skirting a ridge exposing Woodhull and Van Wyck mountains to the southwest. The trail varies in pitch, generally gaining elevation as you go through thin stands of hardwood, climbing through broken rock ledges and taking frequent breaks. Within 45 minutes of leaving the lean-to, you reach a ledge among the cherry trees with a view of Peekamoose and to the south. Several more spur trails lead to the right 20 or 30 feet off the trail, some with worthwhile views. Beware—these are dangerous ledges. Through the trees to the left (north) as you continue, you may see Slide and its neighboring peaks, and, as you gain in elevation, you'll identify Panther, parts of Giant Ledge, Lone, Rocky, Balsam Cap, and Friday.

Within 2 hours of the Denning lean-to you reach Table's summit. There is no view here. The best view of the entire trip awaits. Continue through thick spruce and fir until you reach a spur trail, to the left (east) of the main trail. This side trip may demand considerable exploration, as several herd paths have been created and may confuse you. However, if you've found the right trail, you should reach a rock outcrop within 5 minutes. It is worth your time to search for this spectacular vista. Slide is the long ridge close in front of you to the north. To the right you see Lone, Wittenberg and Cornell, Friday, Rocky, Balsam Cap, Hanover, the Ashokan Reservoir, West Kill and Hunter between Slide and Cornell, the Blackheads, Plateau, and Sugarloaf. Through Pecoy Notch you can see Kaaterskill High Peak. This is nearly the entire Devil's Path skyline.

When and if you've had enough of this rare sight, continue on the main trail to Peekamoose, which you can see before you as you descend. Some faraway views are available along this downhill section of trail—extending beyond the Shawangunks and into the Highlands. Even Anthony's Nose and the deep gulch spanned by the Bear Mountain Bridge can be seen with binoculars, or good eyes.

As you drop into the fragrant, co-niferous saddle between Table and Peekamoose, the trail becomes wet, and within 10 minutes you begin climbing again. You may see a vague Y in the trail as you approach the summit of Peekamoose. Go right to reach the summit, where a large boulder sits in a small clearing surrounded by scrub evergreens. This boulder can be climbed for more views, but they are inferior to Table's.

If you are walking out to Peekamoose Road instead of returning, continue ahead following steeply downhill through a series of ledges and overlooks, following the backbone of a long ridge extending south-south-west. Within half an hour of leaving the summit, following frequent blue trail markers, you reach an outstanding viewpoint exposing the Rondout, Neversink, and Mongaup valleys, Samson Mountain, Bangle Hill, Breath Hill, Little Rocky, and some interesting ridges to the west. Avoid the dotted trail, which leaves this point east of Buttermilk Falls Brook; it crosses private lands. From this point you walk down through a dense, predominantly ash and maple forest with a beech understory. The trail continues amid white violets, huge cottonwoods, and red and white pines as you gradually go downhill, meeting up with a skid or fire road that becomes steadily eroded and finally reaches Peekamoose Road, 2 hours' walking time from the summit. If you choose this way out, you'll be glad you avoided it on the way in.

26

Ashokan High Point

Distance: 7.5 miles

Time: 5½ hours

Vertical rise: 1,980 feet

Map: NY–NJTC Catskill Trails, #43

This fine hike has only recently been included in guidebooks and has risen from considerable obscurity into a popular destination. The trail is not marked and there are no signs indicating the mountain's presence, yet it is one of the most attractive trails and biggest scenic payoffs in the Catskill Range.

The Devil's Path from Ashokan High Point

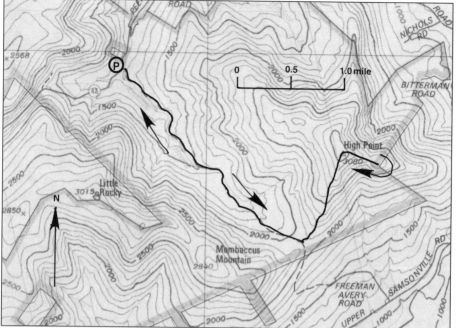

The trail to Ashokan High Point's summit is an old settlement road that has been so well built that it requires little maintenance. The surface is hard-packed dirt and gravel, where few seedlings will hold. It has been so well drained in past years that erosion has caused little damage. Old stone walls and ditch construction protect the trail from the advancing forest. Only the overhanging boughs that you occasionally duck under betray any need for trail maintenance, much of which is done by a few loyal hikers and the Boy Scouts. Because it is not overused, the trail is also very clean. All things considered, it is a rare find in an era earmarked by intensive use and exploitation of the Catskill scenic areas.

The trail to High Point shows on the New York–New Jersey Trail Conference (NY–NJTC) map as a dashed line, keyed as an unmarked trail. The map is accurate to a point. It shows the correct route to the summit but omits some side trails that might cause confusion. Don't let the lack of marking deter you, however. The moderate-difficulty trail is self-guiding in its entirety (except for the short bushwhack to the knob) and it is hard to get lost if you pay attention to the map and text.

Find the trailhead by turning south on NY 28A from NY 28 in Boiceville west of Kingston. Follow NY 28A for three miles to West Shokan. Here, Peekamoose Road (County Route 42) runs uphill along the Bush Kill. After 3.9 miles you see a parking area on the right. State land and forest preserve signs are posted nearby. Cross the road and take the timber bridge across Kanape Brook to access the trail.

Follow the trail uphill through a typical Catskill slope forest of beech, birch, and maple, slowly climbing up and away from Kanape Brook, which is on your right. Within 10 minutes you cross one of several stone culverts that run under the trail, draining the northwest watershed of the mountain. These are structures you ordinarily won't see on Catskill trails. Several are completely handmade; the ditch itself is lined with bluestone drywalls and capped with large, flat stones that you walk over. You begin to see some very attractive bluestone drywalls (not mortared) along this part of the trail, as well as some stone bridges that span seasonal creeks. You cross two such bridges and climb gradually but steadily into an area where mountain laurel appears.

Within 5 or 10 minutes you reach a Y in the trail, on which you bear right, staying on the more established trail. Shortly afterward you pass a small spring on the left that has been dug by hand and built up with stone. In another 10 minutes the trail crosses Kanape Brook into a clearing with a mortared brick-and-stone fireplace. This is a pretty spot—the brook forms a large pool as it flows from the shaded conifer forest upstream. Balsam fir now appear, and shortly afterward some larger hemlocks appear. There are many attractive camping sites all along this trail, particularly through this section.

Keep going uphill, never strenuously, for another 20 minutes through a second-growth forest. You curve gradually toward the east and suddenly reach higher open forest where the trail turns grassy amid the oak and laurel. You may notice a good trail branching to the right at this point. Keep going, until within 5 minutes you reach a T where you are in an airy, forested saddle between High Point and Mombaccus mountains at 2,000 feet. There is a campfire ring here and several flat camping areas. Watch closely for the left turn up the mountain. If you've reached no-trespassing signs, you've gone too far.

Turn left (northeast) here for the 1-mile, 1,000-foot-elevation-gain hike to the summit. Pass a road that goes off to your left slightly beyond the trail intersection, and follow straight ahead, beginning to climb uphill in a moment. In 5 minutes you pass a vague footpath to the trail's right. Continue uphill into a slide-and-ledge area over broken-rock footing. Views appear as you climb through this red oak, maple, and blueberry cover on your way through terracing terrain. From saddle to summit takes not more than 45 minutes.

The summit is a small rock ledge with an east-to-southwest exposure, revealing the edge of the Ashokan Reservoir, the Kingston–Rhinecliff Bridge, the Shawangunks from Mohonk to Minnewaska and down to Sams Point, and beyond into the Hudson Highlands. Carvings from 1878 show in the summit stones, along with several anchor bolts from an early observation tower. North of the summit several trails wander into the woods, one of which leads in 100 yards to an open westerly overlook with good views of Slide, Friday, Balsam Cap, Rocky, Lone, Table, and Peekamoose. This short side trip is a must!

Ashokan's summit has a fine collection of views to pick from, but what will astonish you most is its blueberries, which are everywhere and rank easily as the best of the Catskill patches. The thick bushes cover the entire unshaded summit, and the unusually large berries remain seemingly unnoticed until harvested by frost.

Although it may not seem possible

as you stand on Ashokan High Point's true summit, the views (and the blueberries) are better on the low knob you can see just east of you. This is a short bushwhack, some of it on an obscure and for the most part indistinguishable foot trail. Even without a compass it is difficult to get lost, but it is a good idea for beginning bushwhackers to have one along just in case. This 0.25-mile trip to the eastern summit is so worthwhile that it should not be missed.

To get there, drop down around the summit's north side on a vague footpath that will disappear eventually, sometimes to reemerge looking like a well-trodden deer path. Follow east (a compass bearing would be accurate at 125 degrees with declination figured in) and into a saddle with long rock ledges running north to south. The terrain undulates gently afterward, gradually ascending to bring you out to the open easterly expanse. Figure on about 15 minutes for this bushwhack.

Here you see many ledges and rock overhangs where you can search for more views, but the terrain is easy. In autumn a montage of burgundy berry bushes grows thickly and reaches to knee height. Scrub oak turns the color of brick dust on amber. You can see almost the entire Ashokan, a long, flat strip of indigo amid the valley's greenness, where colors will change in weeks to come. Spun into the scene are the somber, drab outcrops of rock that pockmark the summits and ranges beyond, and the short stilts of battered, nut-brown tree trunks, festooned with the scarlet berry clusters of mountain ash.

Looking left (north) from east to west, you observe Overlook, Plattekill, Indian Head, Jimmy Dolan Notch, Twin, Pecoy Notch, Sugarloaf, Mink Hollow, Plateau, Stony Clove Notch, Hunter, Diamond Notch, and West Kill Mountain. To the north are Wittenberg and Cornell. To the east and beyond the reservoir are the Taconics and the Berkshires. Moving westward is the long Shawangunk Ridge and the flat plain of the Neversink, Rondout, and Mongaup rivers. Suddenly Mombaccus again fills your eye, and you've covered about 270 degrees for what promises to be one of the best overlooks in the Catskill Mountains.

You can also see the roads around the Ashokan Reservoir (New York City's water supply), which provide outstanding views of the range. The hike out from the knob and back over Ashokan High Point will take you about 2 hours. Avoid the shorter southerly access, for it is private.

If you have time after your return, you might want to drive across the dam and causeway on a longer route back to NY 28. Instead of going left when you get to the bottom of Peekamoose Road in West Shokan, go right and stay on NY 28A until you reach a left turn (approximately six miles) that you will see crosses the reservoir, providing views of Ashokan High Point and the Catskill High Peaks.

This huge impoundment has an unsettling history. Its construction required the relocation of 7 towns, 11 miles of railroad, 64 miles of roads, and the valley's 2,000 inhabitants; 2,600 coffins in 32 cemeteries were exhumed and moved, dumps were dug up and disinfected, buildings were burned and sanitized, and recompenses were made. It took 25 years to settle all the claims involved.

If the water table is high, you will want to see the spillway, which you can reach by staying on NY 28A (east) toward Kingston. This is where wastewater from the lower basin finds its way to the Hudson River via the Esopus Creek.

Ashokan meant "place of fish" to the Iroquois, as it does to modern fishermen who regularly catch trout weighing up to 20 pounds below the weir. The Ashokan is the wintering place for trout that spawn upstream in the Esopus, a fact that has made the stream famous for its annual spring run, particularly of the rainbow trout.

27

Mount Tremper

Distance: 5.5 miles	
Time: 4 hours	
Vertical rise: 1,960 feet	
Map: NY–NJTC Catskill Trails, #41	

The trail to Mount Tremper is most direct and interesting from the southwest access along old NY 28, or the Old Plank Road, south of Phoenicia. It is also accessible from Willow, off NY 212, on the longer, blue-marked trail from Jessup Road.

Both trails form a section of the Long Path as it approaches the Devil's Path from the south through Mink Hollow. Switchbacks characterize the red-marked trail to Mount Tremper, transforming this otherwise difficult 2,000-foot ascent into a moderate hike. The path zigzags across the slope, turning at convenient points of terrain to double back on itself, sometimes nearly 180 degrees. Long before hiking became fashionable, the road was used for log hauling and stone quarrying, and later for fire control and maintenance.

The Esopus at low water

The red-marked trail begins on the east side of the Esopus Creek, off County Route 40 (Old Plank Road or old NY 28), 2.3 miles northwest of Mount Tremper Corners or 1.6 miles southeast of Phoenicia. Parking at streamside is ample, and you will most likely be sharing it not with fellow hikers but with trout fishermen who enjoy the long run of water here known as "sleepy hollow."

You'll be taken with the water's clarity and alpine character. You may see dimpling rises of brown and rainbow trout, whose enduring management has made the creek one of New York State's most valued fisheries. After heavy runoff, though, the Esopus assumes an ugly tinge of mountain grit and remains for days the color of chocolate milk. During these periods, when fishermen are scarce and snow sticks reluctantly in the hemlock shadows, the views from Mount Tremper are at their best.

As you enter the forest preserve, don't be deterred by the trail's initial steepness, where logs have been placed to check erosion. It soon levels out, bringing you to the trail register at 0.25 mile. Continue over broken rock and red shale footing, gradually gaining elevation.

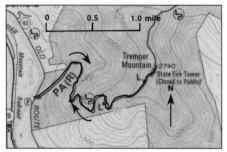

© 1989 NEW YORK–NEW JERSEY TRAIL CONFERENCE

Several larger feeder streams intersect the trail, and a culvert appears as you enter a sparse stand of maturing white pine. Evidence of logging is visible in the abundance of thin, second-growth hardwood and decaying stumps. Yellow paint blazes running north and southwest mark the forest-preserve boundaries. This piece of trail also sports a few of the Long Path's blue blazes.

As the trail steepens to 15 or 20 degrees, you cross another culvert, over an energetic brook that cuts a deep gully in the mountainside as it bursts from an uneven-aged hemlock stand. At this point you are 20 minutes into the hike, or almost 0.5 mile. You will have reached the first switchback when the trail suddenly turns south and uphill, where large maple and ash dominate an understory of young hemlock. To your left (east) and uphill, a long outcrop that has slid in many places starts an interesting visual transition. Water appears from a spring on your left. Fallen rock can be seen below the trail to your right, now heavily covered with moss, the accumulated stuff of ancient forests.

As you come through the next switchback, you see a huge pile of quarry tailings, the broken stone that was shoved aside as longer slabs of bluestone were excavated. It now forms a sort of constructed ridge covered with thin soil and vegetation. The quarry is accessible from a small, over-grown roadbed on the trail's left that ascends gently into the quarry excavation, which covers an acre or two. Follow it to a high, right-angled rock face, where the slabs were removed. Other than this vertical stone wall, only a small foundation and a few rusted iron remnants bear testimony to the once-thriving industry. During your exploration, beware of the quarry-dwelling rattlesnakes, who habitually bask in the warm sun of early spring. (They are shy and wary of you.)

Many of the nineteenth-century hotel owners disliked the imposing quarries. By the early 1880s Major Jacob H. Tremper's Tremper House was competing for business with the Catskill Mountain House, so could ill afford competition with the nearby bluestone quarries that robbed the hills of their peace and quiet. Alf Evers writes in *The Catskills from Wilderness to Woodstock*, "Boarders grumbled at the ugly quarry scars on mountainsides. They noticed with displeasure a conspicuous quarry erupting even before 1880 near the Catskill Mountain House and a short walk from the romantic Moses Rock, and saw quarry after quarry breaking into other mountain forests. Quarries began to threaten the Tremper House from its flanks, while others were unpleasantly visible. . . . In all parts of the mountains boarders never knew when their surries or tallyhoes might meet a ponderous stone wagon driven by a cursing teamster in the cloud of dust raised by its horses' hoofs and its wheels."

After you have visited the quarry, where the dust has long since settled, follow the trail along a flatter section into an oak forest, which turns into the oak and laurel cover typical of higher elevations in the Catskills. At about 1,800 feet above sea level, you switchback about 120 degrees on a steepening grade, where paper birch and an occasional white pine appear. You'll have a few glimpses southwest toward southern high peaks during early spring. Once through the switchback, you can look through the trees at northwesterly views toward Sheridan Mountain.

The trail steepens, heading directly uphill, nearly due east. Within a few minutes you see a lean-to on your right. At this point you are 1.9 miles from the trailhead. Keep a sharp eye out for this shelter if you intend to use it, because it's easy to miss, positioned as it is, downhill and facing south. It is in better condition than the summit lean-to, is more private, and has a water source nearby.

Finally, after one more switchback you climb slightly and walk a long ridge. Just as you expected the summit to appear, you discover that the ridge continues for another 0.5 mile through a canopy of twisted oak, tormented and battered by exposure. After 20 minutes more of hiking, you reach a stand of bright-barked beech trees on your left, and soon after that the second lean-to.

The fire tower just ahead has had its stairs removed and is closed to the public. At this time the New York State Department of Environmental Conservation (DEC) is examining alternative designs and possible rehabilitation of the existing tower because of its strategic location and the 360-degree view it provides. The fire tower was built to replace the one on Slide, after the Mount Tremper tract was acquired between 1906 and 1910. Fires occurred on Mount Tremper in 1881, 1888, and again between 1916 and 1917. The area gave heavily of its hemlock stands between 1836 and 1879, with one local tanner recording an all-time harvest of 170,000 cords of bark. A new trail is also being considered for this wild forest area. The trail would run from Mount Tremper to Silver Hollow Notch, eventually joining the Devil's Path. It would decrease the road mileage of the Long Path and may adjoin additional new trails to Mount Tobias and the Catskill Interpretive Center.

The Tremper House Hotel was built in 1879 near the existing railroad bed at the base of the mountain. It was the Catskill's first railroad hotel, in an era when remoteness was more in fashion, and was visited by so many colorful personalities that it threatened even the popularity of Charles Beach's Catskill Mountain House. Young Oscar Wilde "chose to deliver his aesthetic lectures," according to Evers, "only at the Tremper House and the Kaaterskill Hotel. Wilde praised the Catskills' scenery, but shocked hotel proprietors by stating that their mountain houses are always built in the wrong spots. The top of a mountain is no place for a mountain house . . . it should be put in the valley, there the picturesque and beautiful is ever before you." Decide this for yourself as you return to the parking area the way you came.

28

Overlook Mountain

Distance: 10 miles

Time: 7–9 hours

Vertical rise: 1,250 feet

Map: NY–NJTC Catskill Trails, #41

The most interesting trail to Overlook Mountain begins at the head of the precipitous Plattekill Clove, reached by the harrowing Platte Clove Mountain Road, which climbs 1,400 feet in two miles. In dry weather the road is not much of a problem, but it is closed officially during winter months. Portions of the serpentine surface slide

Overlook Mountain

JOHN HANISLAN

into the ravine 500 feet below, and the road is repaired continually. At the guardrails you might want to pull over to spy down at "the wildest and boldest, most picturesque and romantic scenery of the entire Catskills," in the words of H. A. Haring in his classic *Our Catskill Mountains* (1931).

To find Platte Clove Mountain Road, take NY 212 from its junction with NY 32 in Saugerties, and turn right in Centerville after 2.4 miles, onto Blue Mountain Road. Bear left when you reach a fork at 1.5 miles. Continue straight ahead through the village of West Saugerties and up the mountain road for another 4.5 miles to the trailhead.

You can avoid the steep ascent altogether by coming from the west through Tannersville (on NY 23A), following Spring Street south and Bloomer Road east, which follows into Platte Clove Mountain Road two miles from where you left NY 23A at Tannersville. From here it is another five miles to the trailhead. Coming from Tannersville, avoid the DEC trail signs to Mink Hollow, Twin Mountain, and Devil's Path on Prediger Road. Continue instead to the Catskill Center for Conservation and Development (CCCD) signs, which you will see on the right one mile beyond Prediger Road. Parking is limited here, but there are several spots ahead (southeast on the mountain road).

This is a watershed divide. The northwesterly flowing Schoharie drains Roundtop and Kaaterskill High Peak on the north of its valley and the Devil's Path Mountains (from Indian Head to Hunter) on the south. The Plattekill Creek, flowing east, draws its youthful might from Kaaterskill High Peak, Plattekill Mountain, and Overlook Mountain. From here it flows through the clove to meander sluggishly to the Hudson.

Start your hike by following the green arrows on a white background across Plattekill Creek (tricky during runoff). The trail follows the old Overlook Road, which is washed out and unrecognizable at first but which soon becomes a pleasant bedrock pathway shadowed in hemlock. The arrows are intermittent and finally absent, but the trail is obvious and soon joins the Devil's Path, marked by red DEC trail markers of the State Forest Wilderness Area. An abandoned quarry apparent to the left just before this junction is easily explored. From late spring on, however, beware of rattlesnakes.

Within another 2 or 3 minutes' walking, the red-marked Devil's Path turns right. A series of trail signs marks this junction. Here you proceed straight on a blue-marked trail for the Devil's Kitchen lean-to and eventually Overlook Mountain. Continuing on the blue-marked trail, shortly after this junction, you discover a vague Y in the trail, on which you bear right, arriving at the Devil's Kitchen lean-to on the Coldkill.

Northeast of the lean-to there is a virgin tract of hemlock and mixed hardwood that has been categorized by the CCCD as a unique plant community. The major ground-cover species are alder-leaved viburnum, jack-in-the-pulpit, spinulose wood fern, Canada mayflower, and wood sorrel.

Continuing from the lean-to, on the blue-marked trail, cross over the Coldkill on a wooden bridge, and follow a slight uphill washout until you reach level terrain under oak and laurel cover. To the east you will notice some good views through the oaks to the Hudson Valley. About 1.1 miles from where you crossed the Coldkill

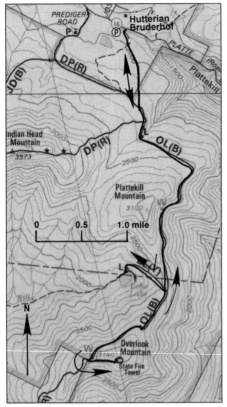

it is an easy hike that allows for overuse by crowds. A rough trail circles Echo Lake, which forms the headwaters of the Sawkill.

The degree of abuse at Echo Lake, at this writing, has been severe; the privy has been torn down for firewood and stuffed with litter, the vegetation ravaged, and refuse widely distributed. But it is still worth the trip to see one of the Catskills' few natural lakes and to observe some of the problems the Catskill Forest Preserve faces. You might even try for the echo, which was a favorite pastime of guests from the Overlook Mountain House days.

At the Overlook Mountain and Echo Lake trail junction, you are only 1.9 miles from your destination. Continuing up around the northwest slope of Overlook, there are good views, in the spring, of the Devil's Path mountains. Indian Head (3,573 feet) seems to have appeared from nowhere and is surprisingly close at three miles. Identifying the notches and peaks will be a good lunchtime activity from Overlook's summit.

Within a half hour on this gentle but steady ascent (after passing a good spring), you reach a trail junction near the ruins of the Overlook Mountain House. The trail signs give the wrong distance of 2.5 miles to Devil's Kitchen lean-to; the correct distance is 3.5 miles. Keep in mind as well that the stated 5.9 miles to Platte Clove Mountain Road, while accurate if you entered on the red-marked trail from Prediger Road, is actually 4.5 miles for those using the CCCD trail, which you came in on.

Continuing to the east following the blue markers, you arrive at the summit in another 15 minutes. The fire tower has not been occupied since 1989 and should not be climbed. The

is Skunk Spring on the right side of the trail. Except for the dry months, this is a great place to slake one's thirst and refill a canteen. The trail is fairly level here, following the 2,500-foot contour on Plattekill's eastern shoulder. On this effortless section of the trail, you notice the appearance of white birch and get occasional glimpses of the Overlook summit and fire tower to the south.

Three miles into the hike you reach the Echo Lake spur (yellow markers) to your right. This trail drops 500 feet in 0.5 mile to the west. There is a good lean-to at the lake and some designated camping sites, but because of its proximity to a trailhead at Meads, summit view is excellent, however, even without the tower climb. (Also on the summit are picnic tables and the small residence for the forest-fire observers, one of whom is reported to have placed rattlesnakes in his dresser drawers after having found them rifled by hiking vandals.) Just as inspiring a view is that of Overlook itself from the valley floor, a sight that merited the brushes of Frederic Church and Thomas Cole and prompted the pen of Charles Herbert Moore. The mountain continues to provide inspiration for aspiring artists from the village of Woodstock below.

From the summit, the heavy haze of the Hudson Valley, during most summer days, limits the view east to Kingston and Saugerties and to the Hudson River itself. On the marvelous clear days of spring, autumn, and winter, though, you can see into Connecticut and Massachusetts. The Hudson Highlands to the southeast can be seen too if the air is very clear.

In 1871 the Overlook Mountain House opened here, but despite its various distinctions, it was not a great success. It burned completely in 1875, was reconstructed in 1878, and burned again in 1924. In 1928, under new ownership, the existing poured-concrete foundation and walls, near the old hotel site, were started. Walls, windows, and plumbing were about all that were completed when the crash of 1929 happened and the project was abandoned.

If you want to hike to the summit of Overlook from Meads, the trailhead begins at the road's height on Meads Mountain, 2.5 miles north of the Woodstock village green. There is good parking space opposite the Zen Buddhist monastery, and the walk is an easy uphill hike of 2 miles following the red markers. Hike back to your car the way you came. At this point you'll be happy that it's all downhill!

29

The Old Mountain Road to Palenville Overlook

Distance: 8 miles

Time: 5 hours

Vertical rise: 1,300 feet

Map: NY–NJTC Catskill Trails, #41

To reach this quiet and isolated pair of overlooks, now marked only as a snowmobile and horse trail, you travel the historic Old Mountain Road through Rip Van Winkle Hollow, which, notes Roland Van Zandt, "was to become the classic approach to the great scenic domain of the Catskill Mountain House for almost all the remaining years of the nineteenth century." The road had its beginning in 1823 as a tannery road and stage-coach route to Charles L. Beach's Catskill Mountain House. It remained a stage route until the railroad came in the 1880s and caused its eventual abandonment.

By 1931 H. A. Haring wrote in *Our Catskill Mountains* that the road "is impassable for any sort of vehicle, but is endlessly charming for the hiker who is equal to an ascent of 2,000 feet within a walking distance of five miles." The road has been repaired since, and new bridges are in place for the modern hiker.

Begin at the western end of the Mountain Turnpike Road, which you will find by turning right in Palenville on Bogart Road, the first right after the light on NY 23A as you are driving west. Follow Bogart Road for 2.5 miles to a four-way intersection with Mountain Turnpike Road at Pelham's four corners (the portion to the right is dirt). There are some old trail signs here that, at this writing, are decayed badly. Turn left, and go one mile to the end of Mountain Turnpike Road, where you can park. You will see the snowmobile-trail markers as the road turns to dirt and curves uphill into Rip Van Winkle Hollow.

As you begin, you follow Stony Brook on the left, which for the first mile of trail skirts a deep hemlock ravine. Continuing uphill over a roadway that is still manageable for four-wheel-drive vehicles, you cross Black Snake Bridge within 0.5 mile. A hardwood forest slopes up to your right toward the

Round Top and Kaaterskill Clove from Palenville Overlook

escarpment, while the ravine, pitching steeply down to your left, slowly rises to intersect the trail at the horseshoe turn in Sleepy Hollow, where you see the old stone foundations of the Rip Van Winkle House. The 1-mile distance to this point will take you a half hour of uphill hiking, so you may enjoy a stop here, the traditional resting place for coach travelers to the Catskill Mountain House.

Every effort was made to assure guests that this was the spot where Rip encountered the strange crew of Henry Hudson's *Half Moon*. Nearby was the rock upon which he took his famous slumber, and a tree could be pointed out beneath which the bones of his dog Wolf were "discovered." Haring recorded that "every summer visitors in hundreds scrambled up the perpendicular continuation of Sleepy Hollow in search of the 'flats' where Hendrick Hudson's gnomes thunderously rolled the balls in their game of ninepins." In fact, Washington Irving is not specific as to the location of the events in the legend, which appealed to the romantic mind for its very vagueness and mystery. He did not visit the Catskills until 1832, 12 years after the publication of the story.

Continue from here on the 0.5-mile-long Dead Ox Hill, going steadily uphill through hardwoods toward the little Pine Orchard and Cape Horn. You reach Cape Horn within 30 minutes of Sleepy Hollow, to find a stone fireplace and rough campsite. From Cape Horn, views to the east are fair, with the Taconics and the river valley visible. Make a 180-degree right turn here, onto the Short Level, which takes you up a moderate grade to another horseshoe bend in 0.3 mile, or 10 minutes.

Now you turn toward the north, then switch back south to Featherbed Hill. This path also is shown on an 1876 map, drawn by Walton Van Loan, entitled "Map of All Points of Interest Within Four Miles of the Catskill Mountain House." You can get a photocopy of the map at the Haines Falls Library. Van Loan's representation of this particular area, specifically from the Saxe Farm at the end of Mountain Turnpike Road to Palenville Overlook, while not entirely reliable, accurately shows this section of the trail.

Many of the trails, however, are rerouted or abandoned. Other maps showing this trail are *Walking News'*s "Hikers' Region Map Number 35" and New York State DEC's "Horse Trails in New York State."

The trail throughout is so well marked that you will have no trouble following it. From Featherbed Hill, you walk the next 1.5 miles uphill through a hardwood forest until you reach a Y in the trail. Take a left at this Y. This point is known as the Long Level, where the grade becomes flatter as it approaches the bend in the road. If you wish to see the bend, continue straight 0.3 mile, but it is no longer a scenic attraction since the destruction of the Catskill Mountain House. There is a limited view of Pine Orchard here. This was the most popular location for painting and etching the Catskill Mountain House as it was seen in detail by visitors on the stage route. The classic scenic points favored by nineteenth-century artists were from the north and above the hotel, in the neighborhood of Sunset Rock and North Point (see North Point, hike 36). Most of the prints can be seen at Haines Falls Library. You'll observe that the romantic painter intensified and exaggerated scenes to produce effect. Thomas Cole believed "the subject [of art] should be pure and lofty, . . . an impressive lesson must be taught, an important scene illustrated—a moral, religious or poetic effect be produced on the mind."

At the Y you follow a steep downhill grade left to the northeast, which switches back almost immediately to the south. In a few minutes you cross the open gash that runs up the mountain—the abandoned Otis Elevated Railroad track. Opened in 1892, this incline railway saved from three to four hours' stage time for the trip to the Catskill Mountain House during the crucial period when the supremacy of Charles L. Beach's domain was being challenged by other resorts. Lack of patronage and the advent of automobile travel caused the railway to be closed in 1918, when its rails and cables were sold to the government for weapons manufacturing. The bare scrape it left in the escarpment can be seen for miles.

After crossing the railway clearing, the trail narrows through a forest of mixed hardwoods and continues along, flat and featureless (except for limited views through the trees to the east), until you reach a fork within 20 minutes. Take the right fork. One hundred feet beyond is a posted trail junction with a sign to Halfway House Lookout (0.45 mile), which is also Palenville Overlook. Follow this trail about 10 or 15 minutes on level terrain, and suddenly you stand over the abyssal depth of Kaaterskill Clove, with the village of Palenville below and remarkable views of Kaaterskill High Peak and Roundtop. To the west is Indian Head or Point of Rocks, which can be reached by bushwhacking along the cliff edge. A rough, unmarked trail exists at this time, but it is not continuous. By keeping the canyon

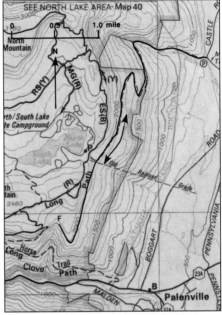

© 1983 NEW YORK–NEW JERSEY TRAIL CONFERENCE

to your left, it is difficult to get lost, though, and the extra diversion is worth the 10-minute walk.

These grassy, open areas are ideal spots for picnicking, sketching, photographing, camping, or simply pondering. The vertical drops are extremely dangerous here, so be cautious.

Indian Head (not to be confused with the Devil's Path mountain of that name) is a profile rock, and from More's Bridge in Kaaterskill Clove (just below Fawn's Leap) it does resemble a head. As you face the south from Indian Head, the bridge is visible on your right, far below. It is the second bridge west of Palenville.

When you have enjoyed this place to your satisfaction, you can return the way you came. Before leaving, if you should wish to rest in the bewitching silence, high above the birthplace of Rip Van Winkle, be careful lest you too should sleep away a lifetime.

30

Kaaterskill High Peak

Distance: 9 miles

Time: 6 hours

Vertical rise: 1,855 feet

Map: NY–NJTC Catskill Trails, #41

High Peak was far more popular 100 years ago during the hotel heydays than it is today. Then the Catskill boundaries were exaggerated by hotel magnates who did everything possible to convince visitors that their establishment was indeed positioned in the heart of the Catskills. High Peak was considered the highest mountain

Looking west from Kaaterskill High Peak

in the range until Arnold Guyot reduced it to a lowly 23rd on the list of Catskill peaks (actually it is 22nd). Guyot's map and report on the Catskills, published in 1879 and 1880, was produced when he was writing textbooks and building a foundation for the United States Weather Bureau. His formidable authority and statements then were considered absolute; at the same time he challenged local belief to the point that many people claimed his findings were in scientific error.

Guyot had believed Black Top, now known as Black Dome (3,980 feet), to be the highest in the range, but in 1871 he assigned that rank to Hunter Mountain (4,040 feet). By 1872 he had determined that Slide (4,180 feet) in fact was king of the Catskills, a finding that qualified the Shandaken Mountains as geological members of the Catskills.

From the Hudson Valley, High Peak does appear to be the highest mountain on the skyline. Its elliptic shape betrays it from north, east, and south, and it can be identified further by its lower westerly neighbor, Roundtop (3,440 feet), which stands like a dorsal fin in High Peak's shadow. T. Morris Longstreth, in his volume *The Catskills,* describes High Peak and Roundtop from the Hotel Kaaterskill as "sublime breakers just ready to topple over in a universal thunder of white foam." James Fenimore Cooper, in his legendary Leatherstocking novel, *The Pioneers,* quotes the hero as stating: "Well, there's High-peak and the Round-top which lay back like a father and mother among their children, seeing they are far above all the other hills."

While it is evident from guidebooks and maps of the golden era that Kaaterskill was a popular climbing destination, the mountain has since enjoyed such inconspicuousness that not even a state-marked trail crosses its summit. At this time a snowmobile trail circles both High Peak and Roundtop, providing access to High Peak's summit trail. Roundtop is trailless. Because there is only a vague (but negotiable) trail to High Peak from this well-defined snowmobile trail, it should be regarded as a strenuous and challenging hike that requires direction-finding skills, a map, and a compass. It also is a very quiet piece of country, even when the neighboring trails to the south and north (the Devil's Path and Escarpment trails, respectively) traditionally are crowded. Camping opportunities are exceptional, water is normally abundant, and the views, although not frequent, are one of High Peak's best-kept secrets.

The trail begins at the top of Platte Clove, which can be reached most easily from Tannersville. Going west out of Tannersville, find the Bloomer Road (County Route 16) on your left at 1.5 miles. Follow this road, heading back east for six miles, passing state trail signs into the Devil's Path Range on your right. Just past the Hutterian Bruderhof site, a dirt road appears on the left with red and yellow snowmobile-trail markers. (Here you will also see the blue-and-white Long Path disks that mark a trail to Palenville.) The best parking is ahead, across a stone bridge with iron guardrails that skirts a deep, dangerous clove. A large gravel parking lot on the right will accommodate several cars.

Follow the snowmobile trail uphill through a dense hardwood forest, mixed with rich stands of hemlock, passing old stone walls on your left, and listening (in season) to a tumbling creek on your right. In about 25 minutes you reach a fork where arrows indicate you turn right, following the snowmobile trail, which is washed out in places but consistently marked. In less than 10 minutes you reach another fork. Go right, through a forest of large oaks and other hardwood, where hemlock, viburnum, yellow violets, and trout lilies form a colorful understory. The trail is relatively level for the next 20 minutes until you reach a short timber bridge crossing into a swampy area between two shallow creeks. Another timber bridge is ahead within minutes, which you cross after passing through this pretty spruce-and-fir swamp on a sodden trail of old corduroy and the spongy root systems of balsam fir.

Leaving the swamp, the trail heads uphill into a hardwood area where you may have to step over blowdowns—normally cleared on a regular basis but rarely in early spring, the best time to climb High Peak. You begin to see beech trees, blue violets, and some remarkably large hemlock and maple. Wildlife is abundant. Porcupines will scuttle away as you approach; owls will scrutinize you with haunting whispers as you rest. Here, amid the spring beauties, you can look south at Plattekill Mountain, and northwest at the shoulder of High Peak. Within 40 minutes of leaving the swamp, including time for a good break, the trail levels out into a birch forest with scattered evergreens. This area, which can be wet, has an alpine quality, with stands of solid conifer, cleared blowdown, and old corduroy.

After 45 minutes of traversing this flat, swampy section of trail, which in spring is uncomfortably wet in places, turn sharply left, still following the snowmobile markers. (If you are hik-

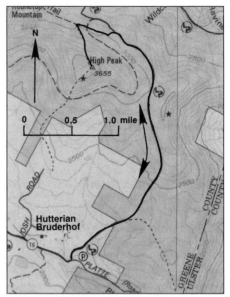

© 1989 NEW YORK–NEW JERSEY TRAIL CONFERENCE

ing the Long Path, the trail to Palenville via Buttermilk Falls and Wildcat Ravine forks to the right off the described route at this point. This trail is significant because it completes the Long Path in the Catskills.) The trail leads uphill here, and within 5 minutes you reach a trail junction with several signs describing the loop around Kaaterskill and Roundtop and the direction back to Platte Clove Road. Turn right (west). There is no sign indicating a trail to High Peak's summit, so at this time you must be very alert to pick it up on your left. Within about 500 feet, blue blazes can be seen off the trail in a southerly direction.

In the spring, when water is running down the mountain and when seasonal streambeds are still visible, you'll find a capillary creek at this junction. Shortly after this creek, you cross another one, and just before crossing a third you see the blazes on your left. Now look into the forest for a couple of hundred feet if you don't see a blaze right away. Once you've found the marks, follow uphill, looking for blazes on rocks and trees, into an area of steep ledges and rock-strewn, moss-cloaked forest.

About an hour of strenuous hiking takes you across several ledges and through many tangled blowdowns as you reach the summit. You will get some views to the north of Kaaterskill Clove and the surrounding mountains, but mainly these are obscured by trees.

You will know you've achieved High Peak's summit when you reach a flat area among the evergreens, where benchmarks can be studied in the stone. To reach Hurricane Ledge and its remarkable views, follow the trail for another 15 minutes. The trail brings you to a large expanse of grassy, open terrain with an east-to-west, south-facing aspect. The view is rare, including a variety of topography from the Hudson River Valley, the Shawangunks, the Hudson Highlands, and the immediate Catskills. The ledge is a fine place to snooze, snack, photograph, or bivouac.

High Peak and Roundtop are often present in Hudson River School paintings of the nineteenth century as background or subject matter, particularly in scenes from the Catskill Mountain House area. One of the finest representations of Kaaterskill High Peak appears in Thomas Cole's *Sunny Morning on the Hudson,* which depicts a highly romanticized version of High Peak from the vicinity of Roundtop. While it can be argued that the peak is not Kaaterskill, climb Roundtop with a photocopy of the painting, and you will have little doubt that it is. Return the way you came.

31

Plateau from Stony Clove

Distance: 6 miles

Time: 6 hours

Vertical rise: 1,840 feet

Map: NY–NJTC Catskill Trails, #41

"If you will believe me that the Stony Clove is a pastoral of lyric beauty with one dramatic climax, instead of the roaring bloody gulch of the fictional folders, I hope that you will also believe that its beauties cannot be more than skimmed by him who trusts only to steam or gasoline for his scenic memories."

So wrote T. Morris Longstreth in his 1918 classic, *The Catskills,* which

Notch Lake in Stony Clove

he promised to be free of exaggeration. No hiker who ascends the steep paths of Stony Clove would disagree.

It is curious also to read Longstreth's impressions of quaint Phoenicia, which you should visit when you descend Plateau's summit. He describes it as the "nerve center" of the Catskills, lying at the "cross-roads of Nature." He likes the "clean" and "painted" shops and applauds the lack of the commercial development that is so typical of some small Catskill villages today, a blight that Longstreth recognized even in 1918. What he says is still true, for Phoenicia, which lies within Stony Clove's southerly access, remains a tidy, scenic, and unpretentious retreat.

Stony Clove notch is a narrow mountain pass with all the rugged visual appeal that Longstreth promises. It is formed by the long ridge of Plateau meeting with that of Hunter and holds at its apex the teardrop of Notch Lake and the Devil's Tombstone State Campground, where the Devil's Path Trail crosses NY 214. To locate the trailhead, drive south on NY 214 from NY 23A between Hunter and Tannersville, and go three miles to the south end of Notch Lake. Or from the south at Phoenicia and NY 28, go north on NY 214 nine miles. Park at Notch Lake and cross the road to the east, climbing the log staircase where you will find the trail sign. Plateau Mountain Lookout is indicated at 1.23 miles, but the mountain's summit is on the east end of the ridge at 3,840 feet, 2.5 miles from the trailhead. What you will discover at the lookout will please you more than the actual summit, which is boreal and enclosed. The Plateau Mountain Lookout is an outstanding viewpoint at 3,600 feet—one that is often ranked in the hierarchy of Catskill vistas.

Begin the climb by going uphill over rocky terrain into a tall forest of young hardwood. A few minutes ahead, take some time to observe a slide to your left with a few large slabs and broken talus heaped beneath it. A short (200-foot) spur trail leads you to it. Continuing on the red-marked trail, you pass another short, unmarked spur to the right, which leads to a good campsite near a stream. After this point the main trail gets very steep, with makeshift stone steps to aid your ascent. In 10 minutes or more, as you climb over roots and rocks, you encounter more slides to your left (which are now stable and safe) and views to your right. Continue amid birch and cherry trees for 10 minutes until you reach an area that has been cleared to provide a view. Several trees have been topped, providing views of Wittenberg, Cornell, Friday, Peekamoose and Table, Panther, and beyond.

These good views vanish as the trail turns north, with spring beauties and red trillium sprinkled sparingly along its edge. If the trillium is in bloom during your visit, you might be surprised at its putrid scent, one that is unbecoming to such a pretty flower. Blooming as it does in very early spring, the trillium's stench attracts pollinating insects in search of decomposing flesh. For this reason it is called a "carrion" flower. All species of trillium are rare, protected, and *may not* be picked. In the spring you also will see in bloom the very pretty viburnum, or hobblebush, with its large, heart-shaped leaves, a favorite deer food.

On this flat section of trail, you can look back west for occasional views of Hunter Mountain. You cross the 3,500-foot mark and perhaps see a sign indicating this point. In another 10 minutes you traverse some ledges, which take you gradually up and onto the very scenic overlook on Plateau's

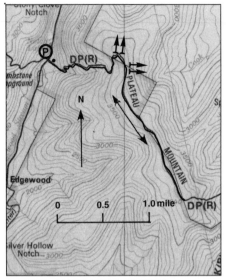

western end. This is a 180-degree view, reaching across the range from Colonels Chair to Hunter, Southwest Hunter, West Kill, the high peaks, and into the Ashokan Reservoir.

There are several illegal campsites in this area, which you pass as you follow the trail around through the east. The New York State Department of Environmental Conservation (DEC) requires that hikers "camp and build open fires only below 3,500 feet." An unobstructed overlook on the ridge's north shoulder surveys the Blackhead Range, North Point, South Mountain, Roundtop, Kaaterskill High Peak, and down into Platte Clove. Hard to your right you will see Spruce Top and then Sugarloaf with its long ridgeline plunging into Mink Hollow to meet the Roaring Kill and Schoharie. At this lookout there is a large, apparently balancing rock upon which a crude rising sun is carved. Beneath it we found a fulcrum stone and a broken timber, suggesting that boulder-levering is not a forgotten pastime. Most of the good balanced rocks were pushed into their present locations a century

ago by visitors to the mountain houses.

Continue on the flat ridge over a good trail for another 5 minutes until you reach an overlook with the same northerly views. Trees here also have been cut to provide an uninterrupted view. Many blown-down conifers lie upon the ridge, much like bleached whale bone against the contrast of verdant life.

Within 5 or 10 minutes you reach an attractive but overused campsite with "no camping" postings. Continue through a forest of large spruce and fir, where the trail switches to the ridge's south side. You begin to go uphill slightly in a few minutes, and within another 10 minutes witness a thick understory of balsam beneath a dead overstory. The trail here is reminiscent of Indian Head but not so enclosed. Whipped winds tear along the thin ridge as you peer through trees into Silver Hollow and Stony Clove. The forest remains coniferous on this long walk to the summit; it lends a somehow nostalgic feel, maybe reminding you of favorite walks in places far away: the Pacific Crest, the Whites, the Maine coast. They all come to mind.

In 20 minutes you reach the summit, just beyond a 90-degree left turn where the trail turns south to east. Follow the trail for another 15 minutes to your final destination—a rock looking east. Jump across a shallow crevasse and survey Sugarloaf, Kaaterskill High Peak, Roundtop, North Point, North Mountain, Overlook, and part of Twin. The view is limited compared to the one you had farther west, but it gives you an intimate feeling for the heart of the Devil's Path. It is a sight unavailable to "him who trusts only to steam or gasoline for his scenic memories."

Return the way you came, and keep an ear open for the "grrroook, grrrooook, grrroook" of nesting ravens.

32

Indian Head Loop

Distance: 6 miles

Time: 4½ hours

Vertical rise: 1,573 feet

Map: NY–NJTC Catskill Trails, #41

Looking south through Jimmy Dolan Notch

Indian Head is a beguiling triad of peaks, which make up a profile mountain that can be seen from afar as a face looking skyward. The profile is more impressionistic than real, more caricature than exact, very much in the cigar-store-Indian style. It is best seen from the north or east, from the Taconics or from Olana, Frederic Church's Persian castle in Hudson, and from the New York State Thruway and the surrounding valleys. Thomas Cole painted it in 1843 in *River in the Catskills,* the mountain set in vague repose beyond the dark ridges running southeast from Kaaterskill High Peak.

Indian Head is a contender for the position of most rugged and intriguing of the Devil's Path mountains. Its summit ridge is so boreal, so completely enclosed by thick spruce and fir, that you are never certain you are on a mountain at all but feel lost in a sea of endless, aromatic brush. The mountain yields its claustrophobic clutches piecemeal, giving you some extra-rugged views every now and then to lure you onward.

To reach the trailhead turn south off NY 23A at the (only) light in Tannersville on County Route 16. At

1.3 miles this road intersects the Bloomer Road, on which you turn left. Within 0.4 mile you will reach a Y where you bear left on Platte Clove Mountain Road. At three miles you pass Dale Lane on the right (trail to Sugarloaf, Twin, Pecoy Notch). Stay on Platte Clove Mountain Road, and in one mile you see Prediger Road on the right. Follow it 0.25 mile to the trail.

Here you will see signs on the red-marked trail to Indian Head Mountain, Jimmy Dolan Notch, and Echo Lake. The mileages shown from the trail junction (Indian Head 3.35, Jimmy Dolan Notch 3.80) are correct for taking the trail from east to west, not from west to east as you will do.

The foot trail leads you into the forest over a timber bridge across one of several lively creeks that will keep you company until higher elevations are reached. Follow the self-guiding and well-marked old road uphill, reaching the trail register within 500 feet. Maps are (at this time) posted here. Within 10 minutes you pass a stream on your right, and a trail junction appears. Bear right on the blue-marked trail, which shows Jimmy Dolan Notch at 2.2 and Indian Head at 2.65 miles.

On the blue-marked trail to Jimmy Dolan Notch, which is a section of the Long Path, you go uphill slightly over a rocky trail with exposed tree roots, an occasional large hemlock, and a few huge cherry trees. To your right, in a northerly direction, you can see Kaaterskill High Peak and Roundtop Mountain through the trees in the spring. The trail is not strenuous yet, as you slowly bend to the south, getting a view of Twin's northerly shoulder up to your right.

The trail becomes badly eroded in places where runoff has created a tem-porary streambed. The various streams you encounter, and the one you can hear in the ravine just west of you, form the easternmost headwaters of the Schoharie Creek.

As you continue along a steeper section of the trail, you'll have a peek at Indian Head on your left (south-east) and will see more of Twin to the right. Climbing higher, about 45 minutes into your hike (1.5 miles), you can look back (north) at Kaaterskill High Peak, Roundtop, and the Black-head Range. Within 10 or 15 minutes more you will be happy to arrive at the notch for some rest before the steep summit climb.

At Jimmy Dolan Notch the Long Path intersects with the Devil's Path, showing Indian Head at (a rugged) 0.45 mile, and Platte Clove Mountain Road (your exit route) at 3.95 miles. Take some time to explore here, and don't miss a walk into the notch, which you can see from the trail junction. Walk into the V as far as you can safely go for a good look at the Esopus Valley and some of the southern Catskills. For less-restricted views to the south, follow the rim of the notch to the west, via a fairly well trodden herd path, to a steep and dangerous cliff that forms the west side of the V on the notch. More views are possible if you pursue the meandering path, which eventually dead-ends. Jimmy Dolan Notch is a local favorite. It is in every sense a classic notch, a symmetrical cut through the mountain that is scattered with large boulders and crumbling rock shelves, an ancient river canyon from which the waters have long since run off.

The trail climbs and eases alternately as you struggle uphill from the notch, going east. After a half hour of this terrace climbing, the trail, thick

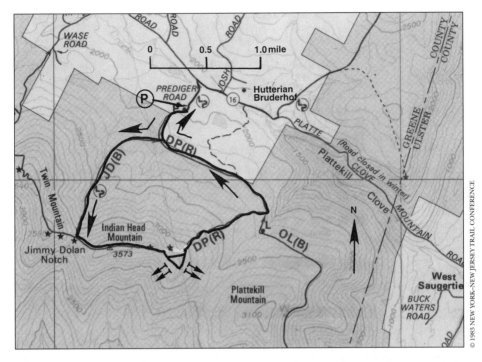

with hemlock and balsam, flattens suddenly. This is the only indication that you have reached the summit, completely surrounded by trees with no view. Within 5 minutes you go downhill slightly, to another flat area where huge, climax spruce trees soar above. A few enticing ledges here and there on your right provide limited views south.

Continue along through a pure evergreen forest. Some restricted views of the Sawkill Valley are available to the south if you want to push your way through the trees and explore a little.

You are now descending to the middle knoll, from the forehead (summit) to the eyebrow of the Indian Head. On the eastern end of the middle knoll, you reach a high overlook that juts out to the east with a vertical, dangerous drop, at 3,200 feet above sea level. A near-180-degree view reveals the Ashokan, Shawangunks, Overlook, the Hudson (part of which is obstructed by the east knoll, or nose) and the Highlands, Taconics, and Berkshires. You are roughly midway through the hike, with 3 miles behind you.

From here follow cautiously down a very steep section of trail into a shallow saddle separating the eyebrow and nose. Within 10 minutes you encounter another thick stand of fir that would be difficult, if not impossible, to walk through without a trail. Going uphill, and leveling out onto the nose, in 10 minutes or so you reach a spot where a view has been cut. The result is an outstanding look at the Catskills high peaks area, running from Ashokan High Point over to Slide and beyond. In this outstanding collection of peaks are also Peekamoose and Table, Lone, Rocky, Balsam Cap, Samuels, Friday, Wittenberg, Cornell, Giant Ledge,

Panther, and many more.

Within a few minutes of leaving this area, you swing toward the north, skirting the nose's easterly rim, which will give you a look at Plattekill's western shoulder. With fair views to the east along the trail, you have the opportunity to look deep into Platte Clove, and within 5 minutes you reach Outlook Rock, which has also been cut over to provide views to the north and a previously unavailable look at the Blackhead Mountains. This is the last scenic overlook before the plunge into the valley.

After 20 minutes or so of hiking downhill, with diminishing views to the east, you may find the trail wet as it terraces down, level for a way, then steep again. The footing is red shale and some broken conglomerate. The majestic stands of large virgin hemlock here, some over 30 inches in diameter, reflect the magnificence that was primordial forest.

The tanbark era in the Catskills, which ran from about 1830 to 1870, resulted in the near-deforestation of such hemlock. Hemlock bark, rich in tannin, was used in leather tanning. Trees could be peeled profitably only to the first branch, so much of the tree bark was wasted, and perhaps less than 1 percent of the lumber was used. Most of the trees were left to rot. In H. A. Haring's estimation, "from three to ten hemlocks were felled to obtain a cord of bark (128 cu. ft.). . . . Probably, in the life of the industry, one hemlock was cut down for each hide tanned into leather. . . . Col. Pratt, at Prattsville, turned out more than two million hides" during the lifespan of his tannery. With at least 60 tanneries running for 40 years, you get an idea of the vast number of trees involved. The trees here are some of the largest hemlocks you will ever see in the Catskills. Chances are they were in their vigorous youth as the industry waned.

Within 30 to 40 minutes of leaving the nose, you reach a trail junction. To your right at 0.2 mile is Devil's Kitchen lean-to, and at 2.8 miles is Echo Lake. To your left, two routes lead to Platte Clove Mountain Road. About 500 feet down this trail, after you've turned left, the red-marked trail dodges back into the woods, going left. Watch closely for this, as it's not too obvious. Don't go straight on the Catskill Center for Conservation and Development (CCCD) trail, or you'll wind up east of Prediger Road.

Turning left, or northeast, and back into deep hemlock woods, the trail takes you uphill slightly. In 10 or 15 minutes you reach a creek with a set of log stairs in place, which you cross, continuing through a fern glade, crossing another small stream and reaching the trail junction where you took the blue-marked trail. The 1.5-mile section of trail from Devil's Kitchen will take you about 40 minutes. Turn right, and you are back at the parking lot in a few minutes.

33

Twin Mountain

Distance: 4.4 miles

Time: 5–6 hours

Vertical rise: 1,680 feet

Map: NY–NJTC Catskill Trails, #41

Twin is one of the Devil's Path mountains, those craggy and tempestuous summits that you see crowding the western sky as you drive between Catskill and Saugerties on the New York State Thruway.

Forming the southeastern shoulder of the northern Catskills is Overlook and its Minister's Face, which

Looking west from the summit of Twin Mountain

juts into the valley, looking from a distance like a coastal headland. The ridge running north from Overlook is Plattekill Mountain (3,100 feet), which is fairly flat for several miles and of the same elevation as Overlook. This continuity is broken as the ridge turns 90 degrees to the west and over the irregular horizon of Indian Head, Twin, Sugarloaf, and Plateau mountains.

This is the Devil's Path. Falling away to the north are the deep, stone-ravaged depths of the Devil's Kitchen. To the south is the town of Woodstock; to the west the path drops suddenly into Stony Clove Notch. Perhaps because they are comparatively easy for the hiker, or because they lack the deep cavernous cloves so feared by the early Dutch settlers, Overlook and Plattekill are not included in colloquial descriptions of the Devil's Path mountains. Instead, the diabolical distinction is given to the mountains that run from Indian Head to Hunter. In recent years, West Kill has been included in the trail system to challenge hikers on what has become the most rugged and longest continuous trail network in the Catskills, with a total distance of 24 miles. This can be lengthened by an additional 5.5 miles to include Plattekill and Overlook, finishing (or beginning) in Meads.

While the Devil's Path in its entirety, from Platte Clove to Spruceton, is a popular and strenuous weekend outing for serious backpackers, any single mountain in the chain can be hiked in a day or less. At the same time, the Devil's Path is aptly named for its tormenting ascents, its profusion of rock, its abrupt visual contrasts, its dark hemlock corridors and false peaks. You will be rewarded on the trail with unusual feelings of isolation and with splendid views.

Many short side trails join the main ridge trail of the Devil's Path, predominantly from the north. They provide not only short hikes into an otherwise remote series of higher-elevation peaks but also easy bail-out routes in the event of emergency or foul weather.

Twin is best hiked from the Pecoy Notch Trail, which ascends gradually from the Schoharie Creek along Platte Clove Mountain Road. From Bloomer Road, 1.75 miles west of Tannersville on NY 23A, travel southeast on Platte Clove Mountain Road to the trail sign on Dale Lane (4.5 miles). Turn right here, and continue straight onto Wase Road, which leads in 0.3 mile to the trailhead. Tannersville can be reached from the south via the New York State Thruway and routes to Hunter (NY 32A and NY 23A) or from Phoenicia and Woodstock, which are both west of Kingston off NY 28, by following scenic NY 214 through Stony Clove and turning right on NY 23A, 12 miles north of Phoenicia.

From the trailhead it is 1.2 miles to Pecoy Notch, where the trail branches west to Sugarloaf and east to Twin, another 0.5 mile. This presents the possibility of hiking Sugarloaf as well as Twin in a one-day outing. Keep in mind the additional 2 miles and a cumulative elevation gain of 2,670 feet. Twin has the superior view, however, and you can save Sugarloaf for a later hike that could include a section of the Mink Hollow Trail and a look at the boreal Plateau Mountain.

Following trail markers in two shades of blue—both light and dark are used interchangeably at this time— walk to the trail register and sign in. Registering is not only a safety precaution but also a vital tool for deter-

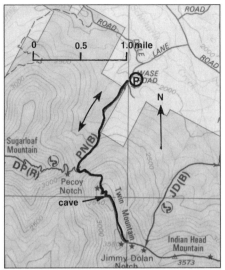

mining public use of the forest preserve.

The beginning of this trail can be wet in early spring, as it follows an eroded gully through a poorly drained hemlock-and-mixed-hardwood forest. Tiptoe across a small bog, which is alive with peepers in April, and continue on higher ground into stands of northern hardwood and an occasional striped maple. Club moss and trillium line the trail. At around the 2,400-foot elevation, less than 1 mile into the hike, you will see a beaver pond 300 feet or so to the right (west). The pond, which may be dry in summer, abuts the relatively featureless footpath and makes an interesting diversion. It can be circled in 15 or 20 minutes, allowing you to rejoin the trail again by turning east at the pond's southern edge. Beaver activity is diminishing in this pond that feeds the Schoharie, but several dams and lodges might be seen still, and the several-acre expanse of rotting timber will be evident for years. The pond has a quiet,

primordial spirit about it, making a welcome stopover. Its waters are contained by a sudden elevation gain at its most southern point, where its feeding creek trickles down from Sugarloaf. As you regain the trail and hike uphill, you begin to get views to the north of Thomas Cole, Black Dome, and Blackhead, left to right, collectively known as the Blackhead Range.

At 1.2 miles, after about an hour of leisurely hiking, you reach Pecoy Notch, and the ridge trail of the Devil's Path. To the left on this section of the Long Path is Twin at 0.5 mile with an additional 830-foot vertical rise.

There is no trail out of Pecoy Notch to the south, only a profusion of tumbledown boulders and twisted logs. This is one of the notches, along with its easterly neighbor Jimmy Dolan Notch, that can be seen as bright bare scrapes from points as far south as the Shawangunks.

Turn left and go uphill over a good trail through scrubby beech, birch, and maple. The incline is steep with a westerly aspect, soon exposing Sugarloaf and beyond it Hunter and its fire tower. You pass a large rock overhang that has been heavily used by hikers and is a convenient shelter in the event of rain. Although steep in places, the trail is easy and interesting to walk, even if you find yourself breathing heavily and resting frequently. Suddenly, through a balsam-thick shoulder of the mountain you see views opening up to the south, the vertical ledges of stone on your path finally subsiding to a series of flat outcrops that form the north summit of Twin.

From this point the view is very good, extending as far south and southwest as the eye can see, but it is blocked to the north and east by mountains in the 3,500-foot class. From this southerly exposure you can survey the southern Catskills' high peaks just west of the Ashokan Reservoir. You should recognize Ashokan High Point, Samuels Point, Friday, Wittenberg, Cornell, Panther, Giant Ledge, Balsam Cap, Balsam Lake Mountain, and Graham, with many lower surrounding peaks identifiable with the aid of map and compass. You will also have a close look at the foreground mountains, Tremper, Carl, and Olderbark (west to east). During runoff, listen closely and you might hear the noisy waters of the Sawkill or Mink Hollow Brook. Cooper Lake, part of Kingston's water supply, is visible five miles south-southwest of you, with Mount Tobias on its right.

The southerly summit of Twin is an easy 0.5-mile hike from here through a saddle of dense coniferous forest, which brings you to another flat rock overlook, facing south. Views to the east are of the Hudson River Valley and much of the river itself. From here nearly the entire Ashokan Reservoir is visible, as well as the Shawangunks. On a clear day, beyond them, you can even see scattered hills of the Hudson Highlands.

You'll want to visit both of Twin's summits to take in the variety of views that one cannot offer individually. If you have a lunch, plan to enjoy it at the more expansive southerly summit. Return the way you came, and while descending the north summit, about halfway down, you can test your lungs against the echoes from Sugarloaf.

34

Huckleberry Point

Distance: 4.8 miles

Time: 3½ hours

Vertical rise: 700 feet

Map: NY–NJTC Catskill Trails, #41

Huckleberry Point is a delightful, little-known, and out-of-the-way day hike in one of the Catskills' quietest corners. This small outcrop of rock hangs over the Hudson Valley, where the Plattekill Creek runs out of Platte Clove. It commands an intimate view of both, and it is seldom visited by hikers who are not familiar with the

A tributary of Plattekill Creek near the Huckleberry Point trailhead

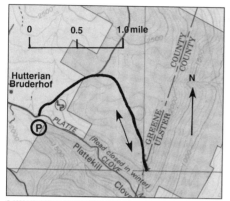

© 1989 NEW YORK–NEW JERSEY TRAIL CONFERENCE

area's secret footpaths. The point is appreciated locally, though, and if you ask around on a sunny weekend, you may be directed to several access alternatives that cross private lands. The only public-trail access is via the snowmobile trail that runs around Kaaterskill High Peak, which you follow for a short distance. (See hike 30 for directions to the trailhead.) Huckleberry is the ideal picnicking point, suitable to those days when an easy hike with a quiet, scenic payoff is the goal.

Follow the snowmobile-trail markers, which are both red and yellow, to an arrow pointing to the right, which you should reach within 25 minutes of leaving the paved road. This trail is also the route of the Long Path. After turning right, you find another turn to the right (in less than 10 minutes) indicating the continuation of the snowmobile trail.

Within 4 to 5 minutes, only a short distance from the junction, the trail begins to turn north slightly. Looking very carefully to your right at this point, locate the white markers with the red dot in the middle. These are markers put up by a group of hikers known as the Nature Friends. The

markers were originally tin-can lids that varied in size, color, and condition. With increased use of this trail, new markers (white with red dot) have been placed and it is now easily followed.

When you have located the Nature Friends' trail, follow it right (east) through a level hardwood forest with a hemlock understory. You see many signs of early settlement: stone piles, walls, and perhaps an old foundation or two. The trail is remarkably clean—free of litter and blowdowns. Within several minutes you go slightly downhill, and you reach a tiny, clear brook that can be several feet deep during runoff. Find a safe place to ford, and continue directly on the other side toward the point. Don't make the mistake of following one of the old overgrown skid roads you may see at this point. Be sure you follow the white-and-red markers.

A few minutes from the stream you begin to climb slightly, into an oak and beech forest with laurel ground cover. The trail undulates easily up and downhill, yielding early spring views of the Devil's Path peaks, including Overlook (see if you can spot the fire tower), Indian Head, Twin, Sugarloaf, and Plattekill.

Within a half hour of starting the Nature Friends' trail at the snowmobile trail, you enter a forest primarily of pitch pine with some red and white pine. Large rocks and a needle-covered forest floor color the scene, which may interest you in camping out. There are several natural campsites here, but be careful with fire in the soft subsoil beneath the pines.

Markers continue through the forest, within moments leading to a southerly bend in the trail, where you begin to sense the abyss ahead. Suddenly, you reach the open rocks of the point, with the ridge running from Hunter visible before you. Overlook's Minister's Face, the eastern tip of the Ashokan, Mohonk, the Hudson Highlands, Kingston, Saugerties, the Taconics, and lands beyond are recognizable.

This is a great place to get close to large ravens, hawks, and vultures who ride the updrafts against the cliff, rarely flapping their wings, oblivious to the rocks that are so rarely visited by people.

To avoid trespassing, return the way you came.

35

Kaaterskill Falls and the Cliff Walk

Distance: 5 miles

Time: 4 hours

Vertical rise: 300 feet

Map: NY–NJTC Catskill Trails, #40

The trails in the North Lake area are the most popular, accessible, and historically significant in the Catskill range. At one time they were the most popular in North America. They encompass falls, cliff walks, and mountaintop vistas, and both North and South lakes, their beaches, and public campgrounds. They constitute much of the 24-mile Escarpment Trail,

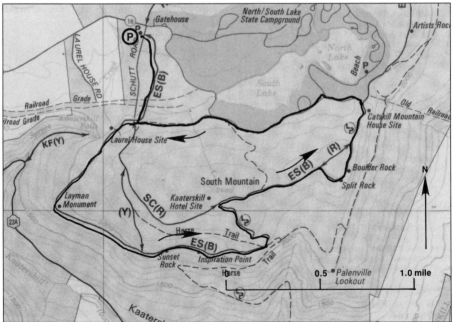

traverse several old hotel sites, and make a variety of day or weekend outings very convenient and satisfying for both dawdlers and aggressive hikers. The views from the North Lake area's trails and popular observation points are famous in and of themselves, embellished in the prose of the romantic era to such an extent that any description of them risks redundancy.

The first and easily the most renowned of these passages can be found in James Fenimore Cooper's *The Pioneers,* in which Leatherstocking (Natty Bumppo) describes the view from Pine Orchard as one containing "all creation." The tale was written in 1823, the year the Catskill Mountain House was constructed. Leatherstocking says, "I saw the hills in the Hampshire grants, the highlands of the river, and all that God had done or man could do, far as the eye could reach—you know that the Indians named me for my sight, lad [Leatherstocking refers to his nickname, Hawkeye], and from the flat on the top of that mountain I have often found the place where Albany stands."

Today, the North Lake trail network is a maze of both new and forgotten paths, roads, and horse trails, which were developed to support lucrative endeavors in tanning, quarrying, hotel building, logging, and railroading, following the earlier paths of hunters, trappers, fishermen, and surveyors.

Probably the most popular spot in the area, if not Pine Orchard itself, is Kaaterskill Falls. It is without peer if measured by the volume of literary and artistic attention given to it, and even Leatherstocking describes the falls as "the best piece of work that I've met within the woods."

To fully appreciate the falls, you must see them from below, where many hikers relax in the gathering mists of Spruce Creek. Because of extreme overuse and hazardous trail conditions, the Kaaterskill Falls access was made a dead-end trail in 1988. If you want to see the falls, park at the public parking area on NY 23A, which is 3.5 miles west of the intersection of NY 23A and NY 32A in Palenville, and the same distance east of Tannersville. Here you will be looking into Kaaterskill Clove and at Twilight and Santa Cruz parks, with a good view of the valley below. Walk downhill (east) to the hairpin turn (0.25 mile), where you'll find the trail signs on the road's north side. Follow the yellow trail markers over a heavily eroded path studded with exposed tree roots and large boulders. Once above Bastion Falls you might prefer to follow the creek bed instead of the less interesting trail. They are close to each other, and both lead to the falls. A round trip to the falls should take less than an hour.

You walk through a stand of virgin hemlock trees before reaching the falls at its lower basin, which is scattered with huge stones and some of the fragmented sections of the higher precipices. At 260 feet, these are the highest falls in New York State, consisting of two runs with vertical drops of 175 feet for the top and 85 feet for the lower run.

It was long ago fashionable, and is still possible today (although foolhardy), to walk behind the falling water of the upper amphitheater. Today this act, without the cabled walkways and stairs of the last century, involves considerable risk and is not recommended. Kaaterskill Falls, once as popular as Niagara, fell out of favor after the

Graffiti—or art? Kaaterskill Falls (top, circa 1825; bottom, circa 1920)

epoch of the great hotels. Now they are so popular that during the summer months you might see over a hundred people picnicking on the upper ledges, which has led to fluctuating levels of litter and rock defacement.

The cliff walk (Escarpment Trail) begins on Schutt Road, several miles beyond the Kaaterskill Falls parking area. Drive uphill (west) about two miles and take the first right, following signs to North Lake. At the end of this road (two additional miles) you reach the North/South campground. Turn right onto Schutt Road, which is just to the right before the campground entrance. Within 100 yards, find the parking area to the horse trail and the Escarpment Trail. Follow the blue-marked trail. This section of trail is also used by horses. Follow it generally downhill through attractive forest cover with several very large white pines, cross an old railroad bed (from which the tracks have been removed) and soon thereafter Spruce Creek (which supplies Kaaterskill Falls). A little farther beyond the creek you reach a four-way intersection. Stay on the blue-marked Escarpment Trail toward Layman Monument and Sunset Rock. You soon come along a long, open series of overlooks on steep rock outcrops, providing exciting views of the entire Kaaterskill Clove, of the precariously perched homes of Santa Cruz and Twilight parks, and of the mountains immediately to the south, Kaaterskill High Peak and Roundtop. You can look west to Hunter Mountain, Colonels Chair, and the East Jewett range. Fifteen hundred feet below you, Kaaterskill Creek flows toward the Hudson.

The view gets better as you continue toward Sunset Rock and Inspiration Point, passing a yellow-marked trail that returns to Schutt Road and the red-marked trail. Sunset Rock is the first large outcrop you reach after the trail junction. If you've timed your visit to coincide with the appearance of the pinkster blossoms, and it is well worth it to do so (mid-May to mid-June), you'll also see swallowtails, bronze coppers, and cabbage butterflies alighting on them and on the many-colored hawkweeds and assorted wildflowers along the way. As you head for Inspiration Point, you dodge in and out of an oak and laurel forest over easy terrain.

After enjoying Inspiration Point, continue through the forest for another 15 minutes of easy walking to reach Shorey Point, which you'll recognize by its horse-trail markers and the trail signs to Schutt Road Corral. Stay on the blue-marked trail toward Boulder Rock (1.2 miles) and North Lake Campground (2.2 miles). There is no view from Shorey Point, and the trail becomes relatively featureless until you reach the Kaaterskill Hotel site on South Mountain, which takes about 15 minutes. The site is neither marked nor obvious—it is an empty grassy knoll adjacent to the trail junction as you turn right toward Boulder Rock. The hotel was built in 1881 and burned in 1924.

Continue on the blue-marked trail to Boulder Rock, and at 0.5 mile you reach a trail junction where the red-marked trail shortcuts off to the left toward the Catskill Mountain House site. Avoid this trail and continue following the blue markers. In a few moments you reach Split Rock, a large rock leaning away from the trail with a deep fissure cleaving it, and, just beyond it, Boulder Rock. Views of the Hudson Valley here are outstanding, giving an idea of what's to come over at Pine Orchard.

You continue to have fine, far-reaching views of the Shawangunks, Taconics, Berkshires, and the escarpment as you hike along toward Pine Orchard. Avoid the several intersecting, older, unmarked trails that now are closed because of erosion and hazardous situations, and keep to the trail. Within 10 minutes you reach the north end of the red-marked shortcut trail, where a sign shows North Lake Campground at 0.9 mile. After a 15-minute walk through cool, dark forests of mixed hardwood, pine, and hemlock, you suddenly reach the large open ledge where the Catskill Mountain House stood. Here you can look north toward North Point, North Mountain, and Sunset Rock. There is a plaque commemorating the hotel, but there are no ruins, as earlier topographic maps might indicate. After being declared a menace to public safety, the Catskill Mountain House was burned on January 25, 1963, at 6 A.M., so it no longer commands its ephemeral view over "all creation."

At this point you have hiked for about 2 hours. To return to your car, you can go back the way you came, or you can follow a faster, shorter route via the North/South Lake service road, which you intercept just west of the hotel site. Follow an unmarked path until you reach a paved road. Go left. Or you can follow the blue-marked trail that continues going north, dropping downhill slightly to the top of the abandoned Otis Elevated Railroad track, which runs up the mountain from Palenville. The road then runs from North Lake public beach along the south shores of both lakes (go left), and continues going west. As you approach the southwest end of South Lake, you see a Nordic ski trail going off to your left. If you'd rather walk in the woods back to your car, follow it until reaching, in 10 minutes, the blue-marked trail on your right, which goes back to the Schutt Road parking area (this is the trail you came in on and is the more secluded option). However, you can also continue on the service road, crossing the earthworks dam at the lake's south end and continuing uphill to the campsite entrance (the parking area will be on your left at this point).

36

North Point

Distance: 7 miles

Time: 4½ hours

Vertical rise: 700 feet

Map: NY–NJTC Catskill Trails, #40

This historic, scenic day hike begins in the heart of the North Lake State Campground and includes some of the best scenery available from anywhere along the eastern escarpment, and maybe the entire range.

To reach North Lake State Campground, turn north from NY23A onto O'Hara Road (County Route 18) in

North and South Lakes with Kaaterskill High Peak and Roundtop Mountain in the background

Haines Falls, and go straight ahead, 2.5 miles, to the gatehouse.

You may begin outside the campground entrance in order to avoid the minimal day-use fee charged at the front gate, but that trail (yellow-marked Rock Shelter Trail) is longer and less interesting than the recommended red-marked Marys Glen Trail, which begins just 0.75 mile beyond the gatehouse.

Limited hikers' day-use parking is located at the Marys Glen trailhead, which you see on the left just beyond the Marys Glen Trail sign. Park and walk back to the sign, which shows Marys Glen at 0.4 mile. There is another location in the North Lake area that has the name of Marys Glen, or Glen Mary, just above Kaaterskill Falls on Lake Creek (Kaaterskill Creek). In both instances the placename remembers Mary Scribner, wife of Ira Scribner, who operated a sawmill on the creek. The Glen Mary Cottage was most likely where Henry David Thoreau, with William Ellery Channing, spoke of spending an evening in the early 1840s.

The glen is a cool, sometimes wet and rocky, but easy trail that skirts a swampy area full of beaver sign. Go left when you reach the bottom of Ashleys Falls (also called Marys Glen Falls) at 0.4 mile, where a spur trail continues for a short distance ahead into the stone rubble below the falls.

Hike along the trail indicating North Point at 1.3 miles, and stop to enjoy the falls before continuing. There is generally no water here in the dry months. The hike in from the trailhead should take only 15 or 20 minutes. Continue on the trail toward North Point, beneath an overstory of white birch, hemlock, and maple for another 10 minutes, which will bring

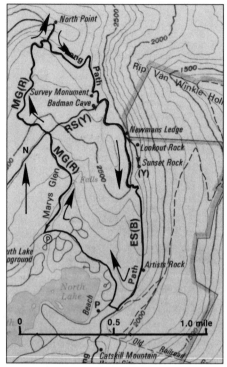

© 1983 NEW YORK–NEW JERSEY TRAIL CONFERENCE

you to a four-way trail junction. Locate the red markers for Marys Glen Trail, which is the continuation of the trail you are on, and follow it toward North Point (1 mile). Passing a long ledge that sports a small waterfall during wet periods, climb above it through more ledgy terrain and into a flat, swampy, coniferous area. The swamp sometimes swallows up a piece of the trail here, and herd detours may be created. You might still get your feet wet in spring. If the foliage allows, you might at this point be able to look high to your left (northwest) and see the ledges of North Point.

Within a half hour of leaving the trail junction you reach another, where the blue-marked trail (Escarpment Trail) on which you will be returning leads back to Artists Rock and the campground. Turn left here, onto the only continuously steep section of the trail. After 15 minutes of strenuous and aerobic effort, you see a white-birch stand that precedes the large, flat rocks and long views from North Point's summit. Investigate views from various parts of the ledge: Windham High Peak, Burnt Knob and Acra Point, Blackhead and Roundtop to the north; the Hudson Valley toward Albany, to the east through the Taconics and Berkshires; and south across the highlands and into the escarpment, where North and South Lakes lie like spilled quicksilver under the shadows of Kaaterskill High Peak and Roundtop.

While North Point was widely known and visited during the hotel days of the nineteenth century, it was not as popular as the lower ledges and lookouts that have been memorialized by the painters of the Hudson River School: Thomas Cole (*Catskill Mountain House*), Sanford R. Gifford (*Catskill Mountains*), W. H. Bartlett (*The Two Lakes and the Mountain House in the Catskills*), and others both renowned and anonymous.

A selection of prints and a detailed history of the area may be studied in Roland Van Zandt's classic text, *The Catskill Mountain House*. Van Zandt expresses his own opinion that the trails in this vicinity are "some of the most beautiful of the Atlantic Seaboard."

Leave North Point on the blue-marked trail you came up on, reaching the trail junction of the Marys Glen and Escarpment trails within 10 minutes. Turn left on the blue-marked trail into a flat walk through birch and hemlock woods with occasional thick spruce and laurel appearing. You will traverse large, flat rocks and blueberry patches in this arboreous,

gardenlike section of trail, with views to the east as it passes in and out of pure scrub spruce stands. In 10 minutes you reach a large, flat, stony area with views of Roundtop, Kaaterskill High Peak, and the river valley to the east. The trail descends into forest, where large rock overhangs eventually bring you to Badman Cave (also a shallow overhang) and the yellow-marked Rock Shelter Trail junction alongside a small wetland. Follow left on the blue-marked trail, over a rocky surface with far-reaching views southward, descend suddenly into a marshy area, and continue to Newmans Ledge, a dangerous vertical wall of a hundred feet or more.

Be cautious, but watch for gliding birds of prey here as you gaze below into Rip Van Winkle Hollow. Look carefully and you might see the Old Mountain Road against the north face of the hollow. A wide view of the valley greets you here, as well as some varied initials and graffiti on the rocks.

Continue along the escarpment's edge and into the forest for 20 minutes and you reach the yellow-blazed spur (left) to Sunset Rock. By all means take this dead-end walk of 10 minutes, for it leads to perhaps the most scenic lookout in the erstwhile domain of the Catskill Mountain House, if not in the Catskills themselves.

The many ledges around Sunset Rock and Artists Rock, the latter lying ahead, were the popular viewpoints from which scenes of the Catskill Mountain House were painted in the highly romanticized fashion typical of their admirers. Thomas Cole could see his home in Catskill from these points, and he would show it to friends from the area around Artists Rock.

The youthful and daring may want to slide back down to the trail anywhere possible to avoid backtracking, or look around for the Bear's Den route, a cavernous tunnel that reaches the trail below. The sharp drop off the south end of Sunset Rock was once the location of Jacob's Ladder, a long wooden ladder removed by the New York State Department of Environmental Conservation (DEC) as a safety precaution. If in doubt, return the way you came.

At the trail junction, turn left and continue south past the long wall of conglomerates of which Sunset Rock is made, wind around in front of the rock wall, and you reach Artists Rock within 5 minutes. Another ledge follows in this fairy-tale forest of flat rock and pine trees that long ago earned the area the name Pine Orchard, which extended to the ledges around the Catskill Mountain House.

The trail drops down into the campground picnic area and bathing beach at this point, where bathroom facilities and telephones are available. Turn right and walk 0.5 mile back to your car at Marys Glen.

To learn more about the area, stop and browse at the Haines Falls Library, which is on your left on O'Hara Road just before it joins NY 23A.

37

Hunter Mountain

Distance: 7.2 miles (add 2 miles for Colonels Chair)

Time: 7 hours

Vertical rise: 1,950 feet

Map: NY–NJTC Catskill Trails, #41

The Blackhead Range from Hunter Mountain

Hunter is a big mountain that is best hiked on the long, gradual trail from Spruceton. The considerable vertical rise of 1,950 feet is distributed evenly over the trail so that it is never too steep from this western approach. The trails from Stony Clove Notch, although interesting and more direct, are shorter and steeper, best reserved for more aggressive hikers or for days when you are more in the mood for an assault than for a pleasant day's outing.

Driving east on NY 23A from Grand Gorge, turn south on NY 42 at Lexington. After 4.2 miles turn left on County Route 6. From the south, NY 42 is reached conveniently by NY 28 out of Kingston, and from Catskill by NY 23 or NY 23A. County Route 6, Spruceton Road, which leads to the trail, takes you through a very attractive upper-elevation flatland with a high-plains character, surrounded by the peaks of North Dome (3,610 feet), West Kill (3,880 feet), Rusk (3,680 feet), and Hunter. Trout fishing is good in the West Kill Creek. Drive past the trail to West Kill Mountain, which will appear on your right at 3.8 miles, and continue for another three miles into the forest preserve access parking area, where there are several trail signs. Locate the blue-marked trail on the road's north side, which leads to the John Robb lean-to, Hunter Mountain, Devil's Tombstone Campsite, and Platte Clove Mountain Road.

Setting out along a well-defined truck trail, you follow what was once the Jones Gap Turnpike, which was built in the late nineteenth century. The road was later improved to build and maintain the Hunter Mountain fire tower, and it is still in good enough shape to be driven by four-wheel-drive vehicles (which are not allowed). After 0.5 mile the trail turns east and steepens gradually. About fifty minutes into the hike you arrive in the saddle between Rusk and Hunter mountains, at 1.7 miles. You see an unmarked trail leading downhill to the north through Taylor Hollow, which is no longer state marked or maintained. This section of the old Hunter Road leads to South Jewett on NY 23A, west of the village of Hunter. Although it still exists, and may appear on older topographic maps, it is not marked and is very difficult to find from NY 23A.

Your trail continues east from here, uphill, reaching a good spring on the right within 0.5 mile. Near the spring, views to the north and southwest are good, with Rusk and West Kill in the foreground. The John Robb lean-to is ahead 0.1 mile on your left at the 3,500-foot mark.

Continue for another 0.1 mile into a flat area of thick evergreens, and you come upon the Colonels Chair Trail, which branches north following yellow markers. This is part of the old Shanty Hollow Trail, which is no longer in use below Colonels Chair, having been erased by ski-trail con-struction. It is still possible, however, to hike out from the summit lodge directly into the town of Hunter, if you want, by following the ski trails.

The mile-long side trip to Colonels Chair and the ski lifts and summit lodge of the Hunter Mountain Ski Area is worth your time. Hunter's chair lift, or "Sky Ride," runs through the summer and is good to keep in mind for quick bail-out purposes (make sure to check schedules), but you'll be very far from your car. The trail descends gently into an open area, with excellent views of North Mountain, High Peak and Roundtop, the Blackhead Range, Onteora Mountain, and the East Jewett range, among many nameless rolling hills. At the lodge you will see on the northwest side a trail sign showing Hunter Mountain at 2.05 miles. If you walk downhill on that trail in a northerly direction, you notice on the rocks the words "Lookout Point" painted in red. Here an unmarked and vague trail leads a short way down to a rocky ledge with more of the same impressive views. The Colonels Chair, so called for its shape, is named for Colonel William Edwards, an early "tanlord" after whom Edwardsville was first named. The village name was later changed to Hunter.

There are picnic tables at the summit lodge, and there are refreshments, food, and communications available year-round. To the south, another 1,000 feet in elevation, you can see the fire tower near Hunter's summit.

After you return to the blue-marked trail, the summit is 1 mile along the trail to your left. The heavily rutted trail leads you through a dense forest of spruce and fir with occasional ledges and views to the northeast. From the Colonels Chair Trail it will take you

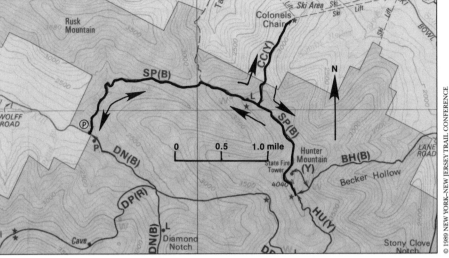

about 40 minutes to walk to the summit. Once you have looked around on this rocky peak and have enjoyed the 360-degree view from its fire tower, by all means continue on the blue-marked trail to the "true summit," where the fire tower and lean-to previously were located. This additional distance takes about 10 minutes and is worth the little extra effort. When you reach the old tower site, where the Becker Hollow Trail descends very steeply into Stony Clove, you'll see a forest of evergreens. You will notice a yellow-blazed side trail to the right, which leads a short way through this forest to a west-facing ledge that has excellent views from the north-north-west to the south-southwest, including West Kill, North Dome, Sherrill, Balsam, Vly, Bearpen, and many lesser peaks. This is the place to rest and have lunch.

T. Morris Longstreth, whose 1918 guide is considered a classic account of Catskill Mountain trails, sums up Hunter's view aptly: "Hunter is a climb-repaying mountain. From the steel tower on the top the entire Catskill mountainland is visible. Stony Clove, the cross-bar of the letter 'H', which is completed by the valleys of the Esopus and the Schoharie, is but a gash in mother earth. The mass of the southern Catskills rises in ranged domes, which on that morning dropped into gulfs made pearl gray by the mists of melting snow. Westward the chain that walls the valley toward Lexington wandered away until it grew soft with lilacs and lavendars [sic]." He suggests that "if you have your nerve with you, climb Hunter some forenoon that promises thunder . . . nowhere else can you find more beautiful concentrations of vapor."

Looking east along the Devil's Path, Longstreth couldn't help commenting on the visual boisterousness of the place. If you do fall prey to a thunderstorm at this elevation, your quickest escape is Becker Hollow, which if you haven't arranged for a shuttle would leave only the devil to pay. A better bet for immediate shelter is the lean-to at Devil's Acre, 1.5 miles south on the yellow-marked trail. A good water source is located there. Better yet, to assure your full appreciation of any Catskill peak, hike only on clear days with plenty of sunshine.

Hunter Mountain is the second highest peak in the Catskills. For a long time it was thought to be the highest, until Arnold Guyot, a Princeton geologist, proved otherwise. It was annexed to the forest preserve in 1930.

From the old fire-tower site you can return to Spruceton the way you came, or use the yellow-marked trail to the Devil's Path for an interesting but longer alternative.

38

West Kill to Buck Ridge Lookouts

Distance: 9.6 miles

Time: 7 hours

Vertical rise: 2,000 feet

Map: NY–NJTC Catskill Trails, #41

This is the longer but gentler approach to West Kill from Spruceton. Although the elevation gain is considerable at 2,000 feet, representing more of a vertical climb than the trail from the eastern end of Spruceton Road (1,780-foot rise), the ascent is more broken up and not such a workout. Also, if you already have hiked Diamond Notch to West Kill Falls, you will have seen the only reason to come in from the

West Kill Mountain

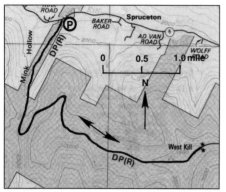

east (the falls) and will enjoy more new country on the western approach.

To reach the trailhead, turn left off NY 23A onto NY 42 in Lexington, west of Hunter. Follow NY 42 toward Shandaken into West Kill. About 4.2 miles from NY 23A you see signs for Spruceton on County Route 6. Turn left here, and go 3.7 miles to the West Kill Summit Trail, which you'll see on your right. This is the extreme west end of the red-marked Devil's Path Trail, which also leads to Diamond Notch lean-to, the Spruceton–Old Hunter Road, Devil's Acre lean-to, the Hunter Mountain fire tower, and Devil's Tombstone, on NY 214.

Go immediately uphill through a hardwood and pine forest. The trail levels out shortly, suddenly turning right instead of following an overgrown jeep road that leads straight ahead. After 10 minutes you find that you are walking the border of a forest transition, with hemlock on your right and hardwood on your left. To your right is Mink Hollow (not to be confused with the better-known Mink Hollow near Lake Hill) and its brook, which joins the West Kill. Large boulders covered in moss decorate the forest. Grouse may burst from dense cover as you walk along.

After 20 minutes or so over rocky, root-covered footing, you meet the creek that runs into Mink Hollow. The trail then veers left, ascending into a rocky hardwood forest. In 10 minutes you hear a spring bubbling beneath the trail, as you look ahead into a gap or opening in the forest where a dry pond (seasonal) sits between West Kill and North Dome. The gap runs south into the head of Broadstreet Hollow and the two ponds designated as Timber Lake Camp on your map.

There are two signs at this pond section on the trail, one indicating West Kill Mountain summit at 3.01 (it's safe to assume this is intended to mean 3.1). The other shows Spruceton Road as back the way you came.

Turn sharply uphill to the north. Continue climbing for 20 minutes or more, over the steepest section of trail you will encounter. The trail eases over grassy, fern-covered flats through ledges and undulating terrain where beech and cherry appear. This pattern continues for another 20 minutes until you descend more steeply than you'd like to. But the drop is not severe or prolonged; it flattens out and the trail climbs again momentarily. Be very careful here while negotiating the slanted slabs of bluestone that the trail crosses. When wet they can be as slippery as ice.

As you ascend to a level walk again, it will take you 20 more minutes through winding flats to climb into alpine terrain where the trail narrows and balsam becomes prolific. At this point, no sooner do you realize you are on a summit ridge, than a sign noting West Kill Summit appears on your right, above a set of stones arranged as a crude campfire ring. You will begin to wonder where the view is—but there is none from West Kill Summit.

Continue for another 3 to 5 minutes, to the ledge of Buck Ridge. This is a view often on the favorite list of hikers, and it is impressive. There is enough room for a dozen people to rest here, poised in midair looking at a 180-degree collection of peaks. From left to right you can see Windham, Thomas Cole, Black Dome, Blackhead, Hunter West with its ski trails, Hunter and its fire tower, Southwest Hunter, Plateau, Overlook and its fire tower (for Hawkeyes only), Slide, Table, Lone, Rocky, Wittenberg, Cornell, Friday, Balsam Cap, Ashokan High Point, the Mohonk Preserve, a piece of the Ashokan Reservoir, and down into Lanesville on NY 214. You can also see a widening in the Hudson River, which is Vanderberg Cove, as well as Olderbark, Little Rocky, Carl Mountain (in the foreground), and Mount Tremper to the right of the Ashokan Reservoir. See if you can find its fire tower.

Before you leave the summit, to retrace your steps, you may want to collect some balm of Gilead—the pitch of balsam fir—to save in a film container. This resin from the blisters of balsam is said to have medicinal value; it does keep bacteria and fungi to a minimum, at least in the tree's case. People once thought that it must also do that for them, recalling the prophet Jeremiah's reference to the balm that ancient Israelites found on Mount Gilead in the Holy Land. Native Americans called the balsam *cho-koh-tung,* or "blisters." The resin was used commercially to create adhesives for lenses and microscope slides until synthetics were found to be superior.

About the only thing you'll want to do with balm of Gilead is stash it with your Christmas ornaments or keep it in a desk drawer as a freshener. Use it to whiff that nostalgic thrill of the holidays or to return to West Kill Summit during times when life's requirements don't let you do so.

39

Diamond Notch to West Kill Falls

Distance: 4.6 miles

Time: 3½ hours

Vertical rise: 1,500 feet

Maps: NY–NJTC Catskill Trails, #41

This is an easy hike that takes you into Diamond Notch via an old turnpike rebuilt in 1937 as a ski and hiking trail. You begin in Lanesville on NY 214, five miles north of Phoenicia. Look for Diamond Notch Road on the left, where there are trail signs. If you come in from Hunter to the north, take NY 214 (two miles east of town), and you'll see the trail seven miles into Stony Clove or four miles beyond Devil's Tombstone campsite, on your right. Go up Diamond Notch Road 1.2 miles to an iron bridge, cross it, and park on the right. There is a better parking area 0.3 mile ahead, just beyond a house and barn, but the road washes out often, and unless you have an appropriate vehicle, you'll be better off walking.

You'll see the blue state trail markers along the trail, which follows a large stone wall on the left. Almost immediately after setting out you discover a wide variety of wildflowers: Dutchman's-breeches, Carolina spring beauties, yellow violets, and purple trillium. You will also notice some of the yellow paint blazes of the New York State Forest Preserve. Pass by a locked steel gate where wilderness-area signs appear, near an unimproved parking area and a rough campsite with scattered fire rings. Entering the trail along Hollow Tree Brook are a few overgrown side roads, most likely logging skid roads, which you may notice as you cross a good timber bridge on stone abutments into a hardwood forest of second growth.

After 15 minutes of hiking, just beyond the bridge, you can make out a high ridge to your left, which is part of West Kill, the ridge that forms the west side of Diamond Notch. At this point some hemlock begin to appear, and the trail becomes heavily eroded and gullied. Soon another bridge crosses Hollow Tree Brook, and the trail begins an even ascent, continuing due north into Diamond Notch Hollow. This is most likely the spot

West Kill Falls

that suggested the development of a ski trail through the notch, but you'll probably opt for the novice slopes of a sanctioned ski area after you look down from above. Look up to your left (west), and you see the rocky, spruce-covered shoulder of West Kill's east ridge jutting out.

About 1.5 miles into the hollow you come across a miniature waterfall on your right and another small kill just beyond it, both running straight down the mountain, crossing the trail. If you rest here, you may get a look at the elusive hermit thrush, the shy bird that Burroughs claimed was his favorite. Some outcrops of thinly stratified sandstone lie ahead, hinting that the notch is not far beyond. Within 5 minutes there are excellent views to the southwest, highlighting (from right to left) Slide, Table, Lone, Peekamoose, Cornell, Wittenberg, and Ashokan High Point. Up to the right is a long pile of landslide talus, with birch, cherry, and maple establishing themselves in its thin soil. Dr. Michael Kudish speculates in *Vegetational History of the Catskill High Peaks* that the slide "might date back to the 1890–1910 era when the area was logged and possibly burned."

An old road descends sharply into the ravine on the trail's west side. Now, 1.7 miles into the notch, you approach its highest point, where the mountains of West Kill and Southwest Hunter come so close together that you can touch them both at the same time (theoretically). Alf Evers, in *The Catskills,* writes that "a man who wants to make the effort can stand today with one foot on West Kill Mountain and the other on a supporting ridge of Hunter Mountain so that he may boast ever afterward that he once stood on two mountains at the same time."

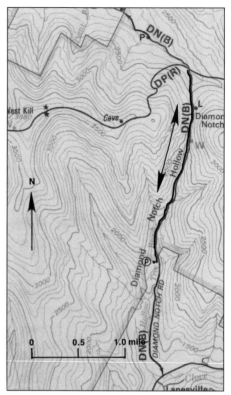

© 1983 NEW YORK–NEW JERSEY TRAIL CONFERENCE

After you have enjoyed the notch and its fine view, follow the trail into an evergreen forest, descending gently to reach Diamond Notch lean-to. The shelter has a wood floor, its site is cleaner than most, and it's in good shape as far as Catskill lean-tos go. Just below the lean-to is a small wetland that contributes to the upper reaches of West Kill Creek. Follow along on what can be a fairly wet trail, with a view of Rusk Mountain ahead and slightly left. To the west of Rusk (3,680 feet) is Evergreen (3,360 feet) and to the east, Hunter (4,040 feet), but neither summit is visible. Within 15 minutes of the lean-to you should reach the junction with the red-marked Devil's Path Trail and the Timber

Bridge over West Kill Falls. Diamond Notch is shown at 0.7 mile back the way you came; your car is about 2.3 miles away; the nearest road is ahead on the blue-marked trail, at 1 mile (Spruceton–Old Hunter Road).

The falls here are very attractive, with several tiers of 10 feet or more and a succession of large pools you might want to slip into. Have a look at the ingenious porcupine-proofing around the map stand near the trail— garbage pail covers. (At this time the system is working fine.) There are good tent sites all through this area on the north side of the falls, and evidence of camping is moderate. At only a mile from the road, the area is subject to inevitable popularity and overuse—a situation not yet out of hand. You will find the falls an ideal place to picnic, camp, or spend a hot afternoon swimming. Hike out the way you came in.

40

Giant Ledge and Panther

Distance: 6.5 miles

Time: 4 hours

Vertical rise: 1,500 feet

Map: NY–NJTC Catskill Trails, #42

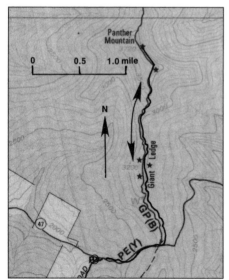

This fairly easy and highly rewarding hike will take you into one of the Catskills' deepest recesses. The long ridge of Panther Mountain, which includes the lower, southerly Giant Ledge, reaches from Fox Hollow in Allaben and south to Winnisook Lake. To the east it is flanked by the extensive wilds of Woodland Valley, and to the west by Big Indian Hollow. It is here that the fledgling Esopus gains momentum, nurtured within Panther's long ridge and the western landscape with its rustic Bavarian-looking homesteads and cozy mountain hotels. Even the placenames sound rugged: Hemlock, Spruce, and Fir Mountains, Eagle Mountain Road, Elk Brook, Lost Clove, Big Indian. As you drive in from the Big Indian you will begin to feel why this valley was the birthplace of legends.

The most famous legend, many versions of which have emerged as happens in folktelling, involves Winnisook—the Big Indian. The general plot in most versions of the legend is that Winnisook, a man over seven feet tall, fell in love with a valley farmer's daughter, who eventually rejected her husband to join Winnisook and his people. This went on for

Isolated winter view from Giant Ledge

several years until Winnisook was eventually shot by Gertrude's jealous husband during a typical livestock robbery; the dying man hid within a hollow tree, where he was later discovered dead by his lover. An account from Lionel De Lisser's *Picturesque Ulster* (1896) offers this summation: "Winni-sook was buried at the foot of the pine tree in which he had been found, Gertrude and her dusky children living near the grave until the time of her death."

Still other versions of the legend maintain that Winnisook became a civilized farmer who was overcome by wolves. In his memory, local farmers carved his statue from a large tree, which stood near the site of his death. No matter which interpretation is embraced, and there are many to choose from, the active imagination will find such events to be plausible, as they are tame in proportion to the obvious fantasy of many period legends. When you consider the history of the Catskills' early wars, pioneer expansion, and frequent confrontations between Native Americans and settlers, the tale is even more enticing. Make up a few paragraphs of your own while you hike into Giant Ledge.

Turn south at Big Indian off NY 28 and onto County Route 47 between Shandaken and Pine Hill, and go 7.3 miles to the hairpin turn on the way to the Slide Mountain trailhead. At the hairpin there is a large parking area on your right. The trail to Giant Ledge begins across the road on your left. It follows the yellow-marked Phoenicia–East Branch (PE) Trail first, intersecting with the blue-marked Giant Ledge–Panther–Fox Hollow Trail in a little more than 0.5 mile.

The hike to Giant Ledge is 1.5 miles. This initial section goes uphill over a rough and rocky trail, crosses a dry streambed (seasonal), and again ascends through a hardwood forest and into some large sedimentary rock gardens. The hike to the blue-marked trail junction will take no more than a half hour, when you reach a long, flat walk with an unmaintained trail going right and downhill onto the private lands of the Winnisook Club. Turn left, and within a stone's throw you will be at the triple–trail junction where the PE Trail joins the blue-marked trail to Giant Ledge.

There is no designation or mileage listed for Giant Ledge itself, which actually is not a single identifiable site but consists of a long ridge. It is an attractive camping spot.

Once upon the ledge, or series of ledges, pick a vacant vantage point (this is a very popular spot) on the east side. You look toward Fork Ridge and into Woodland Valley, with Terrace, Cornell, and Wittenberg to your right (southwest). To the northeast you can identify the lower peaks of Garfield and Sheridan, with Romer to the east and Tremper beyond it, including various members of the Devil's Path Range from northeast to east. On the west side of Giant Ledge, several open rocks make possible views of Hemlock, Spruce, Fir, Big Indian, Eagle, Haynes, Balsam, and Belleayre mountains. There are many isolated outlooks all over the ridge here, so take some time to poke around and explore the many footpaths that run from east to west, leading to additional viewpoints. The ledge is predominantly scrub-hardwood covered, but at its north end there is a virgin spruce grove, which extends to the ledge's base.

You'll have more time to explore the ledge on your return from Panther, which is another 1.75 miles beyond the ledge and an additional 500 feet in elevation. You have another 40 minutes of hiking, going slightly downhill at first and then climbing vigorously through large boulders and thick hardwood forest, passing a spring on the right. You have several views of Slide, Wittenberg, and Cornell as you cross open rock terraces.

The Panther summit is an expanded version of Giant Ledge in terms of views and topography, with isolated openings in the dense coniferous forest, yielding views of the Panther Kill Valley, Fork Ridge, and the village of Phoenicia with its two bridges crossing the Esopus. While the ledges on Panther face mostly to the east, some face west, and you can even look around for northerly views of Sheridan, Garfield, North Dome, Sherrill, and Balsam.

On the north side of Panther, the trail (completed in 1936) descends into Fox Hollow over a jeep trail that would make an attractive cross-country ski run, suggesting that this could be an adventurous two-car loop if you had skiing in mind. The loop ups the trip mileage to 7 total, about 3 of which can be skied if conditions are powdery. There are some breakneck sections where walking would be advisable.

From the summit of Panther you are an easy 1.75 miles from Giant Ledge and another 1.5 miles from your car.

41

Wittenberg and Cornell

Distance: 9.4 miles	
Time: 7 hours	
Vertical rise: 2,480 feet	
Map: NY–NJTC Catskill Trails, #43	

Wittenberg (3,780 feet) is a favorite among local hikers, who praise it as one of the Catskills' most dramatic hikes. Although not panoramic, the view encompasses an impressive 180-degree hemisphere of mountain and valley that reaches north over the Devil's Path Range and the escarpment, east over the Hudson and Taconics, and south over an extended variety of terrain where the Gunks

The Devil's Path from Wittenberg

taper off into endless flatlands. It is in many ways similar to the escarpment view of Pine Orchard fame, the single most lauded overlook in Catskill history. It offers intimate observation of the nearby peaks stretching from Peekamoose to Friday and in its eastern lowlands the Ashokan Reservoir, which is almost entirely visible.

The scene impressed John Burroughs, who visited there after a "long and desperate" attempt at Slide: "The view from the Wittenberg is in many respects more striking, as you are perched immediately above a broader and more distant sweep of country, and are only about 200 feet lower. You are here on the eastern brink of the lower Catskills, and the earth falls away at your feet and curves through an immense stretch of forest until it joins the plain of Shokan, and thence sweeps away to the Hudson and beyond."

The "plain of Shokan" is now the site of the Ashokan Reservoir, which was impounded in 1913 to supply water for New York City. Ashokan is Iroquois, meaning "place of fish." Slide is not visible from where Burroughs stood, but it is included in a collection of good views on the western side, along the trail to Cornell.

To reach the trailhead at Woodland Valley State Campground, cross the bridge from the middle of Phoenicia (just south of the only four-way intersection in town) and turn right on High Street, going under the NY 28 overpass. High Street leads directly into Woodland Valley Road in about 1.25 miles, where you turn south and go 4.7 miles to the campsite. If you are coming east on Route 28, get off at the Phoenicia exit and continue straight on High Street.

Woodland Valley is one of the Catskills' deepest and most romantic valleys. A hideaway for recluse, hiker, and flyfisher, it penetrates into the park's most remote peaks. You'll enjoy the sense of rugged terrain, the intriguing architecture of valley homesteads, and the lively creeks of Panther Kill and Dougherty Brook.

Do not rely on topo maps and earlier guidebooks, which place this trail a mile back to the east, where a suspended bridge led the trail to Terrace Mountain via an old bark and cross-country ski road.

From the hikers' parking area, which is on the road's north side, opposite the trailhead, find the red-marked trail signs and follow them across Woodland Creek. If you are hiking during the camping season, you must first pay the parking fee at the campground entrance. Don't be disheartened by the immediate ascent involved in this 3.4-mile hike to the summit of Wittenberg; the rise eases considerably, before steepening again as the summit is approached. Proceed through a heavily forested and boulder-strewn grove of large hemlock and maple trees. The trail is well marked here, but because of its many boulders, it is not self-guiding. So keep a close eye on the markers as you boulder-hop, or it will be easy to stray off the trail. As the forest type changes subtly into mixed hardwood, footing eases into occasional flat walks through high ledgy terrain and frequent dark stands of hemlock. After a half hour's hike, the trail becomes predominantly self-guiding and remains so until you encounter more rock in the upper elevations.

Within 2 hours of moderate effort, allowing for observation, refreshment, or photographing, you reach a trail junction, where you turn right for the

1.3-mile Wittenberg climb. The ascent is characterized by attractive (albeit steep) terraces, unusual rock formations, and penetrating vertical crevices. The forest cover will have changed notably into spruce and fir, and as Michael Kudish, in *Vegetational History of the Catskill High Peaks,* comments, "On even slopes the transition from slope to ridge forests is gradual and barely noticeable to the observer. But just as frequently, however, a high ledge will create an abrupt break in the topography, creating a likewise abrupt break in the forest. Examples of such rapid transitions from slope to ridge forest occur at the north slope of Wittenberg at 3,000 feet along the trail."

Within 45 minutes to an hour of diligent stalking you will have bagged the summit, which includes an intriguing array of sheltered outcrops and open ledges facing east. There is some evidence of illegal camping (above 3,500 feet) in the surrounding forest, which, however, does not detract from your aesthetic appreciation of the place. Although the profusion of mosses, lichens, and various forest cover is typical of Catskill peaks, it is interesting to note the absence of alpine species. Kudish speculates that these could have been eliminated by the trampling of hikers. Below the summit ledge a short distance is a large overhang that may be convenient in the event of rain.

After lunching and resting on the Wittenberg, you will want to observe some westerly views, which can be done best by hiking the short trail to Cornell via the ridge that connects them, a narrow and interesting rock path that is several feet wide. A short side trail to the left will take you to the summit, which you will find just after you climb the steep cleft in the cliff face. Cornell's

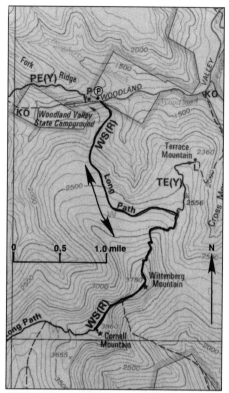

© 1983 NEW YORK–NEW JERSEY TRAIL CONFERENCE

westerly shoulder provides a good view of the slide on Slide's north side, which occurred circa 1820. To see this, proceed west 0.1 mile on the trail as if hiking to Slide. The hike to Cornell from Wittenberg is about 30 minutes. If you have arranged for a shuttle you may choose to hike Slide. If not, you must return the way you came.

This trail dates back to 1880, when Burroughs haunted the range, relating anecdotes of the porcupines in volume six of his complete nature writings, *Riverby.* And if you've dropped your pack off on Cornell's summit to find the westerly view of Slide, don't be surprised to find the omnivorous quill pig investigating your lunch when you return.

42

Slide Mountain Loop

Distance: *7 miles*

Time: *5½ hours*

Vertical rise: *1,700 feet*

Map: *NY–NJTC Catskill Trails, #43*

John Burroughs never would have suspected that the mountain that had so successfully defied his climbing efforts in the early 1880s would become one of the Catskills' most approachable high peaks. In Burroughs's time, Slide was, as he suggested, "probably the most inaccessible; certainly the hardest to get a view of, it is hedged

Slide Mountain from Cornell

about so completely by other peaks, the greatest mountain of them all and apparently the least willing to be seen; only at a distance of thirty or forty miles is it seen to stand up above all other peaks." Yet within a few years of Burroughs's 1885 ascent, the mountain became revealed to members of organized outings by Jim Dutcher, a bark peeler living at the foot of the mountain, who was recognized as its singular guide.

Alf Evers tells us that "Dutcher, who kept a boardinghouse at Big Indian (Panther Mountain House) and served as the hamlet's postmaster, was among the best known of all the mountain guides and the guardian spirit of Slide Mountain."

Dutcher's trail remains to commemorate him, but today only a small section of it is seen by hikers. The easiest way to get at Slide is from the top of Big Indian Hollow. This is also where the trail to Denning is picked up.

Take County Route 47 (Slide Mountain Road) from Big Indian Pass (heading south), pass Winnisook Lake at 8.4 miles on the left, and park at the trailhead lot one mile farther on. Don't get confused by the yellow-marked trail that departs for Giant Ledge and Woodland Valley from the hairpin turn, before you reach Winnisook Lake. This is the same trail that goes to Slide, but it follows the road at this point. Follow the yellow markers you see on trees and telephone poles along the road, to the Slide Mountain parking lot.

Once afoot you immediately cross the upper reaches of the Neversink's West Branch (often dry here), which flows into the Delaware River. Also originating on Slide's northwest watershed is the Esopus, which runs down through the hollow into Phoenicia, the Ashokan Reservoir, and the Hudson. Continuing on an easy uphill and heavily impacted trail through a stand of thin maple and mixed hardwood, you reach an old road that you follow to the right.

After about 5 minutes on this road, you notice a spring on the left side. Soon you come to a junction with a red-marked trail, which goes off to the left. This trail is the old jeep road up Slide Mountain. It is the shortest way up, but it is a rather boring climb. Instead, this road will be used for the descent. Continue straight ahead on the yellow-marked road and cross a wooden bridge over an unnamed tributary of the Neversink's West Branch. From here, the road climbs slightly. In another 15 minutes or so, you reach another trail junction. Here the blue-marked Curtis-Ormsbee Trail up Slide Mountain begins.

Note the interesting stone monument near the junction. William ("Father Bill") Curtis and Allen Ormsbee, for whom the trail was named, both died in a sudden snowstorm on Mount Washington, New Hampshire, on June 30, 1900. They were on their way up the mountain to attend a meeting of the Appalachian Mountain Club at the summit. This beautiful trail up Slide was laid out to commemorate this tragic event.

Turn left onto the blue-marked trail. Soon you climb up a very large rock. In another 15 minutes, after a steep but short climb, you find a beautiful viewpoint to the north. The trail now levels off, soon passing the 3,500-foot sign, above which no camping or fires are permitted. In another 5 minutes, a short side trail to the right leads to an outstanding overlook. Down below ahead of you is the valley of the East Branch of the Neversink River.

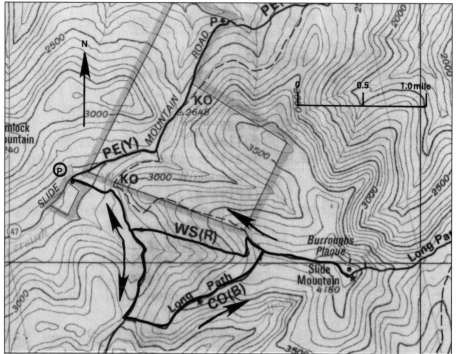

Table Mountain, distinguished by its long, flat summit, is directly ahead, and Lone Mountain is to its left. You'll probably want to rest here for a few minutes and savor the spectacular view.

After leaving the viewpoint, the trail remains relatively level for a while and then continues to ascend. It soon begins to pass through a spruce-fir forest, common at high elevations in the Catskills. After about 40 minutes of hiking (from the viewpoint), you climb rather steeply and come to a junction with a red-marked trail. This is the Cornell-Wittenberg-Slide Trail, the end of which you passed earlier.

Turn right onto the red-marked trail. Slide Mountain is only another 0.65 mile away. This section of trail is relatively flat, and you have only about another 200 feet of elevation to gain before you reach the summit. Take time to enjoy this beautiful section of

trail and to explore the various viewpoints both to the right and to the left.

Within another half hour you reach the summit, marked by the foundation of a former fire tower. Continue ahead to an open rock with excellent views to the east. Ahead of you and just to the left are Cornell and Wittenberg Mountains, and the Ashokan Reservoir is visible behind in the distance. Directly below the ledge, affixed to the rock, is a plaque commemorating John Burroughs, which reads in part: "Here the works of man dwindle in the heart of the southern Catskills."

Slide's summit view includes nearly 70 named Catskill peaks as well as a wide view of the Hudson Valley, Ashokan Reservoir, Green Mountains, Berkshires, Taconics, Hudson Highlands, and Shawangunks. This is the same view that Commissioner Cox, climbing Slide in 1886, pronounced to be "every bit as fine as anything to be seen in the Adirondacks."

Slide was not recognized as the Catskills' highest peak until Princeton Professor of Geology Arnold Guyot published his map of 1879. Previously, Kaaterskill High Peak and later Hunter Mountain competed for the title in the days when a common carpenter's level was the critical measuring tool.

To return to your car, retrace your steps on the red-marked trail, but continue straight ahead when you arrive at the junction with the blue-marked trail. In another 5 minutes, the trail makes a sharp left turn. Here, you may notice a faint trail which continues straight ahead. This trail, laid down by Dutcher in 1886, featured many stone steps.

While some current sources maintain that Dutcher Trail was built to enable three newly appointed forest commissioners and a party of officials to ascend Slide in 1886 to officially designate the Catskills as a part of the New York State Forest Preserve, in fact the trail was developed for women. Even Burroughs commented, in a statement reflecting more the dress and cultural habits than the attitudes of his time, that the rugged and direct approach from Woodland Valley is Slide's "most difficult side," whereas from Big Indian "the climb is comparatively easy and . . . often made by women." This statement was made prior to the Dutcher Trail's appearance. From Woodland—remember that Burroughs was traversing the treacherous 1,200-foot-by-500-foot landslide that earned the mountain its name—he claimed that "only men can essay the ascent."

The Dutcher Trail leads into the private property of the Winnisook Club, which is not open to the public. You should therefore continue down on the blue-marked trail. This section of the trail is very interesting, and has the character of a garden pathway.

Writers and historians have commented on this section of trail, taking particular notice of the presence of white quartz. Where this stratum of rock continues into Pennsylvania, it is overlaid with anthracite coal. Geologists believe that, given another 500 feet in elevation, the Catskills would have contained coal.

The history of trail locations on Slide is vast and confusing. Although some contemporary woodspeople refer offhandedly to the trail discussed here as the "old bridle path," H. A. Haring noted about 1930 that "today both [the wagon road and the bridle path] are completely abandoned, partly engulfed in landslides and at all points densely overgrown. Both are now impassable. Even the footpath follows a different route." Interestingly, T. Morris Longstreth, writing about 1917, makes no remarks about either bridle path or wagon road; he was directed along a blazed trail upon which "there were no footprints." Neither does he make reference to Dutcher. Some details of his climb ("to our left the woods sloped uniformly up, on the right they fell into a ravine") and his telling of following the old telephone wire that ran to the tower, suggest an approach similar to today's.

Continue along on the blue-marked trail, which now descends rather steadily. This section of trail is an old jeep road and affords no views. When you arrive at the old yellow-marked road at the base of the descent, turn right and follow the yellow marks back to your car.

43

Blackhead, Black Dome, and Thomas Cole

Distance: 7 miles, 8.5 if car left at Maplecrest

Time: 6 hours

Vertical rise: 2,450 feet, cumulative

Map: NY–NJTC Catskill Trails, #41

At the age of 24, Thomas Cole, an immigrant from England, had an established reputation as a landscape painter. In 1825, in the company of a wealthy patron, Cole made a first visit to the Catskills, traveling to the House at Pine Orchard, forerunner of the fabulous Catskill Mountain House. Cole was enthralled by the views of mountains, lakes, and forests. The inspiration of those mountains played upon his nostalgic view of nature, resulting in the first major series of

Lunch on Black Dome looking south

paintings of the mountains. The combination also firmly established Cole as a leader in the romantic realism school of painting that dominated the middle of the nineteenth century.

Cole's love of the Catskills was reflected in the paintings he made from sketches done at the scene on many trips into the mountains. His close observations of nature breathed life into his view of the romantic wilderness. He wrote of the view on the trip through the Clove near Palenville and the huge precipices above the village that "frowned over the valley like towers and battlements of cyclopean structure." He declared that the "sun shining in gleams through the tall, dark, spruce forest, upon the velvety carpet" reminded him of "the interior of some Gothic pile, where the sun comes through narrow windows in slender streams, and lights whatever it strikes with a refulgence almost supernatural, amid the gloomy shadows around."

Although he considered the view from High Peak to be the finest in the whole Catskill Range, and spent most of his time in the mountains surrounding the Catskill Mountain House, he was impressed by the peaks in the Blackhead Range. On "an excursion to Blackhead, or the Dome Mountain as Cole loved to call it, one of the finest portions of the Catskills must always continue to be, both to the writer and the painter, one of the luminous points of the past. . . . At noon . . . the moss beneath black fir trees on the summit . . . the descent down the wooded steeps."

It is fitting that one of the peaks in the Blackhead Range now bears Cole's name. And a hike over Blackhead, Black Dome, and Thomas Cole brings the hiker to several vantages from which s/he still can share Cole's vi-

sion of wilderness without the influence of humans.

A two-car shuttle is a must for this walk, which loops over the three tremendous peaks that offer the best of views in the northern Catskills. Both ends of the loop are accessible from Maplecrest, a tiny hamlet in a high valley.

Leave one car at the parking turnout at the end of Elmer Barnum Road at the west end of the valley. To find it turn south on Maple Crest Road at Maplecrest; Elmer Barnum Road is the first left. Alternatively, you can leave a car in the village, for the 1.5-mile downhill walk from the trailhead to the hamlet does not seem to add too much to the trip. Drive east through bucolic Black Dome Valley to a parking turnout at the end of Big Hollow Road, an extension of Maple Crest Road. Two trails depart from this trailhead. You want the southern one, which gives the distance to Black Dome as 1.8 miles; Thomas Cole, 2.5 miles; and Elmer Barnum Road, 5.8 miles. Your walk will be 1.2 miles longer because you also will climb Blackhead.

You cross a small stream and pick up red trail markers at the registration booth. You cross and recross the Batavia Kill, beginning a gentle uphill on a broad, open old road. The brook or its tributary will keep you company with charming waterfalls in spring flood. Beyond a second stream crossing, the grade increases, and in about 0.5 mile the yellow-marked trail to Blackhead continues straight as you turn right, still on the red-marked trail, to follow the tributary more steeply uphill. After walking for 40 minutes, you reach a spring (with pipe).

The trail is even steeper beyond, and Blackhead can be seen through the trees except in summer. After a

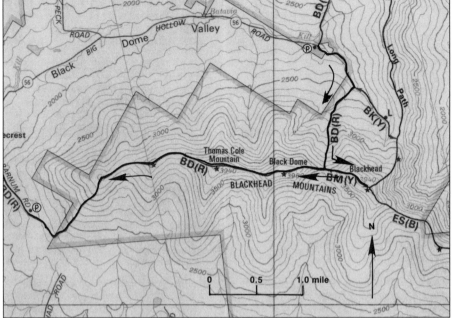

fairly stiff climb, the trail levels out, and you reach a draw between Blackhead and Black Dome, where a sign gives the mileage as 1.7 miles, a trip that probably took you 1 hour and 10 minutes because of the 1,400-foot climb. Blackhead is 0.6 mile from here and so is Black Dome.

The yellow-marked trail heads left up Blackhead, and wonderful views from this trail start almost immediately. The route is steep, with stairs built into the mountainside. At the crest the trail continues across the level top out to the narrow northeastern prong. Here is a trail intersection with the blue-marked trail leading toward Windham High Peak and the yellow-marked trail directly back to the valley, but you will return the way you climbed. First, walk a few hundred feet farther to a lookout to enjoy the views across the Hudson to the Taconics. There is also a western look-out down a small path to the right of the end of the narrow prong with views of Hunter, obvious by its fire tower, across the big, broad valley below.

It will take you about an hour to climb Blackhead and return to the saddle. At this point, take the red-marked trail again and immediately start to climb. Your first impression is a view back to the incredible rock mass of Blackhead. There are several scrambles and a series of ledges before you reach Black Dome's relatively level summit. That climb takes a half hour, and you will find a lovely lunch spot with views to the left of the trail, shortly after it levels out. West Kill is seen to the right of Hunter with Plateau to the left of Hunter. East of Plateau lie Mink Hollow, the Sugarloaf, Twin, and Indian Head. Slide, Wittenberg, and Cornell are seen on the horizon beyond Hunter.

The trail continues across this narrow summit ridge, climbing a few ledges on the way. After about a 15-minute walk, you find a second lookout, this time to the far eastern end of the range with Kaaterskill in full view. You continue across the scrubby summit with no views for another 10 minutes before you begin to descend.

The long, thin saddle between the peaks has been burned, and the twisted stumps give one section an otherworldly air. There are views along the way, one to the west and a second toward the town of Windham and toward Camels Hump. You climb again, this time quite gently, to the summit of Thomas Cole, a point that is 0.7 mile from Black Dome and that, in spite of being a tribute to the famous painter, offers more limited views. The trail crosses the open, wooded summit ridge, then begins to descend through a series of shelves and ledges, typical Catskill terrain. From the first of these knobs, you have views of Windham and Maplecrest Valley. Below a second wooded knob, just as the trail begins a final steep descent, there are more views from an open rock ledge. The 2.65-mile trip down from Thomas Cole to the trailhead, 1.5 miles from the hamlet, takes only an hour.

44

Windham High Peak Loop

Distance: 13 miles

Time: 5–7 hours

Vertical rise: 2,220 feet

Map: NY–NJTC Catskill Trails, #41

This highly scenic and energetic hike follows the escarpment's north shoulder, with Windham High Peak forming the western height of land that reaches in an arch through the east and south. The escarpment is the sudden 2,000-foot rise from the valley floor of the ridge and mountains running from Overlook and north to Windham.

Windham High Peak

From a distance the escarpment looks continuous, yet it is bisected deeply by Kaaterskill Clove (between South Mountain and Kaaterskill High Peak) and its southerly neighbor Platte Clove, between Kaaterskill High Peak and Plattekill mountains. Otherwise, it is visually impenetrable.

The escarpment was revered by local Native Americans, who called it the Great Wall of Manitou. It was beyond this wall that the gods Gitchie Manitou, the spirit of good, and Mitchie Manitou, the spirit of evil, lived in eternal discord. Longfellow leaves us an interpretation of the myth: "Gitchie Manitou The Mighty." (See *Our Catskill Mountains*.)

The Dutch settlers, who sought ground similar to the Netherland's arable, flat lands, had little use for the rocky hinterland beyond the wall, as it was unsuitable for farming and was still, no doubt, the devil's dwelling place. They neither strayed nor settled far beyond the river valley.

The area's beauty was spread by the genius of Irving, Cole, Bryant, Burroughs, Thoreau, Muir, and their contemporaries in art and literature. Later guidebook writers of the twentieth century, H. A. Haring in particular, described the view from the east as one of the "few places in the world where mountains stand out so impressively. . . . The rounded outlines of the range bespeak all the shadowiness and romance with which legend has clothed them, the Wall of Manitou mellows the mountains into soft contours and rounded lines that seem to flow rhythmically from summit to summit."

Windham High Peak is the first "rounded outline" you hike. Coming west on NY 23 from Catskill, turn left (south) on County Route 65 to Hensonville. From there go two miles into Maplecrest on County Route 40. Turn left on County Route 56 (Big Hollow Road) until you reach Peck Road at 1.8 miles on your left. The trail begins within a mile at the end of Peck Road.

Begin on the yellow-marked trail toward Elm Ridge lean-to (1 mile), where you also see red New York State snowmobile-trail signs. Follow a dirt road through vestigial pasturelands, now grown into a forest of mixed hardwoods where stone walls mark the field divisions of early settlements. A side trail branches off to your right into an evergreen stand. Avoid it, continuing to follow the yellow markers. In 15 minutes you should reach the trail junction. Turn right, following the blue (Escarpment Trail) markers indicating Windham High Peak, Burnt Knob, and Acra Point. The Elm Ridge lean-to will appear on your right as you continue. The lean-to is well situated and frequently used. Nearby campsites are plentiful, however, if you are interested in spending the night. One good spot in particular is located on a yellow-marked spur trail that leads left (north) off the blue-marked trail just above the lean-to. It provides a good view to the north-northwest.

After a half hour of hiking, about ½ mile from the lean-to, you pass through some thick, dark, evergreen forests that will spark your imagination. This stretch used to be quite wet in early season, but it has been recently improved by the Appalachian Mountain Club (AMC). The trail then bends gently through hardwood, gradually ascending.

When you reach the southerly shoulder of the mountain at 3,000 feet in elevation, you get a look at the nearby

Blackhead Range and the more westerly East Jewett range. At this point, you are about 3 miles into the walk; turn northeast for the 0.5-mile, 520-foot climb to the summit. During periods of scanty foliage in this birch, cherry, and maple forest, you will be able to look east at Burnt Knob and Acra Point and the long escarpment ridge. The last incline will take you about 30 minutes. Once on the long, level summit, you discover a benchmark and some remarkable views.

The most imposing of these views will be into the Blackhead Range, which feels remarkably close. Down and to your right, or southwest, you see the sister peaks of Round (2,585 feet) and Van Loan Hill (2,500 feet). The westerly views are off to the northwest side of the summit, on a short spur to a rocky area that you will find easily. From this point you see a long line of lesser peaks disappearing into the Schoharie Valley, including Ginseng, Zoar, and Cave Mountain, and slightly to the north, Richmond and Huntersfield mountains with Ashland Pinnacle between them. You can also see the Windham ski area.

The most popular view is from beyond the summit (east), where a graffiti-inscribed outcrop hangs above the Hudson Valley. (These inscriptions are not of the same genre as the North Lake variety, and the few decent initials have been heavily eroded and defaced with the deep and careless scrawls of heavy chisels.) From here you can see the Helderberg Escarpment and, on a clear day, Albany. It is also likely that you'll see Vermont's Green Mountains, the Berkshires, and the Taconic Range. Looking down over the ridge you see Burnt Knob (3,180 feet), the second knoll from Windham High Peak. The precise position of Acra Point is not discernible from here, as it follows a long and fairly level ridgeline around to the east.

Leave the summit, going steeply downhill through hardwood, reaching the scenic col between Windham High Peak and Burnt Knob in 35 minutes or so. The views are similar to those looking south from Windham High Peak, although you are lower and closer to the valley views. Watch for occasional yellow-marked spurs that lead to views. Continue up Burnt Knob, which you will scale in another half hour or so, where more views look both north and south on variations of Black Dome Valley and the expanse of northern lowlands.

You then descend into the 2,800-foot saddle between Burnt Knob and Acra Point, where the red-marked Black Dome Range Trail intersects the Escarpment Trail. If you wish to shorten your hike back to Peck Road via Big Hollow Road, this is the place to do it. If not, continue uphill, gaining several hundred feet of elevation before reaching Acra Point after 25 minutes. Although there are limited views to the north and south, this point offers a wide perspective of the valley toward Hensonville.

All along the ridge from Burnt Knob through Acra Point and south to the junction of the Escarpment and Batavia Kill trails (yellow-marked) there are crude campsites and campfire rings constructed among the balsam. As you travel south from Acra Point, they become bigger, more conspicuous, and more frequent, commanding narrow overlooks with restricted views to the east. There are no views to the west along this ridge, which will take perhaps an hour to hike. At some points you will be able to peer down the escarpment to the south. The Black-

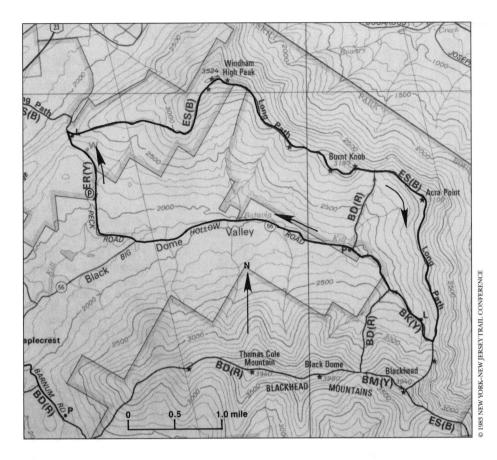

heads will be visible periodically also, ahead through the trees. If the yellow-marked Batavia Kill Trail seems long in coming, don't worry—it's hard to miss it. You descend nearly 200 feet (in 0.5 mile) to reach the junction, where you turn right and drop another 200 feet to the Batavia Kill lean-to, which is no more than 10 minutes beyond the junction.

Hike out, picking up the red-marked Black Dome Range Trail, which comes in on your left within 15 minutes. At this point two creeks converge. You are now only 0.5 mile from the road, and you must walk it back to Peck Road unless you've arranged for a shuttle or can talk someone into giving you a ride—which by now your feet will appreciate.

45

Dry Brook Ridge

Distance: 7 miles

Time: 4½ hours

Vertical rise: 2,000 feet

Map: NY–NJTC Catskill Trails, #42

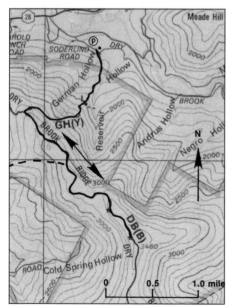

© 1983 NEW YORK–NEW JERSEY TRAIL CONFERENCE

The Dry Brook Ridge Trail provides a short but fairly strenuous outing that will give you a look at the scenic valley of the Delaware's east branch, Cold Spring Hollow, and the long line of Mill Brook Ridge.

The trail has several access points. The Mill Brook Road trailhead, which is the longest access, is also the ridge's busiest, being close to both the Mill Brook and Dry Brook Ridge lean-tos. This southerly access to the ridge is also where the northerly access to Balsam Lake and Graham mountains is located, just uphill of Furlough Lake, which flows east into Dry Brook and north to join the Bush Kill in Arkville. Both creeks drain into the Delaware.

The northwest access is located in Margaretville, where the trail crosses the Pakatakan Mountain for the 9.4-mile ridge hike. Still another access, which is the shortest and most interesting approach, is the yellow-marked trail through German Hollow. In the summer of 1993 a loop trail was constructed that joins the ridge from Benecke Road to the west.

The German Hollow Trail begins at the end of Chris Long Road (Soderling Road on the map), a short dirt dead end that you'll find 0.25 mile south of Arkville off Dry Brook Road. Arkville itself is on NY 28 west of Kingston, between Margaretville and Fleischmanns.

Don't be fooled into thinking that you'll save 1,000 feet of elevation by beginning the hike at the Mill Brook Road trailhead; you will make up for it in the undulating terrain of the ridge, while covering a good deal more distance.

Follow 0.25 mile to the end of Chris Long Road, where the trail starts at a parking lot and runs between German Hollow and Reservoir Hollow to join the ridge trail. You begin immediately uphill over a rough jeep trail, encountering the trail register on your left. Continue uphill, passing a long, crumbling stone wall on your left, and climb through a pleasant hemlock grove.

Within half an hour you reach the German Hollow lean-to, where the trail switches back nearly 180 degrees. Located in a stand of tall, thin ash, the lean-to provides no view, but it has a sturdy stone fireplace, a good roof and wooden floor, and a nearby spring that produces even in dry weather. You are advised to carry your own water, however. You can find the spring by walking directly out of the lean-to and down a short spur trail for 100 yards.

As you continue your ascent from the lean-to, within 15 minutes you reach another spring, marked by a tall cairn on the trail's right side. By now the forest cover is predominantly hardwood, as it will remain for the rest of the hike. The trail is self-guiding and well marked, over a combination of mineral soil and broken stone. Once you reach the junction of the German Hollow and Dry Brook Ridge trails, which is not much more than a 25-minute hike from the lean-to, you see several trail signs. Follow to the left on the blue-marked trail in the direction of Mill Brook Road. You won't be going the entire 6.35 miles to the road, however. The views are located at elevations of 3,300 and 3,400 feet, at the ridge's summit, which is 2 miles ahead.

The trail is flat for a stretch until it returns to its old tricks, running steeply up and down for 20 minutes, then leveling out through ledgy terrain and some wet areas where the trail can be soft. You walk through a consistent distribution of beech, birch, and maple, with a corresponding appearance of moosewood, pin cherry, choke cherry, hop hornbeam, hobblebush, oxalis, woodfern, viburnum, blackberry, raspberry, and blueberry.

After climbing another ledge, you reach a boulder with limited views and, following it, weaving in and out of trees along the western ridgeline, you at last reach a 150-foot-long exposed outcrop with lots of blueberry bushes and some fine views to the west. As you look straight out into the valley you see Cold Spring Hollow directly below you, with its Huckleberry Brook reaching for the Delaware. To the left, beyond Mill Brook Valley, is the long Mill Brook Ridge, running east-west from the vicinity of Woodpecker Ridge and the unseen Balsam Lake Mountain. You can see the Delaware's east branch as it flows from Margaretville and into the Pepacton Reservoir, a New York City water-supply reservoir that is known for producing record brown trout.

You are at the ridge's summit, and although one or two more views are available to the west, they are lesser versions of the same westerly exposure. Regrettably, there are no views to the east. Return the way you came.

Delaware County is a highly scenic and heavily farmed setting of low, gently sculpted hills spotted with rich, cultivated fields and long vistas. It has over 900 miles of trout streams, has led New York State from time to time in the annual deer harvest, and supports native populations of wild turkey, grouse, woodcock, and snowshoe hare.

While in Arkville you should take advantage of the Delaware and Ulster Rail Ride, which runs from Arkville to Fleischmanns and Highmount. Railroads came to the Arkville area in 1871, fostering the great resort boom that followed. Riding the "Red Heifer" (a combination diesel, mail, freight, and passenger car called a brill) through this scenic territory will give you appreciation for the easterly upper Delaware Valley that cannot be seen from the heights of Dry Brook Ridge.

(For more information on the rail ride, call 914-586-3877 or write Delaware and Ulster, PO Box 243, Stamford, NY 12167.)

46

Balsam Lake Mountain Loop

Distance: 6 miles

Time: 4½ hours

Vertical rise: 1,123 feet

Map: NY–NJTC Catskill Trails, #42

Balsam Lake Mountain and Graham Mountain are sister peaks, in the south-western-central Catskills. Many hikers, particularly those wishing to join the Catskill 3500 Club, bag both Balsam Lake and Graham in a single outing. The hiker not tallying peaks might avoid Graham because of its one serious drawback: The view is limited unless you climb the old concrete-and-steel frame of an abandoned microwave station. It is also private, but its owner allows hiking. Local rangers ask that hikers do not camp on these lands. It is always advisable, if it can be done, to ask permission to hike private property. Unless an easement exists or a precedent allowing hikers to use such lands has been set, this guidebook does not describe or en-

courage the use of trails that cross private parcels. Including Graham in this outing adds another 3 miles to the hike, lengthening the total distance to 9 miles and involving an additional 620 feet of vertical rise.

The views from Balsam Lake's fire tower, on the other hand, make the trip a worthwhile one for both peak-baggers and touring hikers, many of whom you'll encounter on the trail during a sunny weekend. (Be cautious on this tower. It is scheduled to be replaced in the near future.) If you feel energetic, climb both peaks.

To reach Balsam Lake Mountain, go in from the north, off Mill Brook Road. From Arkville, find Dry Brook Road (County Route 49), which leaves NY 28 and heads south. From NY 28, go six miles south on Dry Brook Road, straight through Mapledale to Mill Brook Road. Take Mill Brook Road to the right, and go uphill 2.3 miles, where you find the well-marked trailhead on your left. Blue trail signs here indicate directions to the Balsam Lake Mountain fire tower, the lean-to (there are two), and Claryville. Be sure you take this trail, not the one on the north (or right) side of the road that crosses Dry Brook Ridge.

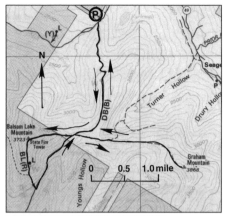

found in open pine woods and bogs.

In 10 minutes or so you see a good spring to the right and downhill (indicated by a sign) among a series of sedimentary boulders, many of which are covered with rock tripe. When soaked for several weeks in water, this lichen renders a purple dye that has some popularity among textile artisans. Rock tripe is also edible, if not entirely wholesome. The dried-up, curled disks of lichen resemble very moldy potato chips. Eat them if you must, but remember that it is illegal to remove any plant life from the forest preserve.

In another 20 minutes you pass a grass-covered trail on your left that leads to Graham's summit. In a few moments you encounter several trail signs. Take the red-marked trail to your right, which goes to Balsam Lake Mountain fire tower (0.85 mile). At this point a sign prohibits entry of any motorized vehicles.

Continue going uphill over flat rocks where glacial scratches can be seen. The trail includes some vigorous ascents broken up by more moderate inclines, hedged in blackberry, bunchberry, and spruce-fir thickets.

After 20 minutes of continually thinking that each rise will produce the summit, you at last see the fire tower and observer's cabin come into view. If it is safe to do so, climb to the top of the tower (without which there would be no view), where you can see in all directions. In general, be careful climbing fire towers in the forest preserve—many have been removed and those that remain are old. Normally, the first flight of stairs is taken out when the tower shows signs of decay. Later, time allowing, the stairs are either fixed or removed. (There are plans to rehabilitate this tower and staff it with a seasonal observer.)

You will find the first section of trail easy to hike and legally driveable; however, only four-wheel-drive vehicles should attempt it; the road is barricaded before the summit is reached. The road is maintained only as a foot trail. Immediately you notice a forest of beech, birch, maple, and cherry over cinnamon ferns, oxalis, and virburnum. In 5 minutes you reach the trail register on your left.

Follow along through a flat section of the trail, which is paralleled by the fire tower and observer's cabin telephone lines, to an uphill section that allows occasional views across Mill Brook Hollow to the west. Ascend gently through a few switchbacks, which can be seen on the map. Look for trailside specimens of jack-in-the-pulpit, Solomon's seal, wolf's claw club moss, and haircap moss. The upright, branched, and densely leaved stems of wolf's claw club moss are used commercially for Christmas decorations. (Picking them in the preserve is prohibited.) The moss is widely distributed through the Catskills and northern North America. It can be confused with the similarly distributed tree club moss, or ground pine, which is usually

Balsam Lake Mountain and Graham Mountain

Below the tower, and running north, is the Dry Brook Ridge. To the northeast on a clear day you can see as far as Bearpen Mountain, 15 miles away. Closer at hand is the ridge on the east side of the Dry Brook Valley and its series of peaks. From left to right are the masses of Belleayre, Balsam, Haynes, Eagle, and Big Indian. Between the latter two, the summit of Panther can be seen. Due east of you is the range that includes Slide and Table. The two neighboring peaks are Graham and Doubletop. To the south and west are the rolling, seemingly endless lower peaks of Delaware County, which includes some of the most sparsely populated lands within the Catskill Park.

Just off the summit, in an impenetrable tangle of blowdown, is a unique plant community: a bog. Researchers call this bog unique because it contains more sphagnum than other bogs in the Catskill region. A hurricane on November 25, 1950, caused extensive blowdown in the northeast half of the bog, which was followed by a heavy second growth of balsam fir. It has been hypothesized that this bog may never follow a bog's normal growth pattern because of the infiltration of acid rain, which acts to decompose peat. Water is retained, and the bog stage remains rather than progresses. Balsam Lake's summit has recently been the site of acid rain studies, a question that has come of age in the Catskills, despite the profusion of its limestone, which acts to buffer acids.

The trail continues downhill past an outbuilding with signs indicating the lean-to at 0.45 mile. Follow downhill, passing an open, primitive campsite with a fire ring on your right. You will see a lean-to on your left shortly thereafter; it's in rough shape, with a dirt floor. A more inviting lean-to is beyond it to the east. It is in much better shape, with a wooden floor and an interesting quarter-loft for stowing packs and possibly sleeping. Views to the south are available here beyond the lean-tos.

Descend toward the blue-marked trail, passing a spring just below the lean-to area, and within 20 minutes you intersect with the blue-marked trail once again. Go left in the direction of Mill Brook lean-to, and follow this pleasant, grassy road uphill for 20 minutes to the junction of the main trail to Balsam Lake Mountain (blue-marked). Five minutes ahead of you is the grassy trail to Graham, which is unmarked but obvious on map #42. If you wish to take it, descend slightly, reaching the intersection in 10 minutes, and go right. The trail heads uphill from here, and brings you to the summit in about 40 minutes. Although it is easily followed, the trail is not well maintained, and should the thick, overhanging boughs and bushes become wet, so will you.

While Graham's summit provides only a limited view into Dry Brook Hollow, the view from atop the concrete television transmitting building (now a shameful mess) is equal to and perhaps better than that from Balsam Lake Mountain. You see the patchwork of farms and hedgerows of Dry Brook Valley, whose shading and brilliance is much like what we see for October calendar pictures entitled "Vermont." As if such beauty only existed there!

The next peak is Doubletop, whose twin summits are covered with balsam fir and spruce, looking foreboding and desolate on a dark afternoon. Beyond Doubletop, still to the east, the peaks running between Slide and Table are clearly visible. Peaks of Cornell and Wittenberg can be seen to Slide's left and, of course, there are southerly valley vistas. But it is the view down into Dry Brook Valley that makes the trip worth the extra effort.

From the trail junction of the Balsam Lake Mountain and Graham trails, you are 50 minutes from your starting point on Mill Brook Road.

47

Bearpen Mountain

Distance: *6.5 miles*

Time: *5 hours*

Vertical rise: *1,600 feet*

Maps: *USGS 7½' Prattsville; NYSDT Prattsville*

Bearpen gets little attention from hikers because it is outside the Catskill Park, does not have a state-marked or maintained trail, and is seldom discussed in books or by hikers other than those of the Catskill 3500 Club.

The trail is an easy but uneventful walk until you reach the summit, where long views of the Schoharie Valley and the Delaware County farmlands make

On Bearpen Mountain

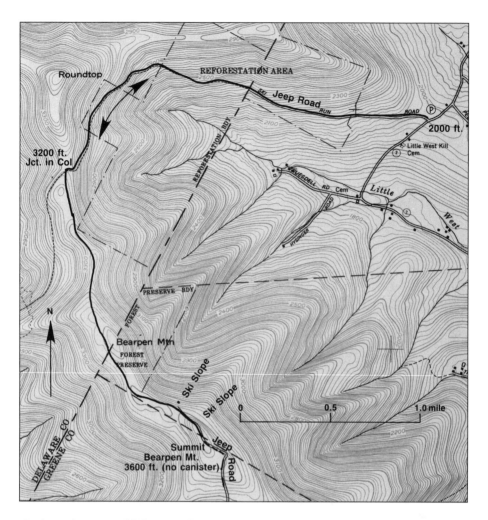

the long jeep-road hike worthwhile.

John Burroughs looked upon the western slopes of Bearpen from Boyhood Rock in Roxbury, where he was born in 1837. He is buried near Boyhood Rock, and his summer home, Woodchuck Lodge, which you can visit on the same day you climb Bearpen, can be seen from the road and is open to the public during summer months. Boyhood Rock is a short hike into the fields. Both places can be visited in less than an hour once

you get to Roxbury.

To reach Bearpen, follow NY 23A until just east of Prattsville, where County Route 2 goes south. Turn here and immediately cross the Schoharie Creek over an old iron bridge. Once across the creek turn right, and bear right at the first fork you encounter a short distance ahead. Within a mile of the bridge, bear left, uphill over a paved road, turning away from the creek. After 1.2 miles, go right at the T (left is a dead end). In another 1.9

miles of scenic driving, with Bearpen and Vly Mountains visible on your left (south), you will reach an intersection.

Turn right at this intersection; the road climbs for 0.6 mile, reaching a jeep trail on your left at the crest of the hill (Ski Run Road). This is the trailhead. Parking is available here in a grove of maple trees where you can look south-southwest at Bearpen's summit.

Start hiking on an easy road that ascends consistently, passing stone walls on the left and right. In 10 minutes you reach state land (you have been hiking a public easement), where you may see blue paint blazes along the trail. The road is so good that it needs no marking.

The trail here is relatively featureless and not terribly exciting, but you will see a profusion of white violets, jack-in-the-pulpit, spring beauties, rue anemone, and Dutchman's-breeches, which may take the edge off your impatience. You also will be serenaded by what seems an unusually high population of songbirds. The ovenbirds cry "teacher, teacher" as you try to locate them. Rose-breasted grosbeaks and phoebes flit curiously above as you walk. Myrtle warblers and red-winged blackbirds betray themselves amid the green leaves of popple and maple.

In 45 minutes or more of this steady incline, with only occasional views through trees to the east, you reach a junction where a road leads to the right. Bear left, toward Bearpen. You are walking south now, through blackberry patches, where the trail is literally lined with spring beauties in early season. Within 35 minutes you reach a flat, open area where the summit is visible ahead of you. Shortly thereafter you reach a pond. From here the summit ridge is still ahead, up a short, steep incline.

Once you reach the summit ridge, the actual summit is ahead of you. From various points on the summit and its approach, Utsayantha can be seen to the west, as well as (from right to left on the southerly exposure) Balsam Lake, Graham, Doubletop, and the Highmount and Belleayre ski areas (left to right, respectively). Continue going east until you reach abandoned ski trails, the second of which approximates the summit.

Bearpen's summit is deciduous, predominantly maple, birch, and cherry. On the ski slopes facing north you find platforms of several old lifts, which were powered by old automobiles whose carcasses appear here and there. The views to the north and east are good, mostly consisting of low, nameless peaks, parts of the Schoharie Reservoir near West Conesville. You can see as far east as Windham High Peak and Thomas Cole Mountain in the Blackhead Range.

It was here, inspired by the expansive terrain beyond, that Bleecker Staats, number 272 of the Catskill 3500 Club, recited his memorable insights on the Catskills, his favorite "movable feast." "You can taste it," he began. "You can hear it; its birds moving and singing in the trees, its breezes; its streams falling over rocks. You can feel it—the surface of the trees, the hair cap moss; you can smell it in the herb green fields, the summit ferns; in its balm of Gilead, and in the pines. You hear the barred owl at night, the scarlet tanager by day, the haunting white throated sparrow."

Below, to the northeast, is Prattsville, which you might want to visit for no other reason than to see the amazing sculptures at Pratt's Rocks, a short hike from the road. Zadock Pratt was a tanlord, one of, if not the, most successful and influential tanners in America. His story is told in stone by a series of carvings cut by a journeyman stonecutter whom Pratt befriended. Many of the carvings are larger than life. There is a bust of Zadock Pratt, a hemlock tree and horse, and a likeness of the tannery building he finished in 1824. Beneath this an inscription reads, "One million sides of sole leather tanned with hemlock bark, in twenty years, by Zadock Pratt." A roadside visitors' booth explains the family history and further exploits of this remarkable man. The sculptures are set in vertical rock walls above a visitors' picnic area.

You can visit both the John Burroughs memorial and Pratt's Rocks in the same day that you visit Bearpen, if you get an early start on the mountain. Consult your map for directions. An understanding of both men's contributions to the area's economy and culture will add immeasurably to your appreciation of the western Catskills. Return the way you came.

48

Belleayre Mountain

Distance: 5 miles

Time: 4 hours

Vertical rise: 1,175 feet

Map: NY–NJTC Catskill Trails, #42

One of the easiest and most scenic approaches to Belleayre Mountain is via Cathedral Glen, a tricky-to-locate trail running from Pine Hill south to the summit. Pine Hill is a scenic, quiet little community between Big Indian and Highmount on NY 28.

The Rondout and Oswego was the first railroad to penetrate as far as

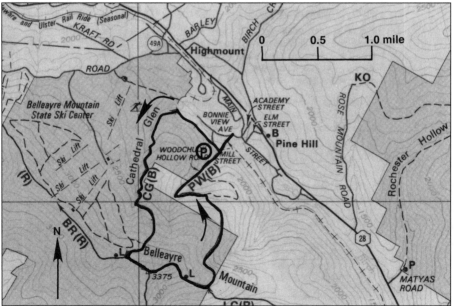

Pine Hill, but only after serious controversies over its construction. Some argued that the railroad from Kingston would threaten the livelihoods of teamsters. On July 4, 1866, the Kingston *Argus* wrote that the road would "strike ruinously at our wagonmakers, our blacksmiths, our harness makers, our flour and feed establishments, our merchants and dealers generally."

The opposite point of view was held by tanners and businessmen along the proposed route, who could see only profit in railroad development. In any case, in 1870, the Rondout and Oswego opened for passenger service as far west as Mount Pleasant. The line later changed hands and took the name of Delaware and Ulster in 1875. Part of the same line can be traveled today via the Delaware and Ulster Rail Ride, which runs west of Pine Hill from Arkville to Highmount.

The railroad's passage through Pine Hill presented some engineering challenges, which resulted in the double horseshoe curve that you see on the map just west of the Cathedral Glen Trail. Prior to the curve's construction, the idea of tunneling through the mountain was popular, but a grant authorized by the legislature was vetoed by then-Governor Hoffman.

One of the more ambitious offshoots of the Delaware and Ulster was the Grand Hotel, which the railroad built and owned. Opened in the same year as the Kaaterskill Hotel (1881), the Grand was positioned in Highmount, on the Delaware and Ulster county line, with views of both the Catskills' highest mountains and the lower pasturelands of Delaware County. Proprietors of the Grand, located in two towns and counties, had the unusual power to move both the bar-room and hotel office when liquor and tax laws made such moves profitable. The hotel was noted for Diamond Spring, which was praised for its wholesomeness and purity by the hotel's management—and recommended by its physician.

While Arnold Guyot was hurriedly elevating the Shandaken Mountains from little-known peaks to the very tallest of Catskill summits, the Grand Hotel was busy promoting itself. This shifted considerable attention from the erstwhile nucleus of the Catskills: Pine Orchard and the Catskill Mountain House.

In Pine Hill on NY 28, turn west at the bus stop and then right on Main Street. Several hundred feet ahead, go left on Bonnie View Road. In another few hundred feet or more you will see a state trail sign on Mill Street. Cross a small creek, continue on a dirt road, go under a railroad bridge, and take the first right, into an open area. Park here, where the railway bed slips into the woods going west. (An official parking area is scheduled to be built here.)

You will hike along the abandoned railway bed of the original Rondout and Oswego to come out on the trail that ends on Mill Street (Pine Hill–West Branch Trail). There are no trail signs along the tracks at this point. You still have a 10- or 15-minute walk to a small pond on your left, where on the far side there is a shed belonging to the Belleayre Mountain State Ski Center. The pond is shown on the map at the trailhead. On the east side of the pond the trail departs from the tracks and heads uphill to the south. You may have to look around for a few minutes in order to find the blue trail markers, which follow along the eastern ridge of the

Hiking on the old Rondout and Oswego railroad tracks

bowl created by the pond excavation. These blue trail markers (there is no trail sign) lead to an easily walked jeep road beneath an overstory of large hemlock.

Travel through this climax forest of hemlock, the spires of which may well have inspired the name Cathedral Glen, and within 5 minutes the trail assumes the character of a foot-path. Shortly you enter a hardwood forest. After another 20 minutes you reach an open field with a snow fence erected along its edges. You are at the bottom of a ski trail. The trail markers continue uphill, placed sparingly on trees to your left. Keep an eye on the blue disks, for suddenly you reach an ease in the trail where another ski trail goes off to the right. Look to your left and you see the blue-marked trail going into the woods in an easterly direction.

Be glad you can avoid climbing the steep ski trail ahead of you. The wooded trail, which is much gentler, will bring you to the red-marked Belleayre Ridge Trail in 10 minutes or so. When you reach the red-marked trail, the ski slopes are to your right and the summit is to your left. Go right at least as far as the lean-to, which will take you only 5 minutes. There is a view here—and there are more views farther to the west from the ski trails. The aspect is always north and east from the ski trails, with long views including North Dome, Sherrill, Balsam, Halcott, Rose, and Monka Hill.

The hike to the summit from the lean-to takes about 15 minutes. The terrain is flat over a service road. On the deciduous summit there is a picnic table and fireplace and a group of trail signs. At this junction the Pine Hill–West Branch Trail departs for Balsam, Haynes, and Big Indian mountains and the Neversink Valley. To your left the Lost Clove Trail goes to Big Indian, intersecting a short way down with the Pine Hill–West Branch Trail's northern leg, which you will take back to Woodchuck Hollow Road and the clearing where your car is parked. Views are limited from the summit.

A short way down the Belleayre Ridge Trail on your left is a lean-to with a latrine on the opposite side of the trail. In less time than it took you to get from the summit to the lean-to (about 15 minutes), you reach the blue-marked trail again, where you turn left, descending on an easy road bed, in 20 minutes entering an obvious logged-over area with private postings. The owner has granted an easement here to allow the hiking public to cross these lands. Pass a large logging "deck"—an area where tree-length logs are dragged by a skidder to be loaded onto trucks for transporting. The hike out from here is flat and easy, leading you to a paved road, past the dump on your left, and back to the parking area.

49

Vroman's Nose

Distance: 2 miles

Time: 1 hour

Vertical rise: 760 feet

Map: USGS 7½' Middleburgh

The Nose is a trip you save for a lazy afternoon when you'd rather watch than walk. From this geologically unique cliff, 600 feet above the Schoharie Valley, there are fine views of the lowlands and the long ridge of the northern Catskills.

You won't have to work too hard to visit Vroman's Nose, and the hike itself is very easy. It may be harder to find the trailhead. The trail itself is well marked. Vroman's Nose is west of Middleburgh, which is about half an hour southwest of the Albany–Schenectady area, at the intersection of NY 30 and NY 145.

Just south of Middleburgh on NY 30, at 0.6 mile on the right, is Middleburgh Road, which runs into West Middleburgh. Vroman's Nose is obvious; its vertical cliffs rise above NY 30 in front of you. The trail starts north of the hill, to your right as you look south at the Nose. Turn right on Middleburgh Road and go 0.6 mile to a point where Line Creek crosses the road (the town line between Middleburgh and Fulton). A few hundred feet beyond the bridge, park on your left, where you notice a rough parking area with room for several cars.

A wagon road runs south through a hay field from here, into a forest of large pine and hemlock, turning right as it leaves the field. This trail has recently been improved with waterbars and grading. Green, red, and blue Long Path markers appear, but there are no state trail signs, as this is private property belonging to the Vroman's Nose Preservation Corporation (VNPC). The goal of VNPC is to keep the area forever wild and open to the public. The path is self-guiding, and a steady climb over easy terrain (steep in places) takes you through a hardwood forest to the "summit." You actually can cover the distance in 20 minutes, but take your time to enjoy the views of the Catskills that will open up toward the south. The overlook, a long and dangerous cliff, is located approximately 50 feet southeast of the

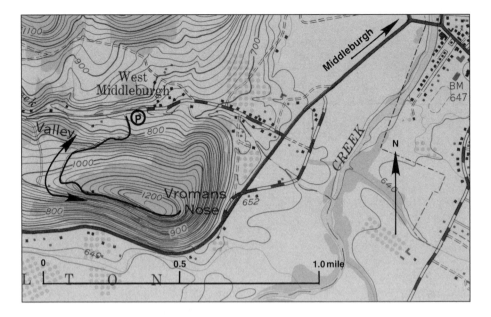

summit, a wooded plateau of roughly 10 acres. The area of flat stone near the precipice is known as the Dance Floor, for dances were actually held there in the early 1900s during the prohibition period.

The heavily scored summit of Hamilton sandstone shows evidence of its past in scratches (*striae*) and chatter marks of an advancing glacier, which moved from the northeast about 50,000 years ago, forming the present topography of the Schoharie Valley. The cliff is heavily engraved with initials and ugly painted graffiti, to such a point that it has an erosive effect. Several concrete fireplaces have been built to help prevent the assembling of fire rings by visitors. Fortunately, there is very little litter surrounding the few crude fireplaces people have assembled nearby.

Trees such as oak, hickory, pine, and cedar thrive on the plateau, which is covered in bearberry (called *kinikinick* by the Native Americans).

The early spring flower, fringed polygala, also appears.

Dr. Vincent J. Schaefer comments on the presence of brachiopods, pelycepods, and trilobites that characterize the Middle Devonian–period thin sheets of Hamilton sandstone. Flagstones from Vroman's Nose were used for sidewalks in cities such as Troy, Albany, and Schenectady.

Early in 1942 Dr. Schaefer visited the Nose while an employee of the General Electric Research Laboratory to photograph the testing of artificial fog generators, ultimately used for the screening of ships, personnel, and cities from air attack during World War II. He pointed out a curious atmospheric phenomenon that generates a strong thermal updraft against the cliff. "The dark-colored rocks of the cliffs of Hamilton shale and sandstone become quite warm whenever the sun is shining on them. This produces a massive upcurrent of heated air. Light objects such as grass, small

Vroman's Nose

twigs, and similar objects when thrown away from the cliff edge are carried upward and toward the north."

You may notice birds, notably turkey buzzards, taking advantage of this free ride. This presents an opportunity to get some good pictures of them as they circle lazily out of sight with no wing movement.

The long, open fields of farmland to the north, east, and south of Vroman's Nose were settled originally by Native Americans, who left evidence of campfires under its thin soils. It was a Schenectady farmer, Adam Vroman, who established the first farm here in 1713. He was followed by German palatines who originally settled in the lower Hudson River Valley. Crops common to the valley today are corn and carrots. In the past, hops were grown successfully in the alluvial flats along the Schoharie.

Dr. Schaefer originally conceived of the Long Path in 1931, then planned to cross Vroman's Nose. The path's purpose is the same today as then: to link the outstanding scenic, geologic, prehistoric, and historic features of the area traversed. Dr. Schaefer died in the summer of 1993. He will miss the completion of the Long Path as it forges its way north to the Adirondacks, but his memory is inextricably bound to it and to those who use the trail. The section that crosses the Nose was dedicated in October 1993.

Beginning at the George Washington Bridge in New York City and ending in the northern Adirondacks at Whiteface Mountain (ultimately), the Long Path comes up from Gilboa, following old roads on the valley's east side. From Keyser Kill Falls, through Panther Creek to Brouck Falls, and into the high country beyond Fultonham and Watsonville, the Long Path follows hill roads near Patria and then descends the ridge to Vroman's Nose. From there it drops down to cross the Schoharie at Middleburgh, goes east through the village, follows a woods road to the top of a rocky cliff east of town, and heads for Dutch Billy's Hill in the Helderbergs.

Although its founders originally intended to construct Adirondack-type lean-to shelters a day's hike apart along the Long Path, these ambitious plans were interrupted by World War II. The Long Path still has its enthusiasts, however, whose mission it is to maintain and continue the trail to its planned destination.

Those who have walked sections of the Long Path may have been frustrated by the sparingly applied blue blazes that designate it. Unlike present hiking trails, the trail originally was meant to be unmarked except on topographic maps. "Thus," to quote Dr. Schaefer, "a hiker must know how to read a topographic map. Such a route eliminates most of the difficulties of trail maintenance and marking, overuse, litter, and the host of other problems that are inherent in the present trail systems. The Schoharie Valley and especially the Vroman's Nose area is a perfect example of the Long Path idea."

Looking south you will have fine views of Windham High Peak and the Blackhead Range, beyond long esplanades of furrowed ground, a geographical contrast that is as unique as Vroman's Nose itself.

(For more information, write to Vroman's Nose Preservation Corporation, 34 Davis Lane, Cobleskill, NY 12043.)

50

Thacher Park and Indian Ladder

Distance: 0.5 miles (plus options)

Time: 45 minutes

Vertical rise: Insignificant

Map: USGS 7½' Altamont

Indian Ladder is a short walk, best enjoyed along with a picnic to John Boyd Thacher State Park and strolls through its lovely grounds, which cap the Helderberg Escarpment. The trail, less than half a mile long, explores one of the state's most striking geological formations; here is a wonderful place to view the accumulations of sand and lime-mud that have been compressed into rock, uplifted, and eroded to form the mountain bastions bordering the plains that much later became the site of the sea of Albany. These light-colored ramparts derive their name from the Dutch, *helder,* meaning bright or light, and *berg,* meaning mountain.

The uplift of these mountains in the Early Tertiary period and later

glacial actions expose a long segment of the earth's history, so a trip to study these formations makes an informative outing. Combine it with the view from the amphitheater formed by the cliffs or a picnic beneath the shade trees of the Paint Mine or Indian Ladder picnic areas, and you have a day in a pastoral setting unlike any that exists in the lowlands before you.

This is a nice getaway spot for a lazy summer afternoon when you are not quite up to a strenuous hike. Be warned, though, that weekends here can be very crowded. The park is easily reached from the capital district. Coming west from Albany from NY 20, take NY 146 into Altamont where NY 156 branches to the right. Follow NY 156 to the junction of NY 157 and a sign pointing left to the park, five miles distant. There is plenty of parking. You will find good directions to the trailhead, whose starting point is just north of the Indian Ladder picnic area, behind the park's administration building. A comfort station is located here also. With some allowances made for conditions, the Indian Ladder Trail is open from May 1 through November 15. Numerous hiking trails exist south of Route 157,

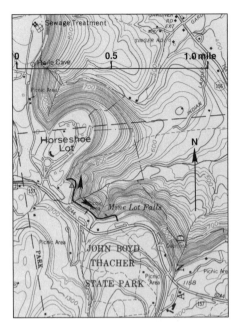

and the entire escarpment can be walked on the informal Cliff Trail, which runs from Hale's Cave Picnic Area to Stone Lot Picnic Area.

Verplanck Colvin, the surveyor who mapped the wilderness areas of northern New York, wrote about the Helderbergs in 1869, shedding some light on the origin of the name Indian Ladder. "What is this Indian Ladder so often mentioned? In 1710 this Helderberg region was a wilderness; nay all westward of the Hudson River settlement was unknown. Albany was a frontier town, a trading post, a place where annuities were paid, and blankets exchanged with Indians for beaver pelts. From Albany over the sand plains . . . 'Schenectada' (pine barrens) of the Indians . . . led an Indian trail westward. Straight as the wild bee or the crow the wild Indian made his course from the white man's settlement to his own home in the beauteous Schoharie Valley. The stern cliffs of these hills opposed his progress; his hatchet fells a tree against them, the stumps of the branches which he trimmed away formed the round of the Indian Ladder."

While it may be that an old Indian Ladder once leaned against this cliff, it has been replaced by the heavy steel staircases that now serve a curious public. This first section of trail follows what was originally the Indian Ladder Road, constructed in 1828 from Albany and westward into the Schoharie Valley.

The upper layers of rock are the youngest, known to geologists as the Coeymans Limestone. That formation takes its name from the nearby town where it is well exposed. Of the two limestone formations in Thacher Park, the Coeymans is the thickest, averaging 50 feet from top to bottom. Look closely here and you may find the preserved remains of small sea creatures. These hard-shelled fossils of *Sieberella Coeymanensis* and other invertebrates date from the Late Silurian and Lower Devonian periods, about 415 million years ago.

Continuing down the trail you notice thin layers (two to three inches) of alternating light and dark beds of a "ribbon limestone," which is softer than the Coeymans and recedes beneath it as a result of erosion. This is Manlius Limestone, a formation used extensively in the manufacture of cement at Manlius near Syracuse. Those thin limestone ribbons form a 50-foot-thick layer that also contains the preserved remains of invertebrate sea creatures and algae. Part of the formation also contains a two- to three-inch layer of waterlime, which has been used for making the Portland cement that will set up underwater. This forms a ledge known in the park as the Upper

Indian Ladder trail

Bear Path. At the base of the Manlius formation is limey mudrock known as Rondout Formation. It is a waterlime that is well exposed near the Ulster County town of Rondout. It was used to produce Rosendale, or natural cement. This formation is less resistant to erosion and has eroded back to form the Lower Bear Path, the ledge you are standing on.

The presence of limestones in Thacher Park, and their characteristic ability to dissolve in rainwater, has caused such phenomena as disappearing streams, sinkholes, caves, and underground streams. The erosion underground can form caves, which occasionally collapse to form surface depressions called sinkholes. The Karst topography is named after its frequent appearance in the Karst region of the Dalmatian Alps. Nearby Thompson's Lake is a sinkhole, which drains through a subterranean cave at its south end.

Once in the large amphitheater, which is called Indian Ladder Gulf, you will see Outley and Minelot creeks. Together they have been responsible for the erosion of this impressive embayment. When the water table is high, these two creeks form spectacular falls that you can walk behind on the trail. The talus slope beneath the cliff consists of rock that has been broken off and that has fallen from the cliff face. Along the Indian Ladder Walk, watch for the small, limestone-loving ferns, such as cliffbrakes and spleenworts.

The view from cliff top encompasses the Adirondack foothills, Vermont's Green Mountains, the Berkshires of western Massachusetts, and the Taconics. There are paths at cliff top with views or shaded paths behind that you can follow to extend the 45-minute walk along the Indian Ladder into a fair day's outing.

The park welcomes groups, and facilities include picnic areas with covered pavilions, fireplaces, water fountains, and modern comfort stations. There are also refreshment stands, swimming pools, baseball diamonds, and areas set aside for paddle tennis, handball, and basketball. Pets are allowed on leashes. No rock climbing is allowed.

Winter activites include cross-country and downhill skiing (no lift), snowshoeing, tobogganing, and snowmobiling. There is a vehicle entrance fee. For information call the John Boyd Thacher State Park office at 518-872-1237.

BIBLIOGRAPHY

Adams, Arthur G. *The Hudson Through the Years*. Westwood, NJ: Lind Publications, 1983.

Bedell, Cornelia F. *Now and Then and Long Ago in Rockland County*. New York: Arno Press, Historical Society of Rockland County, 1941.

Cole, The Rev. David. *History of Rockland County*. New York: J. B. Beers & Co., 1884.

De Lisser, Richard Lionel. *Picturesque Ulster County*. Kingston, NY: Styles and Bruyn Publishing Co., 1896.

Evers, Alf. *The Catskills from Wilderness to Woodstock*. Reprint of 1972 Doubleday edition with additions. Woodstock, NY: The Overlook Press, 1982.

Goldring, Winifred. *Guide to the Geology of John Boyd Thacher Park (Indian Ladder Region) and Vicinity*. Albany: New York State Museum Handbook 14, 1933.

Haring, H. A. *Our Catskill Mountains*. New York: G. P. Putnam's Sons, 1931.

The Hemlock (Catskill Center News). Cosponsored publication of the Catskill Center and Mountain Top Historical Society, Box 263, Haines Falls, NY, 1980.

Hoffer, Audrey, and Elizabeth Mikols. *Unique Natural Areas in the Catskill Region*. Arkville, NY: Catskill Center for Conservation and Development, Inc., 1974.

Hopkins, E. M. *The Sunk Mine*. May 1887. Copied by Olive Adams, Nelsonville, June 1957, papers in the library of the Putnam County Historical Society.

Kudish, Michael. *Vegetational History of the Catskill High Peaks*. Ph.D. diss., State University College of Forestry, Syracuse University, 1971.

Laird, J. R. Dunham. "Dunderberg." *South of the Mountain* (Tappan Zee Historical Society) 8, no. 4 (October–December, 1964).

Longstreth, T. Morris. *The Catskills*. New York: The Century Co., 1918.

Lossing, Benson J. *The Hudson: From Wilderness to the Sea*. Facsimile of the 1866 edition. Somersworth, NH: New Hampshire Publishing Company, 1972.

MacCracken, Henry Noble. *Old Dutchess Forever!* New York: Hastings House Publishers, 1956.

Mack, Arthur C. *Enjoying the Catskills*. New York: Funk and Wagnalls Co., 1950.

Myles, William. *Harriman Trails: A Guide & History*. New York: New York–New Jersey Trail Conference, 1992.

Mylod, John. *Biography of a River: The People and Legends of the Hudson Valley*. New York: Hawthorne Books, Inc., 1969.

New York–New Jersey Trail Conference. *New York Walk Book*. New York:

Doubleday, 1984.

Newman, Joseph. "Recollections." *South of the Mountain* (Historical Society of Rockland County) 13, no. 1 (January–March, 1969).

O'Brien, Raymond J. *American Sublime: Landscape and Scenery in the Lower Hudson Valley*. New York: Columbia University Press, 1981.

Posselt, Eric. *The Rip Van Winkle Trail, A Guide to the Catskills*. New York: Storm Publishers, 1952.

Putnam County Historical Society. *The Last 100 Years*. Third Workshop, 1957.

Quinn, Louise Hasbrouck, The Rev. A. Elwood Corning, Joseph W. Emsley, and Willet C. Jewell. *Southeastern New York: A History of Ulster, Dutchess, Orange, Rockland and Putnam*. Vol. 2. New York: Lewis County Publishing Company, Inc.,

1946, p. 942 ff.

Ransom, James M. *Vanishing Ironworks of the Ramapos*. New Brunswick, NJ: Rutgers University Press, 1966.

Reed, John. *The Hudson Valley*. New York: Bonanza Books, 1960.

Rockwell, The Rev. Charles. *The Catskill Mountains and the Region Around*. New edition. Cornwall, NY: Hope Farm Press, 1973.

Snyder, Bradley. *The Shawangunk Mountains: A History of Nature and Man*. New York: The Mohonk Preserve, Inc., 1981.

Van Zandt, Roland. *The Catskill Mountain House*. New Brunswick, NJ: Rutgers University Press, 1966.

———. *Chronicles of the Hudson: Three Centuries of Travelers' Accounts*. New Brunswick, NJ: Rutgers University Press, 1971.

INDEX

Books from The Countryman Press and Backcountry Publications

The Countryman Press and Backcountry Publications, long known for fine books on travel and outdoor recreation, offer a range of practical and readable manuals.

Hiking Series:

Fifty Hikes in the Adirondacks
Fifty Hikes in Central New York
Fifty Hikes in Central Pennsylvania
Fifty Hikes in Connecticut
Fifty Hikes in Eastern Pennsylvania
Fifty Hikes in Lower Michigan
Fifty Hikes in Massachusetts
Fifty Hikes in the Mountains of North Carolina
Fifty Hikes in New Jersey
Fifty Hikes in Northern Maine
Fifty Hikes in Northern Virginia
Fifty Hikes in Ohio
Fifty Hikes in Southern and Coastal Maine
Fifty Hikes in Vermont
Fifty Hikes in Western New York
Fifty Hikes in Western Pennsylvania
Fifty Hikes in the White Mountains
Fifty More Hikes in New Hampshire

Walks & Rambles Series:

Walks & Rambles on Cape Cod and the Islands
Walks & Rambles on the Delmarva Peninsula
Walks & Rambles in Dutchess and Putnam Counties
Walks & Rambles in Rhode Island
More Walks & Rambles in Rhode Island
Walks & Rambles in and around St. Louis
Walks & Rambles in Southwestern Ohio
Walks & Rambles in Westchester and Fairfield Counties
Walks & Rambles in the Western Hudson Valley

We offer many more books on hiking, walking, fishing, and canoeing plus books on travel, nature, and other subjects.

Our books are available at bookstores, or they may be ordered directly from the publisher. For ordering information or for a complete catalog, please contact:

The Countryman Press
c/o W.W. Norton & Company, Inc.
800 Keystone Industrial Park
Scranton, PA 18512
http://web.wwnorton.com